SALOON

SALOON

A Guide to America's Great Bars, Saloons, Taverns, Drinking Places, and Watering Holes

Toby Thompson

Grossman Publishers
A Division of The Viking Press
New York, 1976

Library of Congress Cataloging in Publication Data
Thompson, Toby.
  Saloon.
  Includes index.
  1. Hotels, taverns, etc.—United States.
  I. Title.
TX909.T53   647'.9573   76-26549
ISBN 0-670-61622-2

ACKNOWLEDGMENTS
Crazy Horse: "Krishna Provides" by Ken McCullough; reprinted by permission. Harold Ober
Associates: from *McSorley's Wonderful Saloon* by Joseph Mitchell (Grosset & Dunlap, 1943),
Copyright 1938, 1939, 1940, 1941, 1942, 1943 by Joseph Mitchell; reprinted by permission of
Harold Ober Associates Incorporated.

Printed in the United States of America

"Out with the truckers and the kickers and the cowboy angels . . . a good saloon in every single town."

—*Gram Parsons*

Contents

WEST

EAST

Introduction:
Varsity Grill Drag

That same week, Arthur Bremer shot Governor Wallace in a parking lot at Laurel, Maryland. I had spotted him. Bremer was leaning ramrod straight against a post near the far end of the bar, and he was grinning that hysterical grin. The Varsity Grill was crowded; later there would be violence—motorcycles ripping through the discothèque, rental police macing and pistol-whipping patrons at will, poleaxed coeds slathering walls of the ladies' room *Stick Pigs* with their own dumb blood. This was the night previous to Wallace's appearance, and they were packed twelve deep at the beer window, punching and shoving to get nearer a drink. Bremer had caught my eye and I remember thinking, Lord could I know that psycopath?

For a second I mistook him for the Nazi, a German political science student of my acquaintance (also blond, also blue eyed) who was kinky about drinking beer in his dead father's fatigues. The Nazi wore this Storm Trooper ensemble at the Varsity Grill to lure feisty barmaids into arguments about historical determinism. He was rarely fussed over. Two or three large Jews occasionally muscled him to Route One, but the Nazi was not without a sense of humor and would always crawl back in a mellower mood, dripping from nose and tooth, dad's helmet tucked humbly under arm. Bremer had worn civvies when I encountered him, but there was something in his manner, in that sickest of smiles which telegraphed a similar persistence. After I'd read Bremer's diary in *Harper's* I understood perfectly; his actions had little to do with the Varsity Grill, or even violence-torn Prince George's County: Bremer was a writer who was having trouble getting published.

The Varsity Grill had long attracted writers—bovine poets, crapulent novelists, gouty lyricists and other chronically tortured folk who whiled away time with the pen and pad. It is not difficult to imagine why Bremer was drawn there. From 1967 until 1971, the Varsity Grill proved intriguing as any drinking spot in America—each evening, a vast territory of unrealized possibility: cavernous back room, the discothèque, warehousing an awesome sound system and scores of twitching, hunching bodies; wainscoted middle room, with tables for couples, milder music to permit conversation; and a cacophonous front barroom, seismic, cabalistic, chaotic with every manner of discordant epicure in the culture. At College Park, half-way between Laurel and Washington—or, on a grander scale, midway between the lumberjack fiddle parlors of Fort Kent and honkytonk shrimper saloons of Key West—the Varsity Grill squatted in a neon half light from Route One like the amorphous gob of shingle and red brick it was . . . sighing as doors opened, closed, and the big trucks roared by.

We were tired. Plumb tuckered, if the truth be told. Our racquets logged spilt beer from a third large pitcher, and peanuts, like shucked nodules, swam along the flow to befoul otherwise spotless tennis whites. Our table was filthy; our match rained out. We huddled near a window in the last light of a purplish afternoon, and pondered. Though barely four thirty the front room was jammed: with bottomfeeders, their rainsoaked leathers exuding a frightened animal stench . . . as if an entire herd of soon-to-be-slaughtered cattle had been showered and shuttled into the Varsity Grill for one final drink. An off-duty security cop lurched past our table, his flaccid belly pink against the dampness of a rayon shirtfront, hogleg .38 flopping off a wide expanse of blue serge. He waddled like a butcher. The bottomfeeders shuffled closer to the bar, their heavy soles skree-skreeing through peanut shells and aluminum pop tops. Here and there a fatted flower child hung her lesioned buttocks out of raggedy hiphuggers and passed an empty pickle can for spare change. A nearby intoxicate sucked cold cheese from a desiccated pizza—red and yellow dreadful spilling to dirty the QUAALUDES ARE FUN! lavender tee. A waterfall of rainbow spansules pulsed from his leather sleeve with the cadence of a loose I.V. Peppering the filth beneath his chair. Old black "Captain" staggered from table to table swigging other folks' wine and moaning, *My name is yo' name!* Somebody smashed a bottle into the glass face of a pinball machine, and everyone wondered why.

Colonial Williamsburg had been a bust. So had historic Richmond; Charlottesville was nice. Now we were afraid again—anxious to fight, flee, or quickly parry. The air was full of projectiles. Each of us bore scars. Only a dullard could have missed it, but College Park had lost face. S. Jack raised his battered calves and nestled ochre Pumas into the seat of a shattered ice-cream chair.

"George Mason," he said. "Colonel William fucking Byrd."

"Patrick Henry," I replied.

"George Washington: Whoring and gorging."

"At Chowning's, the Raleigh Tavern, Wetherburn's."

"Where are they now?" S. Jack shouted, slamming his fist against our table. "Tobe, you'll follow through. We were *lost* out there. You'll find them—"

"The great ones, S. Jack?"

"Top of the stack!"

I knew he meant bars. It had blossomed into an obsession. One month had passed, or was it two? But the memory of four desperate days in eighteenth-century Virginia lingered like a foul virus.

A sentimental trip, launched innocently enough: Swing south through Charlottesville, seat of an alma mater, to visit old friends and introduce S. Jack (a Missourian) to Virginia's architecture and countryside. Cross leisurely toward Williamsburg, with a brief luncheon stop in Richmond, having gassed at Short Pump, to sleep peacefully in John D. Rockefeller's restored capital and explore the Tidewater. But our trip had turned sour. The days were full and fresh, but our nights . . . feverish! No place to drink—not one worthy saloon. The Varsity Grill, rancid as it was, had spoiled us. She knew no equal in the Commonwealth. Our last evening at Williamsburg culminated with a howling stomping war dance from a William and Mary teenhall at one end of Duke of Gloucester Street, past restored taverns long closed at that hour, to a snow-flecked, moonlit Capitol where we stalked the ghosts of braver men and cursed our luck at being bored in a barless town.

The inspiration for a guide soon followed. At Ocean City, to be exact. After a windshook run across Cape Henry's Chesapeake bridge–tunnel and that cold, lonesome pull up Virginia's desolate eastern shore, Ocean City, Maryland—empty of tourists—was predictably bleak; but we located a neighborhood barroom on the south beach side: warm lights, comfortable clientele, soft Nashville music on a venerable Wurlitzer shored up by twenty-year-old Peggy Lee/Louis Prima tunes. Old men, dressed in bright deer shooter's caps and kapok vests, slouched together on chromium stools and joked about the weather.

The book began to take shape. S. Jack, philosopher by profession, possessed a mind which worked easily around the more complex issues at hand. We swilled ice cold Michelob and laid out the bare bones of our project.

A guide to Great American Bars—the basic idea that, no matter what section of the country a person might be traveling, he could consult our book, confront a steambeer and weirdpiss description of Great Bars in his area, and judge for himself if either stop or special sidetrip was warranted. The criterion for greatness would be, not necessarily the quality of food, drink, or music at a particular spot— this not to be specifically a restaurant/entertainment guide—but how well the bar fulfilled its primary function: that of relieving loneliness, boredom, and dread. Included would be essays of varying length: truly great bars, featured in depth, others treated perfunctorily, in the usual tourbook fashion.

Our book would be largely a *road* guide to Great American Bars, geared to the driving traveler's proclivity to ramble. It would offer various routes for tours of Great Bars in odd sections of the country. And it would stand as cash in the pocket against dry scrapes of particularly dull road. Every drinking traveler . . . especially the *driving* drinking traveler . . . knew there was little in life more threatening than to find himself at strange crossroads, desperate and alone, with zero hope of relief unless a decent bar could be located. A traveler who carried our guide would own a good chance of being covered.

"You need a title," S. Jack said—for now we were home at the Varsity Grill, and final authority had been delegated to me. As I'd known it would. "This will be a work with serious American overtones."

"How about . . . *Drunk!*" I offered. "It's light, yet self-assertive. It's unassuming." S. Jack tossed his shaggy head and groaned.

"*Drunk!* is smooth. It's earthy, like Chaucer, yet polemical. It's dry. *Drunk!* has a definite Chaucerian ring."

"Well, I'm worried about it."

I worried about the Varsity Grill. What had brought it, and us, to this strange conflux of violence and despair? Did the clue hide in its history? Nestled under stacks of Black Sabbath and Kinky Friedman albums, or in a sinkful of vomit in the men's john? Was it faulty architecture? Or interior design? The Grill's stench was truly awful—a purée of dried beer, stale urine, and consumptive spittle. All underfoot, and many patrons continuing to scuffle through, shoeless as a day in May, circa 1968. Ice-cream chairs were smashed, as were most of the bar stools. Impossible to find a safe spot to sit without being sloshed from your own pitcher at a table with three legs, or jostled and bruised from any number of staggering, brutal motorcycle types who had haunted the Varsity Grill for over a year now—transforming it into a kind of bloody, brain-ravaged twilight zone for Quaaluders. The fear factor was extremely high. A private police guard had been hired. Five or six burlies worked the Grill's main rooms on a good night; they were rarely bored. The guard was heavily armed and used its chemical mace and riot sticks freely. At least once a week, Prince George's Police were summoned to break up vicious melees in the discothèque. A two-o'clock wail of ambulances and squad cars, hurrying along Route One to the Varsity Grill, had become a fixture in College Park. Many citizens were angered at what they felt to be a soft line taken by Prince George's Police. (Though no one who had lived through a police raid on the Varsity Grill, fending off clubs, dogs and screaming slashing bikers, would attest to that.) Bomb threats were common. And taken in stride. Rarely was the building evacuated. Citizens grumbled among themselves and swore to take the Grill some dark night, by fist or firepower.

A Quonset hut, architecturally: discarded by the Air Force and converted in 1940 to a combination beerhall, cafeteria, and Greyhound Bus terminal by Mr. Zalzac . . . a man of vision who refused to partition off one inch of original space, thereby preserving the Quonset's cheerful sense of "style"—adding, as his personal touch, the cozy filigree of squawking jukebox and Greyhound ticket counter. Charley Bontempo, a bartender and ordinary language philosopher around College Park since 1948, reported that the Grill "went Greek" in that era. Whole hog. Fraternity/sorority clientele: clean fun, low budget, booze your brother under the table, beat up a Negro, vomit on your date, and sleep it all off at The House. The Grill stayed Greek until the mid-sixties, when an early disco craze swept the nation: Beatle bop, Dave Clarkism, the Jerk, the Freddy, and other hysteria attendant to the British invasion ushering in a revival of the dance hall as a commercially viable enterprise.

Regrettably, disco at the Grill attracted a seamy element—one which an older generation would dub "roughneck," still another "low rent," but which neither foresaw as cause for alarm. Leon Zeiger had acquired the Varsity Grill by that time, and capitalizing on the new dance craze, outfitted his mammoth back room with go-go girls, disc jockeys and a substantial sound system. All this hip-slinging buttwalking nigger music was fine for business and the coeds seemed to thrive on it; but—it drew that element. I recall slouching into the Grill's discothèque as early as 1965, with a young lady who had dragged me there not to drink, not to dance, but to "watch the greasers move." This working-class cotillion from

Hyattsville and outlying Prince George's County, with its duckass hairdos, gabardine codpieces, and sateen shirts wide open to the navel, worked a positive magic on my old date: hysterical couplings ensued in deserted playgrounds and the back seats of family cars. The Varsity Grill remained a personal favorite. Its greasers were a minority, but they had crashed in on a wave of musical populism which was masking as class acceptance. What harm could they do?

Leon Zeiger was no fool. A Harvard lawyer and something of an entrepreneur in the bar business, he had grandfathered three of Washington's most successful nightspots: Blue Mirror, Casino Royal, and the Speakeasy. Blue Mirror, in the late forties, had attracted big name entertainers such as Ella Fitzgerald and Billie Holiday. The fifties and early sixties saw the peak of Casino's popularity—followed by a steep decline. The Fourteenth Street corridor had the inner city blues: big movie theaters were pulling out; department stores moving to the suburbs. People were terrified to walk the streets after about noon. Fourteenth Street became "the Strip," an unsavory row of burlesque joints and sailors' bars. Zeiger opened the Speakeasy downstairs in the Casino Royal, to trap what small overflow remained—of college kids and bored tourists looking for a cheap mug of beer, free peanuts, and the chance to get laid downtown. The Speakeasy was a respectable skin shop, though: sequinned bimbos seesawed overhead on velvet swings, presumably dusting their eager admirers with clouds of acrid beer farts.

Zeiger let the Varsity Grill have its head. He saw big money in the changes to come (flower power, a new tolerance toward drugs), and with the exception of two or three grass-befuddled managers who overdid it in the free pitcher department, he encouraged hip insanity, packed the Grill every night, and raked in the profits.

This was the Varsity Grill's finest hour: new music, strange drugs, easy sex, and a maelstrom of cheap beer to slosh it around. Anything was possible; everyone accessible. Regulars drank alongside bus drivers, historians, short order cooks, famous philosophers, garbage men, debutantes, FBI agents, CIA, old second-story men, young car thieves, bluegrass vocalists, ex-nuns, Congressional secretaries, and dignified representatives from every stratum of American life; plus select members of the Washington diplomatic corps. Montana poet Ken McCullough published an ode to the Varsity Grill in *Crazy Horse 9*, titled "Krishna Provides":

> In GENTS, over clatter of dishes
> hear Richey Valens sing *La Bamba*—

> The rubber machine at eye level—
> Just enough gas to make it home.

An article appeared in the *Washington Post* about a Playmate of the Month who had been interviewed at the Grill: dwarfs swarmed in by the tens and twenties. The author had mentioned casually that dwarfishness was a characteristic of certain patrons who frequented the front room—and now the place was jammed with them, everyone barking his shins on them, everyone stumbling over them in the toilet, contorted around urinals in sickening postures, trying to hit the puck. They needed love; the Varsity Grill provided. It was a generous time.

New politics hunkered in the wings, and when campus violence erupted after 1970's Cambodian invasion, everyone secretly welcomed the presence of National Guard troops, a curfew, the Grill cordoned off, and its periodical hosing down with tear gas. Dissenters stumbled through broken glass and burning trash cans along Route One, to drink at the Grill whenever possible—damp handkerchiefs over eyes and noses, grass in the lungs, meth in the veins, acid in the head, and a curious levity about the heart. It was all such a game. Riot tanks and armored personnel carriers rumbled through College Park, aircraft spotlights played across the face of the Grill, choppers throbbed overhead, and battalions of shivering National Guard troopers waited in the cold for closing time and a chance to crack their quota of rank, longhaired pates. *Helter skelter, happiness is a warm gun, four dead in Ohio* . . . on we drank, oblivious, excited, stoned out of our socks, waiting for the bombs to drop or the shooting to start, like characters in a Hemingway story about the Spanish Civil War.

The shooting started later. Violence had worked its subtle drawing card at the Varsity Grill for years. Even during the fraternity era, fisticuffs of an unbrotherly cast were standard operating procedure. A fine local photographer was beaten one evening by fraternity boys who gouged out his good eye and stomped it into the cement. Christenings with empty beer bottle and broken pitcher handle were *de rigueur*, and the sight of severely lacerated patrons leaving discothèque or middle room, via rescue-squad stretchers, was not uncommon.

Times changed for me one night while seated with a tableful of strangers in the discothèque: Prince George's Police poured in both entrances, pistols drawn. Jesus, I was thinking when a fellow next to me hit the floor, who's the hunted now? They hustled my companion away without firing a shot, and the big beat never slowed. Everyone was armed. There were shootings. The Grill hired its own police guard. Dangerous bouts of cutting and cudgeling occurred every evening, but still the regulars partied. Violence was an undercurrent which threatened to become undertow, cold and insistent. Ecstasy outweighed the horror, but a police guard was alarming. How could a bar with so much potential for equanimity deteriorate into such a pighanger?

The dissenters reigned through 1971, and for a time it was pleasant to block Route One, diverting to run crazily from police and National Guard—yet not so delightful to be caught. Everyone carried his sixteen-ounce Black Label into the streets and wept from tear gas, arm in arm. Then the bikers came. They took over the Varsity Grill like Brando's wild ones, and yes, that was exciting for a while. Zeiger freighted in a downhome crazysick manager named Tony, from West Virginia, and we had Tammy Wynette on the turntable instead of Joni Mitchell . . . Faron Young, Mel Tillis, Dolly Parton, Ernest Tubb, Don Reno, and a chorus of ceaselessly reverberating *haw haw haws* from the outlaw clientele. Much shoulder punching and playful headlocking, a lot of skullcracking, but still plenty of an acceptable brand of excitement. It was swimming with hammerheads, and a lot of us got out of the water. But never for long. Zeiger was seen more often in the front room, stumblelimping around on his gimpy leg, dressed in three-hundred-dollar Stubby Kaye suits and outrageous white shoes, patting patrons on the back, encouraging them to stay, arguing that soon everything would be all right—and actually helping waitresses clear empty beer bottles off what was left of the table tops. Casino Royal had folded and so had the Speakeasy. Except for one or two porno supermarts downtown on the rancid side of Fourteenth Street, Zeiger had the Varsity Grill to test his shimmering business acumen, and that was it.

Then something else died, and even the bikers left. Classy ones, that is: with family. Bottomfeeders loped in, losers all, junkies to the man, doped down and surly on reds . . . unpredictably vicious. A seventies edition of the gabardine greasers I had danced with in 1965. Some looked familiar: fat, obscenely bloated from barbiturates, every one of them overweight and morbid after the ecstatic leanness of the sixties. Zeiger hired and fired, threatened and cajoled, shooting for that precise meld of management and staff which could handle the shift in clientele. A few of the old crowd lingered, to see what might develop. Nothing developed. A stench of hideous decay filled the front room, permeating its fixtures. The discothèque had been boarded up; long closed. Few of the toilets worked, and puddled detritus lay two inches deep along the floor of the men's john. Health and liquor violations closed the Grill a month here, three weeks there. When open for business, it was often deserted; and murderous when full. The Varsity Grill became that sort of bar where you are constantly afraid for your Achilles' tendons—one sharp kick from a motorcycle boot, properly directed, sending them rattling and flapping around your kneecaps like a pair of loose window shades. S. Jack and I fled to Virginia. We were exhausted. Now we plotted and schemed in the filth, scaffolding the façade of our portentous undertaking.

The glebes had me—silverhaired ones, in wire rim glasses and herringbone suits. I hadn't told S. Jack. But I'd traded my measure of beer and warm terror at College Park for the bitter logic of a Macke coffee vendor in a Library of Congress snacketeria. An historical precedent existed; of that I was convinced. Surely, some other visionary had conceived and documented a search . . . the Great American Bar, whatever, wherever she was, had been charted and lovingly sketched; I remained confident. A definitive study of seventeenth- eighteenth- nineteenth- and early twentieth-century bars was mine for the borrowing.

Such a volume was not readily located. Books on eighteenth-century taverns, yes: Taverns as inns, taverns as museums, taverns as restaurants, taverns as Revolutionary phenomena, taverns as gift shops, taverns as literary excuse for scholarly DARs to wallow in our Glorious Heritage. But saloons? Sissy bars? Garbage dumps like the Varsity Grill? No study had been published. Slim tomes on Prohibition and Repeal, yes. Catalogues of temperance groups, sure. Travelogues on where to lunch in New Hampshire, or sleep it off for sixty dollars a night in Carmel, you bet. But not one volume breeding dust motes in Library of Congress stacks, about *Bars*. Glebes tracked me through corridors of the main reading room and photographic archives: wheyfaced, Grumman scalped, interloping glebes . . . shiny at the seat, frayed at cuff, hunched as schoolmarms, and moaning "We *need* this book." I did eight or nine hours of research per day and stumbled zombielike, at eventide, to comforting Senatorial wino bars which dotted Capitol Hill.

The Federal City had me whipped. Only one spot provided solace; that was Old Ebbitt Grill, at 1427 F Street—around the corner

from the White House. Old Ebbitt was one of the first bars of which
I possessed a clear recollection. My father had taken me there as a
boy. He was house physician for Washington Hotel in the early
fifties, and on weekends, after hospital rounds and calls, we would
often lunch at Old Ebbitt. It was the oldest bar in Washington, established well before the Civil War. Crusty Irish waiters
ran the place; we would sit at the 1850 front bar on Saturdays, amidst hardwood paneling dating to 1872, and toughskinned
Irish bartenders would call me junior and offer steinsful of autographed baseballs for perusal. No one was supposed to touch
them. Senators' greats such as Walter Johnson, Bucky Harris and
Bobo Newsom had signed Old Ebbitt's horsehides, and I regarded
their signatures with awe. A stuffed buffalo's head glowered behind
the bar, alongside a stuffed boar's head, a stuffed walrus's head, and
genuine elephant foot humidors. A carved mahogany bear stood on
hind paws, mutely roaring at bartenders and boisterous clientele.
Stuffed dolphin and tarpon, yellow with age, swam across the wainscoting. A mangy fox. Elk horns. Gargoyles perched just below the
ceiling, and chambers above and in back of Old Ebbitt were rumored to house gamblers, bookies, and Lord knows what. It was a
fascinating saloon, more like some musty exhibit hall at National
Zoo than a place to wait, bored and frustrated, for a father to drink.
Though Old Ebbitt had long since changed hands and its caustic
Irish waiters been replaced by a younger, less-hip mélange, the bar
drew me back to its coffined interior and a recollection of boyish
hours—which lay draped around stuffed animals, as a shroud. Old
Ebbitt's wildlife was less dangerous than the Varsity Grill's; after a
brutal day at the Library of Congress, a good meal and two gallons
of beer at Old Ebbitt were all which could relax me.

That and its fixtures. Something dwelt there, in ancient mahogany, polished brass, hardwood ice chests, front bar, paintings,
stuffings and paneling. Something like order. Famous men had siphoned dread at Old Ebbitt Grill; it was, after all, Washington's
foremost saloon. The drinking spot of presidents. Ulysses S. Grant
had been a favored customer—strutting from 1600 Pennsylvania,
sword rattling, waddle-tipsy to the bar. Presidents Johnson, Cleveland, McKinley, Teddy Roosevelt and Harding, plus "many other
famous statesmen, naval and military heroes too numerous to mention," the menu stated. Old Ebbitt's bear had been imported by
Alexander Hamilton when he was first Secretary of the Treasury, as
ornament for his private bar. The steins which had held autographed

baseballs of my youth were reputedly members of the most valuable private collection in America: cast in 1575. An enormous clock which stood high above the doorway was over two hundred years old, and still kept time with its original wooden wheels . . . signifying another era, a fixture transfixed through faithful service to weary revelers, a ticking heartbeat of a bar clock which had survived. Old Ebbitt was vital to Washington. And me? How many generations of ancestors had wined there? Old Ebbitt's saloon was to the nineteenth-century capital of Washington City, what Chowning's or Raleigh's taverns were to eighteenth-century Williamsburg.

I had become fascinated with design. And architecture—as cultural expression, the whys and wherefores of its eccentric history. Language was important. The terms: saloon and tavern. Language existed as a first confusion of form as well as its final attribute. Its last shape. Saloon, my research told me, meant something different from tavern, night club or cocktail lounge. Night club and cocktail lounge were twentieth-century terms; saloon nineteenth century, tavern seventeenth and eighteenth. That followed. But "tavern" had been forced back into the language in 1933: imperiously. One word, which had done more to eradicate the aesthetics of traditional bar and saloon life in America than ugly terms like "temperance" or "Prohibition Party" *ever* had.

TAVERN

read the special February 1934 edition of *Beer and Bar Equipment:*

> the very word calls up a picture quite different than any that the lately deceased word in our language—*saloon*—could ever hope to bring to mind.

How true. How sad and FDR and the New Sophistication true.

> That word "tavern" is in fact one of the strongest proofs that the legalization of beer and the repeal of the 18th Amendment have resulted in a new deal which cannot be separated from the *merchandising habit of mind* which has grown so greatly with American businessmen in the last two decades.

American bars were never to recover from these rendering effects of Prohibition and the Depression years. . . .

> Use of this word tavern is in itself a *good piece of merchandising*, since it is at once evidence of the general desire of the country that we should create establishments that could not be associated with

the old saloon, and a constantly repeated assurance that this is the case. . . .

The point of all this is that the world isn't the same world that went into the World War. It isn't the same world that went into the whoopee era, either. *It's a world that has settled down to counting its blessings.*

The eighteenth-century tradition of a tavern as combination restaurant, inn, and drinking spot was fated to be resurrected in the 1930s as a Frankenstein geek in chromium/formica drag. With the advent of New Deal politics and the new democracy, I'd learned, plus a post-crash public whose faith in Big Buck was still shaky, Modernism and the International Style had found easy converts in bar manufacturers and trend-conscious magnates of bar interior design. For as the trade mags preached, America was not the same youngster who had swept off to World War with a Cohan song on the lungs and a slug of rye underbelt . . . as it was no longer the cocky little nation which had conquered the West, harnessed the power of Industrialism, and sailed eagerly to Cuba with Bullmoose TR in that gayest of nineteenth-century conflicts. America, in the thirties, was panting from a middle-aged shortness of breath, tired, distraught and tight in a gut which should have been slack with the paunch of responsibility and success. The country was ready for anything. Anything new, that is. Anything that did not smack of nineteenth-century Industrialism and a foolproof free enterprise system, which had promised much and let so many down; of a Wild West, which had virtually been closed and whose dangerous mannerisms had been relegated to the safety of a motion picture screen; and of that lawless decade of the twenties, which had taken the Constitution and its sacred (though wrongheaded) proclamations for a whizbang kidnap ride through the gangsterlands of New York, Chicago, and Kansas City, forcing unprecedented political compromise. The booze business had understood this. Entire issues of trade magazines previously devoted to a soberer side of industrial craft turned with gusto to the new challenges of Repeal. Design? No question about it, historical eclecticism of any sort was out. Art Deco, Modernism, the International Style, or whatever was the ticket. Chromium was king, formica his blowzy consort, driving cabinet makers from one end of the country to the other to drink alone in the horror of a more personal depression.

You can no more find today a bar interior with the appearance and inconvenience of 1916 installations than you can find a bartender with a walrus mustache.

Of course, new laws had much to do with the new design. Repeal brought with it a fen of blue law ensnarements and general inconvenience for the bar drinker which remains today. We may never be entirely free of what Prohibition did to us. The new restricted hours, restricted days, restrictions in some states of no booze whatsoever under any circumstances . . . these are our legacy. But the most ignoble restriction, as Ohio's Liquor Control Commission happened to state it, was this:

No customers will be permitted to stand at a bar, and all service must be made by waiters to persons seated at tables.

The "food dispensation" as it was called, wrought the big havoc; there was simply no longer a need for the bar as it had previously existed—as a counter at which a man could stand and drink whisky. Now he must drink in a restaurant, at table, from a barstool, or some such ridiculous compromise as the management saw fit to circumvent or comply with the law. This paved way for endless variations on the eighteenth-century tavern tradition, some of them chic, ingenious and of fantastic vitality. But whatever they were—tavern, taproom, cocktail lounge, night club or café—they were certainly not bars.

The classic American bar, or saloon, was of nineteenth-century invention. While the easy agrarianism of seventeenth- and eighteenth-century America allowed for a rigid code of tavern service rendered at specific hours of the day—meals at breakfast, dinner, and suppertime, ale and spirits with food or after supper, *always* served at table—the more hurried schedules of nineteenth-century America with its split and staggered shifts, its drink-now-for-tomorrow-we-work philosophy toward the still limitless possibilities of the continent, called for a more pragmatic method of service. Why bother with food or a table if all a man wants is a quick beer between shifts, or a snort of Wyoming rotgut after roundup? Give that Wall Street tycoon a stylish room with a back bar done in the true spirit of an industrial Gilded Age, where he can gaze at the properly reflected image of his prosperity and drink standing up like a man in forward motion should. To hell with a lot of food.

American architecture in the late nineteenth century was nothing if not paean to Big Buck. And to the freedom of action that Big Buck inspired, the certainty that at last history was under some sort of control, that this time "rugged frontier individualism," coupled with a new technology, would carry the day for American democracy. Democracy meant—well, *cash*, the pursuit of it and a free place at the starting line for all. Hadn't that been the point of Civil War? It was a man's duty, Lord his destiny, to get out and scrape for all he was worth; to ride that wagon West and stake out a claim, invent a better factory gadget and put his patent on it, sell out his best friend at a profit if there was chance for a shrewder investment farther on. All the great nineteenth-century architectural styles, from Second Empire to Eastlake to Châteauesque to Beaux Arts Classicism, shouted this credo; for like Renaissance styles they so often aped, they were created largely at the behest of a merchant/banker class as testament to the permanence and all-power of money. The miner standing in a saloon in Virginia City, Nevada, could not articulate this, but he sensed that the new bar shipped in today *overland* from God knows where back East meant—something important; meant class, a touch of high style, that his camp was prosperous, that there was silver underfoot he'd be shoveling up tomorrow if his strength and determination held. A Vanderbilt or an Astor contemplating progress on a multi-million dollar cottage against the rocky coast of Newport (that most unpleasant and forbidding of spots to find a resort) must have stuffed his hands away from the cold, turned up a collar, and *known* he was doing something right with his life.

The crash finished that sort of heavy architectural statement, however, and interior design soon followed in its wake. Bar styles had started changing during Prohibition when speakeasies found it obligatory to fake some sort of restaurant or teahouse front for a pass at sobriety. As a result, the new bars discovered chefs in their kitchens and customers at table, who in the gayety of a "dangerous" evening, didn't much mind an excuse for a meal. And of course, to the more discriminating restaurant patron, the speakeasy was the only place in town where wine could still be enjoyed with supper. For the first time in American history it was not uncommon to see *Social Register* types entertaining and being entertained in low public. They too were reveling in new fun of the Jazz Age and were determined to miss none of it. All the chicest people were coming down to the speakeasies, theater stars hobnobbing with railroad barons, landed bluebloods with arriviste automobile nabobs. And the crash shuffled the cards for a final trick. Big Buck was dead, no one had the cash to entertain at home or hotel in the old fashion, so why not? Into the streets with this . . . rabble, who seemed to be having such a marvelous time.

After Repeal, things changed even more drastically. It is easy to imagine the plight of legitimate "tavern" owners. How to comply with new regulations and still attract the old crowds? How to deal with this new drinking class who could be categorized by no other name but "café" society, as they knew no propriety, no geography, and had little in common with each other's blood lines. The speakeasy was what this public had become used to; it was an obvious solution to the problem of design, if not the most attractive: just throw up an establishment which mimicked what had been the real thing down the street. But then there was this other public, that untapped generation of law-abiding citizens and young drinkers out for a first fling, who did not wish to be reminded of the past decade. They wanted something in step with what everyone, aristocrat and rumbum alike, believed to be a new age of democracy—not that of Wide Open Spaces and untrammeled individualism . . . but of a country, a world, pulling together. New social orders and the assembly line, "scientific" method and a mild federal totalitarianism—not the debacles of free enterprise and Industrialism, that monomaniac— would save the day. Teamwork was the touchstone. Together we could erase all memory of a slump, and why not have a good time while at it? The Gilded Age was dead. Bury her in a formica casket finished nicely with chromium handles.

New photographic techniques had much to do with the new interior design. By 1934 it was no longer necessary to lug bulky, impractical magnesium flares inside a bar to take a clear picture, nor to be satisfied with the fixed poses such stilted apparati insured. The age of Candid Camera was born with fast film and the flashbulb, and a new social journalism with it. Newspapers found a huge audience for the glamorous's carrying-on in cafés. Café Society, with its relaxed social code, permitted an unprecedented naughtiness to shine through for the rotogravure. If one's name did not appear in café columns at least three times a week, one might as well have left town; and if one's mink-draped carcass wasn't premiered two-stepping out of The Stork or El Morocco as often—well, one wasn't so classy as one thought.

Bar interior designers soon realized that free advertising was theirs for the taking with a backdrop bizarre enough to stand out smartly in the new photos. El Morocco was the paradigm, with its unique zebra-stripe interior of blue and silver palm fronds, which fairly howled the premises' name without necessity of its mention in a caption. Rooms all over the country stole this idea from New York cafés, and a jungle of carousel lounges, floating bars, and candy cane decor sprouted thickly from Cleveland to Kansas City and back up and around again.

Lucius Beebe's anecdote in *The Big Spenders,* concerning the Grand Closing at 42 West 49th Street, had always seemed to me an overly gruesome epitaph, though it aptly drew its point. Jack Kriendler and Charlie Berns, in the years before their move to a larger "21" West 52nd Street, had prospered nicely as speakeasy proprietors in an old brownstone originally owned by the Puncheon family of once considerable wealth. John Whitney, Peter Arno, Rudy Vallee, Avery Rockefeller, Ernest Hemingway, Robert Benchley, Otto Kahn, William Vanderbilt, Beebe himself, and Benedict Quinn, Yale '26, of the original Puncheon family, were a few of the regulars. "Puncheon Grotto" was what Jack and Charlie called the place in those days, and late in the twenties when they finally decided to move around the block, with the inevitable Grand Opening of a new club, Benchley proposed the idea for a Grand Closing. All the old fixtures were still in place at "Puncheon," mirrors, the mahogany bar, crystal chandeliers, and none was scheduled for transport to new quarters. A variety of reasons was offered—out of style, too difficult to move, not in step with what Jack and Charlie planned for the new atmosphere . . . so the regulars demanded their day. On a given evening a handful of wealthy curmudgeons whom Beebe described as a "synthesis of Dun & Bradstreet and the *Social Register*" were issued an assortment of fire axes, crowbars, and other wrecking tools, and given free rein to smash what they could. Not a piece of furniture nor a fixture was left intact. "By virtue of social and financial primacy, Whitney was accorded the honor of smiting the first blow and chose as his objective a twelve-foot expanse of plate-glass mirror behind the back bar." The horror was soon complete, and "When at last the main stairway was sawed through leaving Benchley and Roger Wolf Kahn stranded on the second floor and cut off from the basis of supply, it was agreed no greater disaster could be contrived, and everybody went up the street to the new address." * Damage was later assessed at between $25,000 and $40,000. Jack and Charlie sent out

---

* Lucius Beebe, *The Big Spenders* (New York: Doubleday, 1966).

engraved announcements of the opening at their new speakeasy, which read:

LUNCHEON AT TWELVE,

TEA AT FOUR

AND UNTIL CLOSING

The golden era of "21" was just beginning, but something larger had passed, something ripped from the soul of a vast drinking public. The saloon was dead.

Or so it seemed. Old Ebbitt offered hope, but here at the Varsity Grill any question of "design" was eclectically moot. Bottomfeeders formed a sort of gross, expressionistic *tableau vivant:* Zeiger the sculptor/choreographer, caulking it all together, desperately, with paste pot and palate, mortar and machination, like some Bauhaus Toulouse-Lautrec. But Old Ebbitt. Were there others of her ilk? Less haughty; less glamorous perhaps, but pre-Prohibition—if not in years, certainly mood?

Two decades earlier, Jack Kerouac in *On the Road* had tolled a death knell more embittered and oppressive than Beebe's, for its all-inclusiveness:

> The ideal bar doesn't exist in America. An ideal bar is something that's gone beyond our ken. In nineteen-ten a bar was a place where men went to meet during or after work, and all there was was a long counter, brass rails, spittoons, player piano for music, a few mirrors, and barrels of whisky at ten cents a shot together with barrels of beer at five cents a mug. Now all you get is chromium, drunken women, fags, hostile bartenders, anxious owners who hover around the door, worried about their leather seats and the law; just a lot of screaming at the wrong time and deadly silence when a stranger walks in.

"You won't reconsider." I prodded S. Jack. "Take a month off, maybe two?"

"Nah," he said, glancing quickly aside. "I'll hold the fort. Something may break. Something . . . here," he snorted, with a tired gesture toward the room.

The rain had finally stopped. Across Route One, a Little Tavern hamburger joint flashed red blue green, blue red, green blue, against the charcoal sky—a College Park rainbow. Zeiger limped fiercely from table to bar, grimacing and twitching, filling his arms with beer bottles and mumbleshoving Chinese out of his path. Zeiger'd aged like Richard Nixon. The Chinese were everywhere: students, guests, adversaries, faculty, and friends. Red Chinese were ping-ponging at Cole Field House this evening, and exotic splinter groups, from Reverend Carl MacIntire's evangelists to Formosa's kung fu freedom-fighters, had packed College Park—and tangentially, the Grill. Violence was on the card.

"Varsity Grill could stand a bit of ping-pong diplomacy," S. Jack said, swinging stiffly out of his seat. "College Park sure as *hell* could."

I didn't know if I could handle the excitement. Chuang Tse-tung was in town, coaching, and rumor had it that tonight he'd perform. Chuang was a childhood idol—several times world table tennis champion, a giant of the game. I was eager to see him. But a political confrontation was slated: Red Chinese versus Formosans, Carl Mac-Intire versus everybody, students foulmouthedly versus Secretary of State Rogers and baby Tricia, who were sheduled to appear. I was exhausted. Research had left me limp and I had little backbone for politics, none for foreign policy. The Grill was out of control. At every table students clutched tiny red "Quotations" of Chairman Mao. One or two militant clumps outshouted Zeiger's stereo and practiced revolutionary anthems in Chinese, accompanied by stiff-armed salutes with Mao's book. Still, I longed to see Chuang. I'd used one of his special Western paddles (butterfly attack surface) for years. Bottomfeeders looked on in stuporous disbelief, ready to strike or join ranks for the match. Difficult to gauge their mood. S. Jack and I hustled together our tennis gear and threaded gingerly through bloated flotsam to Route One and a breath of fresher air.

"*Fuckin commies, man,*" I overheard a female bottomfeeder mewl, as we departed the front room. "*Fuckin commies in the Grill.*"

Tomorrow the road?

MIDWEST

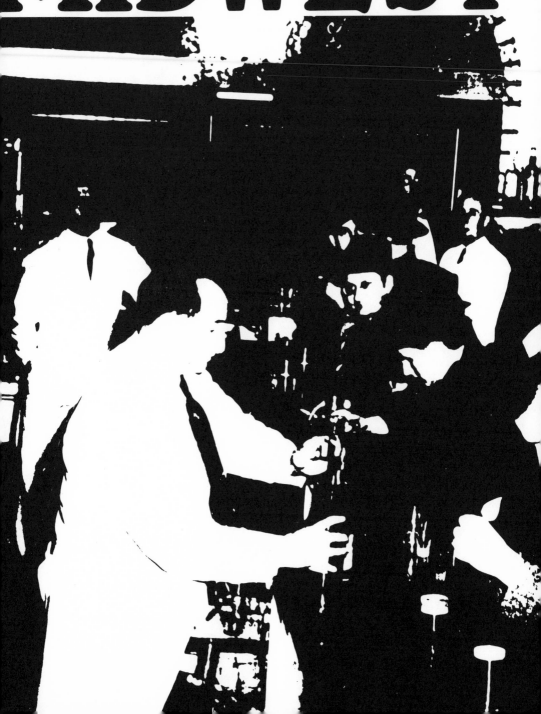

First Hundred Days

It has become increasingly clear that what I seek in a Great American Bar is *form* to frame or isolate chaos. Let me outline one basic field procedure: I study the exterior of a strange bar, its façade and architectural demeanor, to decide whether I might risk a step inside. I examine the bar and the bar's poise within its geographical setting (upon which I have already made aesthetic judgment) and the whole to my practiced eye is a place mat properly or improperly laid. Crucial moment, for a Great Bar and its architecture is not unlike that fine crystal spheroid . . . a paperweight if you will, or a child's toy in crib . . . which houses make-believe snowstorms. Snowstorms are the chaos; you *want* storms. But a proper glass ball is needed to contain them. Same holds true for interior design. You want a landscape sufficiently fixed in mood—sentimental, existential, or whatever—to keep chaos at arm's length and in a kind of check. Variables, such as whether with a lover, a friend, the gang, do not change basic landscape. They only fill it up. Front and back bars, furniture, paintings, and pool tables are the primary artifacts of an interior landscape. Like tiny log cabins, snow-covered sleighs, reindeer. You shake your crystal ball as hard as the mood dictates. Or another something, faceless and edgy, shakes it for you.

There are no Great Bars in the geographical center of North America. There is Virg's Lounge and Bottle Shop, a dank formica-lined cave off Highway 2, jammed this afternoon with hard-drinking farmers, swarthy barmaids, one or two businessmen in coarse black suits, and me: Afraid. Ghostly pastel steers, lumbering through decayed falsefront towns, gawk out at us from their velveteen canvases. A bluish mist hangs in the air. There is the scent of wet manure. A thirty- to thirty-five-year-old waitress keeps muttering *We wouldn't change much if we had it all to do over again, would we boys?* Gusts of wind lunge off the windows and the earth itself seems to tremble. A red-faced man in a soaking CAT cap tips it roguishly toward a barmaid, and the top of his head from his eyebrows back is whiter than a mushroom.

Rugby, North Dakota, may brag on its permanence as the wheat-combed belly button of the continent, and rightly so, but Virg's

3

Lounge and Bottle Shop is just another shaky barroom in the vortex of a bad blow.

Everything has been frighteningly green today. The sky an intense off-Kelly, "exact damn shade as the cab of a John Deere thresher," someone noted. A rain-bitten wind flecked with luminescent yellow hailstones has battered my Volkswagen about all afternoon like the little wooden ball in a *Foosball* machine. I have been on the road and in and out of bars since ten thirty. At noon my windshield was shattered into an annoying crushed ice pattern by stones disgorged from an oncoming cattle truck. I have been dodging tornado warnings and what look to me like surefire death spirals for hours, and my nerve is wasted.

It is impossible to relax in this country. The elements are too fierce, the landscape lonely and harsh. And people are angry. I have driven day before yesterday straight up from Texas with the notion that I might learn an important lesson about American bars here. The geographical center of the United States—Junction City, Kansas—had offered little, although it was Sunday when I passed through and everything closed. But I could tell. After one hundred days and 16,000 miles in search of the Great American Bar, my instinct is finely honed. I *know* when I am near a Great Bar. I can drive down the main street of some obscure Western town and pick the finest saloon in a line of six or eight without missing. There shouldn't be slips at this point. At twenty to thirty bars a day for one hundred days, I had better not miss.

But for the past forty-eight hours I have been wandering around the northeast and central parts of North Dakota like a crazy man. I cannot accept how bad the bars are. I had hoped for truly *great* bars nested here in the hackles of the country, bars in step with what I believed I'd find: a mood of endurance, heartiness and downright good will toward any man fool enough to stray through such primitive territory. The spirit of an Allagash, Maine, or a Silver City, Idaho. Small chance. To this moment my working criterion for Greatness in a bar has been how well an establishment fulfilled what S. Jack and I had determined to be its primary function: that of relieving loneliness, boredom, and dread. These people and the extraordinary texture of their lives, however, have rendered a generality like that meaningless. A bar I researched last night in Minot, North Dakota, is a prime example . . . maybe the ugliest bar in America. I have never visited worse. It was on Main Street, downtown Minot, and was called Covered Wagon, or perhaps the Corral.

I'm not sure; I seem to have blocked out the name. It was one of those spots I normally avoid at first sight because it boasted a very corny covered wagon façade, plus a pool table directly behind the front door so that you had to stumble over players and their sticks before you could approach the bar. Bartender was a double for the Beagle Boys, and the first thing I saw him do was recap a bottle of Budweiser somebody had misordered and stuff it back in the cooler. Distressing. Only five or six other customers occupied the place. Except for a hopelessly stoned Indian seated next to me at the bar, they were *all* screaming at each other in random fashion and jogging back and forth across the room. The Indian boy, with whom I tried to communicate, was entranced by a white "exotic dancer" of about nineteen years—a dimestore mutation between Janis Joplin and Little Orphan Annie. She was miming Barbra Streisand tunes on stage, faking all proper Broadway kicks and Baltimore bumps and grinds to the music of a three-piece Indian band, who between numbers kept slipping nervously into Hank Williams' tale of a wretched cigar store Indian who had never had his wooden mouth kissed and would never know what he missed. The Indian band was utterly intimidated by the crowd's behavior (which may have accounted for their repetition of this palliative number), particularly that of an octogenarian couple seated just below the bandstand, who, although formally attired and of respectable mien, kept lashing out at each other under their table with viciously well-placed kicks to the shin and groin. "I've ruined my *life* with you!" the old woman would scream, sobbing into her arm. A tiny human being, barely five feet tall and emaciated, she had the toe of a Lou Groza. "You shit," her husband would moan, "you're going home with *me!*" Another customer, oblivious even to this, raced about the barroom in a shovel-faced stupor cursing staff, band, and anyone else who would not turn away. A good fight would have aired the place, but frustration was too thick for direct physical action. There could be only words. On top of all else, the covered wagon motif had been carried to the bar's interior. Canvas had been hung across the ceiling and was cinched up with steel ribs, the whole producing an effect not so much like the inside of a wagon, but of some mammoth large intestine . . . complete with peristaltic contractions and dilations regulated to a windblown "sail away with me" rhythm, sucking the customers along. Each of us was aware of this in our own way, and I am convinced it contributed largely to our behavior. I stayed in the Covered Wagon for five or six drinks and several out of tune sets, to stumble out finally around two a.m. with the old couple and one of the bouncers.

Why remain as long as I did? Why endure that kind of humiliation? Other bars were in walking distance, I didn't *have* to stay. The Covered Wagon held some fascination for me, had awakened some guilt instinct for social masochism that I am unable to name. A saloon I had researched earlier that afternoon—Andy's Friendly Bar on Third Street, Langdon—hadn't proved much easier on the nerves. But a crucial difference urges me to mention it in passing. Langdon's central business thoroughfare consists almost entirely of honky-tonks and saloons, crowded to an unnatural degree of daylight hustle and bustle. Third Street fairly explodes with both vehicular and pedestrian traffic, and Langdon being not a large town by anybody's standard, the feeling of activity is sharpened. In fact Third Street is so wild it called to mind nineteenth-century photographs I have seen of Cripple Creek, Colorado, and Idaho City, Idaho, shot at the peak of their mining hysteria . . . indeed, of Virginia City, Nevada, when by official tally of 1876, over 140 retail liquor establishments were found to be doing business over the Comstock Lode.

I picked Andy's Friendly Bar from its mates with my usual flair for realizing the exceptional, though there was little exceptional about Andy's exterior. The name was writ large in hand-painted letters across Andy's front window and I could see old men clustered about tables which partook of that light. Old men are a constant for choice mid-afternoon bars. A good bar always shows its stable of garrulous old men in the early afternoon. They represent order and tradition. Not that one doesn't wish the company of younger men and women; they are *crucial* at other hours—for they represent everything to be done, what has been doing today, and the mysteries of future and time-out-of-time. But old men are your most compelling barmates in early afternoon. They are the world's true romantics. They are what has been done *yesterday* and they love to tell stories. The life of a fine romantic mind is rarely more than twenty years, and matures around ten. It's tough to beat an old man of, say, seventy-five. He is prime entertainment.

A cloud of thick North Dakota dust followed me into Andy's; several oldsters near the door coughed and spat at the wooden floor. I took a stool at Andy's bar: a nice Victorian affair with turn-of-the-century back bar, big mirror, Doric columns, sturdy entablature

. . . the works, but in fairly poor shape. The bartender served me a 25-cent draft, and I asked him if he knew any other old bars in the neighborhood. His expression softened; I thought he might smile.

"Folks are hard on things," he said. "Ain't much that lasts." In fact, Andy's had the only old back bar he knew in the northern part of the state. "Farmers up here are rough," he grunted. "When they go to town drinking, want something modern to rest they elbows on. Plastic. With colored lights. And government people never did care for nothing."

"Government?" I asked.

"Certainly. What you think?" He stared at me. "It's that ABM." I must have looked startled. He did smile then.

"We're smack in the heart of missile-silo country." He laughed; then his eyes narrowed. "You didn't know?"

I shook my head. A man standing next to me, neither young nor old, touched my shoulder and offered to buy a drink. I accepted. The bartender's remarks had left me wobbly. There was something so obvious in what he'd said—for I *must* have known the geographical center of the continent would be where the missiles hid —and so full of simple truth, like every death message, that my earlier conceit of Langdon as an old Western boomtown alive and kicking in 1972, left me weak from the irony of its presentiment. I felt that numbing terror of the Eisenhower years. It welled up in me like a souvenir from adolescence. Which it was. I remembered to be cranky about nuclear war.

Glancing around the room, I took in things that previously I'd failed to notice. People were all potato faced . . . a result of hard work, hard drink, and inbreeding, I conjectured. But it seemed more than that. Their clothes were rough as East European peasants' and they were all drinking heavily. To a man they were without style, clutched together in groups of four or five, hardly smiling. They balanced on Andy's fixtures, with a foot locked around a rung or a knee beneath a table, as if to keep from floating away. Those at the bar hung on with both hands, staring straight ahead into Andy's back mirror.

The man who had bought me a beer introduced himself as Cal Peters, "Registered Barber from South Dakota." Presently unemployed. He had journeyed to Langdon in hopes of locating work as a part-time electrician's helper, but had been up and down Third Street all morning checking saloons instead. He was fascinated by my search for Great Bars. Particularly great interior bars, those hand-carved Second Empire and Romanesque wonders of the last century, so difficult to find. But I was to be reassured.

"Plenty of them things in the West." Cal sputtered. "You look for old boomtowns. Ones that got rich quick and stayed rich for a time. There's fancy bars in them towns. Still. Hell, I'd follow the wagon trains! Head out on the Bozeman, Oregon, and California trails for a starter. Check out ghost towns, get a goddammed map. Stop folks anywhere and ask em what they remember, whether they know bout any hid away in sheds and such. Follow the Mississippi from ass-end to elbow, both shores. Many a fine bar come up that river. They can't all been busted." His eyes drew far away.

"Lord almighty. If a man had a semi and a few thousand bucks he could make hisself a fortune."

I ordered another drink, hesitating to confess that for the past three months I had followed Cal's plan to a T. Never deflate a single dream in the palace of euphoria; but then never let a man take the upper hand when it is undeserved. I outlined a few highlights. Cal snapped back as if his very prayers had been answered.

"You're an *angel* from heaven. Now, just to make certain, you saw that Bucket of Blood Saloon in Livingston? Where Calamity Jane used to drink?" He shook his shoulders and took a long pull off his double shot. "Montana has *the* finest bars in the West. Dale Evans got a spot in Livingston too, called the '10 & 1/2.' Plus there's the Sport and a Stockman's there that's good. And a Longbranch. Down Highway 89 in Emigrant you saw the Old Saloon, didn't you? And over in Columbus, the New Atlas? They got *two* back bars there pretty as any you'll see, and they got old gambling tables—keno, poker, got all of em. Stuffed calf with dual heads, too. Don't forget Virginia City. That Bale of Hay on Main Street is exactly how it was at the turn of the century. Stayed shut for fifty years or something. They got gambling tables there plus all these picture machines, hand cranked, with beaver shots in em that are the real McCoy. Dirty as hell. But they are antiques. Filmed *Little Big Man* or parts of it in the Bale of Hay. Pioneer Bar up Main Street in Virginia City has the only blind bartender I ever run acrost. Don't ask me how he makes change but damn if he don't. Get up to Missoula, see Eddy's Club. And Butte, there's a hellbuster town if ever I seen one. Check Luigi's One Man Band and his House of the Dancing Dolls. Will bug your eyes right out, that dance of the dayglo spiders is a *miracle* to behold. Whole bar's rigged with mechanical insects and when Luigi starts to play every one of em dances in time. Get to Dillon before daylight and go in the Moose. Don't ask for Steve Logan the owner, though. Steve's a mite rough. Likes to dress in black, wear a black hat with a silver band, and carry a gun. Mostly for show. But few years back some fellow put a quarter in the jukebox after Steve had rung last call, and Steve shot him dead. Spent two years inside for that, but . . ."

Of course I had heard it all. And researched every bar Cal named in Montana plus a hundred others to boot. Cal seemed to sense this. He slowed his rambling for a gesture toward the street. "These people ain't like us," he proclaimed, lowering his voice. "They'll do anything in this world for a buck. It's in the blood. They been scratching and pulling since this land was settled. Now it's winter wheat deals with Russians and ABMs nobody understands and quick cash in the pocket. Seasonal wages, just like always but ain't nobody wants to face that. I could not live in this country. Say I find work, it'll be one or two months and so long." Cal jabbed me in the short ribs, swiveling to face the room.

"*Look* at these people. Only past they got is what's set up for business in this barroom." His toe beat angrily against Andy's brass rail. "And they'd tear that apart if you give em half a chance."

I wasn't sure I agreed. On the contrary, physical facts of Andy's— its bar and back bar and card tables in the sunlight—were the only obvious reasons anybody should bother to drink there. They appeared in little danger of being abused. They were more likely to be defended, if expressions and gestures hinted much. And if what Andy's bartender said was true: that people here, like so many Americans, preferred new-and-shiny at any cost to the seasoned dignity of an old bar like Andy's . . . well, why weren't these men drinking up the street?

I paid minimal attention to the rest of what Cal Peters had to say. I was adrift. The beer had left me sleepy, Andy's was overly warm; Cal's voice toxic. My thoughts kept slipping back to a bar I had visited last month: The Montana saloon, on Main Street, Miles City. In my dreams . . . it was always four thirty of a Friday afternoon in Miles City, Montana. I stood at the bar of the Montana saloon, drinking cold draft beer alone. French ceiling fans spun above me, their polished brass blades flashing signs. The oak bar I leaned against and its matched back bar and booths were a hardwood cavalry at attention. With brightwork gleaming: brass spittoons, bar rail, flanges, knobs and handles. The Montana's tile floor had been wiped so white I was tempted to stoop down and lick it. Outside, real cowboys hurried through the city, their cheeks scraped slick and red as apples, shirts starched, pompadours damp . . . the Miles Howard Hotel next door was already fast at business. The Montana's back bar and I commiserated. A six-foot spread of longhorns, cut and set in 1902, drooped from behind the old bar's mirror. A bison's head not far away. I drank deep, marveling at the polished hardwood, shiny brass and achingly bright tile which was the Montana. In the men's room, even brass tubing on the huge trough urinal had been buffed to a high sheen. Other saloons up and down Main Street—the Range Riders, Trail's Inn, Bison, Stockman's and Golden Spur—were brimming with Montana cowboys off early for a night on the town. Soon the Montana itself would fill, wild to the rafters with every kind of Western action. But for a moment there was peace. We stood alone, the fixtures and I, waiting.

Not much consolation for me on a stormy day in Virg's, the wind easing a bit but rain still slicing down in steady sheets. It is bothersome for me to sit here in the geographical center of what was once an entire new world, drinking with people I have little faith in; even afraid of the warheads around me, of energy encapsulated by their form—energy for depression rather than elation. To look at the citizens of Rugby, North Dakota, and dwell upon their lives . . . of what they've relinquished to the shaky stability of copper wire and plastic, of electric eye and magnesium . . . of a euphoria to be reflected in the bleak stares of pastel cattle with Tijuana eyes, drunk farmers with mushroom foreheads, and waitresses who *"wouldn't change one damn thing."* Here the land might be to blame. But I think not. It is in the people's relation to the land. Plainsmen were never meant to be agrarian. They are nomads, by definition. The Indians never had this trouble. They knew enough to move along when the weather got bad; when meat was running out. They lived to follow the buffalo. The miners got out. They lived for something else, and they would follow that. Big farmers will get out when the plastic melts, when the land has dried up and wheat deals with starving nations of the world have started to fall through. Nothing will remain but the superhighways, Delphic sculptorial testament to the white man's modernism, snaking out as turnpike belts of graveled energy bound loosely in tar, atomated galaxies of pure matter which once rushed effortlessly through space and time.

After one hundred days in search of the Great American Bar, I have hard memories to get me through this afternoon. Hard memories and the expensively acquired knowledge that many of America's Great Bars still exist. That if ever I wish to drive thirty-eight miles through Idaho desert–lava at the snail's pace of ten m.p.h. crawling high up into the Owyhee Mountains on a dirt road of carriage width so deeply rutted that my hub caps scrape at each turn, the Idaho Hotel Bar in the ghost town of Silver City will be open and waiting, run by the only two residents mad enough to stay all year. For fifty cents they will let me sleep in the 1863 hotel—on the floor, in my own bag—and if I am thirsty enough to ride in after the snow has come, on a snowmobile, only way, they will be open yet. If I am in Seattle's Pike Place Market after hours, when everything seems dead but the big rats and a few snoring bums, I will know where to duck down to the Victrola Bar or the Pigalle, both alive and rocketing their odd Skid Road ecstasy over Puget Sound, late into the night. If I am in Denver, that most oppressive of Western cities trying so hard to be East, I will know that Ollie's Roundup is the choice for hot cowboy music and a little innocent hugdancing, and (since city fathers tore up Larimer Street, supplanting its great saloons and saintly tramps with boutique groovies and ice-cream shoppes) Johnny Guitar's Rio Grande Bar is a best bet for mingling with what's left of Denver's hip society. In Taos it is the El Patio bar down that certain back alley off the Plaza; I know not to mess with the parrot, nor take my eye off the bartender while he's mixing margaritas. One mile north of Woodbridge, Virginia, it is Hillbilly Heaven for slick country hoofing, and outside of Carson City, Nevada, it's Cal's Saloon for free supper several evenings a week and a reliable selection of fancy ladies from the Kit Kat Ranch next door, one of Storey County's three or four legal whore houses. In San Francisco I have learned which North Beach bars to avoid, sticking to old stand-bys like Vesuvio and the "1232," and down Market Street I know that for me it's either Breen's or the Hoffman. In Fort Kent, Maine, I have learned which Main Street taverns sport the best Canadian fiddlers and where I should expect to be spoken to in French; as in Key West, Brownsville, or Nogales, saloons where I should count on offering some Spanish. In New Orleans I know which curb to squat on in front of which Bourbon Street club, drinking from my own bottle, digging the endless parade of French Quarter demoniacs and soaking up what's left of the best of New

Orleans music; as I know where to sneak away from tourists, for a plate of beans and a beer at black Buster Holmes for less than seventy-five cents, a draft beer for twenty-five cents in that tiny bar with no name off St. Phillip, or a slightly more expensive glass (thirty-five cents) at the Seven Seas just down the block, only bar I've ever patronized with its own ping-pong table. In Kansas City I know to drive directly to Kelly's Old Westport Inn, a cavernous structure on Westport, the oldest building in Kansas City (1837), which among other historical attributes once served the wagon trains as a trading post, outfitted by one of Daniel Boone's grandsons. In Wilmington, Delaware, I may be found at Hagea's; in Washington, D.C., the Old Ebbitt Grill. In New York, Billy's of First Avenue; in Baker, Oregon, Scotty's Tavern on Main. In Detroit I choose my bars where the gentlemen make the cars: Blue Ridge or Savoy, both on East Jefferson Street, shift workers drinking eight hours on, eight hours off, two of the last real workingman's bars of the industrial age. In Champaign, Illinois, it's the Deluxe Lunch, beer and bean soup, and that delicately hand-painted front bar. In Finland, Minnesota, I drink with the black bears, at Bank's Store on the south shore of the Baptism River, two huge German shepherds half-wolf (half at least!) guarding Bank's door. In the center of the Finland State Forest. Near the famous Finland dump. With Bohunic Billy Woods. The list goes on. I can still feel good.

I am trapped by aluminum beer cans, black-lighted chromium and formica for the moment, but the road is out there. The good old American road. What could I do without her? It's wet and misty, my visibility is shot for the day, and I won't be dipping down into Montana as I did just two months ago . . . ramping off North Dakota's Highway 2 toward the Big Sheep Mountains, horsing my car over that forty-eight miles of unimproved road between Circle and Terry, up and down, over ruts, through dust and flying gravel as fat as your fist, a bucking bronco ride at fifty m.p.h. past utility vehicles slowed slightly to let me pass, cowboys swilling beer and waving the cans as I careen crazily by, gearing down their engines as everybody takes a bump, the road cut *into* the land in nose-thumbing defiance of Freeway's cameo skim . . . cowboys working cattle to my left and right, a bisected film set in red bandannas and chaps, men cutting out steers with horses not helicopters, working up a blue denim thirst like *me* for that big evening ahead in Miles City, last of the historic Montana cattle towns. The Montana saloon waiting—

But that, as they say, is another story. Getting out of North Dakota is my first priority this evening. I will pay my check and think but one thought: that there are bars in America I have not *imagined* yet. So. Up off my ass, out of the center; back toward the whole.

IOWA

Donnelly's

119 South Dubuque Street, Iowa City

Despite Cotton Clubs, Pump Rooms, Leon & Eddie's, and Tiny's Tokay Palaces mushrooming up around the country in those first years after Repeal, a few visionaries of the old mind were coming off the lam. Harold Donnelly was such a man. Sometime during Prohibition, Harold had obtained by hook or by crook a matched mahogany front-and-back bar set which in 1859 had sailed up the Mississippi from New Orleans, bound for Colorado. Another set identical to Harold's actually made it, and according to Iowa City legend still renders proud service in a saloon in Central City. As it was illegal even to *own* a bar in Iowa during Prohibition, Harold stashed his find in a barn outside Iowa City, awaiting the inevitability of Repeal. On December 5, 1933, the 21st Amendment was ratified and by early 1934 Harold had his barroom. The 1859 bar with its slim Ionic columns and big back mirror was lifted into place, and Donnelly's "Tavern" soon opened for business.

Harold Donnelly was faced, however, with the same basic problem as his contemporaries: how to attract an old, pre-Prohibition bar crowd without alienating the new. He did not procrastinate. His immediate decision was to *politicize* the place, taking into consideration a burgeoning social awareness of his Iowa University clientele while offering a forum for the old farm and labor set who might not see eye to eye with students on every issue. The 1859 back bar was the kicker of course, for not only did it provide order by the simple magnificence of its presence, but it lent historical perspective to the inevitable clash of ideas to be argued before it. The question of what may or may not have been best for America in the recent past was not skirted by Harold Donnelly with an interior design repressing all painful memories in some formica mantle of futuristic mock concern. That would have been easy enough to do. Just as it would have been easy to let his beer glasses alone, rather than label them "Democrat" for a large draft and "Republican" for the small. Controversy, with other Old Saloon values of individualism, physical prowess, gunfighter shootouts, love of the land, and that long holy trek West were too attractive for even a New Deal Iowan like Harold Donnelly to exclude from his "tavern." He would obey the law, he would not serve on this day or that, in this way or that, sitting down standing up without food or whatever, but damned if he would give up . . . the *feel* of how it all had been before.

Business was good. It is still good. Although currently threatened by urban renewal, Donnelly's is a saloon where poets and farmers, businessmen and academics, men and women, can for example stand together and watch a political convention on television until three in the morning with no more commotion than a healthy argument or two. It has always been like that. The fear factor is very low, for Donnelly's is a saloon where Dylan Thomas ("First hippie we ever had through here") and Jack Dempsey ("Stopped by on his way driving West one year, with two most beautiful girls, they must have been his daughters") could stand before the 1859 bar and drink feeling safe, perhaps not aware of each other's presence. It is an establishment where on any given evening in the thirties, Grant Wood might have wandered in feeling mean enough to trade a painting for a case of beer and maybe one or two extra shots on the house. It is a new American saloon whose spirit made the hop from pre-World War I to the uncertainties of Repeal, without so much as soiling an apron in the taste gap which intervened.

An Edward Hopper / Grant Wood timelessness infuses Donnelly's interior. It is dark, musty and the smell of spilt beer hovers about the fixtures. A chocolate-brown bridge in a sepia sunset, painted on glass, hangs toward the rear of the saloon. Donnelly's wooden booths are comfortable, and Harold serves customers there himself. Dylan Thomas once spent three days in a Donnelly's booth. "Man drank," Harold Donnelly recalls. "Was here in the early fifties. Something to do with Writers' Workshop, I suppose." Grant Wood lived several blocks from Donnelly's. "He died in that house," says Donnelly. "His paintings weren't the style then." A mechanical pool table near the men's room is one of a few modern amenities Harold Donnelly permits. Plus a jukebox and a television, rarely played. The jukebox is stacked with current selections. Quite loud, on a busy night. Grant Wood might have painted many of the gaunt Iowa faces observed any afternoon at Donnelly's mahogany front bar; but on an average evening poets and fictionists, professors and Writers' Workshop types people a more contemporary frieze.

A Democrat, Donnelly's large draft, is the bargain at thirty-five cents; likewise, a Republican at twenty-five. A bottle of Guinness stout is seventy-five cents. Jack Daniels is eighty-five cents a glass and Donnelly's bar whisky (Jim Beam) is a mere sixty cents. Mixed drinks are not popular. They are rarely ordered. Tipping is virtually unknown. "Forgot your change," Harold Donnelly has been heard to say, skewering an out-of-towner.

Charley, Harold Donnelly's acerbic lieutenant of many a season, is more direct. He'll screech at drunken poets on a hectic evening, "Don't you have a home?" Or, "What's the score?" Poets fear Charley and ascribe his wit to a brainlessness induced by World War II shell shock. Charley twitches and flinches, emitting occasional "Oooh!"'s with a puckering of his hawklike features—as if touched in some secret anatomy by an icy finger. Charley is awed before politics, and during the 1972 campaign was simultaneously horrified and intrigued by the prospect of Shirley Chisholm for President. "She'll change your luck," Charley snickered bitterly. Ted Kennedy also appeared to annoy Charley: "It's Kennedy/Chisholm," Charley quipped with appropriate ticks and grimaces. "In '72, he can drown her too."

Both bartenders and helpmates wear white shirts and long white aprons while serving drinks. On Harold Donnelly, with his snowy hair and pink facial tone, this starched effect is disturbingly patrician: sleeves folded twice above the wrists, stern smile, both palms flat and pressed firmly against the 1859 bar, Harold Donnelly is a nineteenth-century, daguerreotype saloon keeper. When questioned about Iowa City's cancerous urban renewal program, Harold is not bitter but insistent. "We're fighting it," he'll say. No one else in Donnelly's likes to face the prospect of Iowa City without its oldest saloon, and conversations swerve quickly to less painful topics. Harold Donnelly calls the majority of his regular customers by name, and doles out fatherly advice or discipline when either is warranted. For poets and poetasters, famous novelists and hacks, farmers and Iowa cowboys, old ladies and construction workers— Donnelly's is the only saloon in America (and Iowa City the only town) where a farmer can be overheard exclaiming vehemently to a longhair: "Theodore Dreiser *sucks*, friend."

The Mill

420 East Burlington Street, Iowa City

The Mill is monument to Iowa City's late fifties, early sixties folk renaissance, even as Donnelly's is testament to pre-Prohibition and

Repeal. Keith Dempster, Mill's six-foot, three-hundred-pound owner, caroms about this cavernous barroom with a harmonica in his ear and a jug at his elbow. He is wont to blow either. Acoustic guitars, banjos, bluegrass hog callers and Italian cuisine are the Mill's major attractions. That, and an ocean of beer. "Our average patron is twenty-five or twenty-six, is or has been in graduate school," Dempster states. And probably plays a musical instrument. The Mill has been a musician's saloon since its inception as the Coffee Mill, on Dubuque Street, 1962. Second incarnation from 1967 to 1972 as the old Mill—more biker/construction worker/intellectual elite than at Dempster's new location, opened in 1972 because of a space crisis that increased old Mill's capacity from 120 patrons to new Mill's 325.

No cover charge at new Mill, though music is the name of the game. Such folky hangovers from the jejune nineteen-sixties are normally cloying to a serious bar drinker, but new Mill is exceptionally spacious; enough so to creep away from performers and stage noise, for a quiet conversation. Food is tasty and inexpensive; most meals can be had for under two dollars. Draft beer is ice cold, under forty cents, and available in either lager or bock. Liquor is not served.

A handsome mahogany front bar frames the rugged drinking section of new Mill—an iron grist mill at one side. An aquarium showcasing what appear to be piranhas is situated along the back bar, and antique guitars and other musical instruments dangle from the walls. Bluegrass and folk–country jukebox; some rock. Dempster is a congenial fellow in his thirties whose easygoing personality and eccentric background—as motorcyclist, house painter, U.S. Steel employee, White Tower chef, bouncer in Spanish sailor bars, promo man in Copenhagen, car waxer in London—lend a relaxed air to his establishment. In no way does the Mill qualify as a nineteenth-century saloon, but its fear factor is acceptable and dread is quickly assuaged.

Outside: Interstate 80 circumvents Iowa City like a freeway overpass, continues through Nebraska in similar fashion until it is slowed and dropped below land by Wyoming's Rocky Mountains. Dip down and off the overpass of Interstate 80, into Iowa's rich, bar-drinking heartland. Route Six, America's longest highway and first transcontinental auto route, runs parallel to most of I–80. Many fine saloons dot Route Six's serpentine course; many lovely nineteenth-century towns. Iowa is a prime bar-drinking state, its citizens friendly, talkative, and minus a sense of either sarcasm or irony. The reason is in the land, I believe—a soft river of forest and field, of corn, grain, and grass. People flow with the rise and fall of Iowa's landscape as mountain people harden to cliffs; as desert people bloat suctorially, driven to excise any or all from powdered stone. Or as plains people stiffen in a rain frozen to incessant wind, opening themselves only with zippers to the flesh—unreliable, wanting lubrication, always half stuck.

Kessler's Tavern
230 East Main Street, Solon

About eleven miles north of I-80, at the intersection of Highway One. A sweet smell of silage and manure; Solon is one of those Iowa towns that pops up out of feed corn and pigshit like some misplaced oasis of wild roses. Kessler's is a barber shop, tackle shop, bait shop, and saloon. Plus assorted hardware. You can buy a twenty-four-hour fishing license in Kessler's (to use at nearby Lake Macbride: fishing, boating, free camping) for a dollar, a short glass of Drewry's beer for twenty cents. Drinks at Kessler's average sixty cents. There is fishing tackle stacked behind the bar: nets, stringers, monofilament, sinkers, camp stoves, and a second-hand chainsaw for sale—hanging from Kessler's ceiling and dripping oil on the cash register. Kessler's has wooden booths, a plain oak bar, with exuberant farmers in field-soiled coveralls and railroad caps, guffawing, slapping the bar hard. Friendly. An old Seeburg jukebox of 1930s vintage squats in the center of Kessler's barroom—a fat red, neon silo. Five plays for a quarter. Hand-printed labels, mostly country tunes. A fine country saloon. The afternoon I drank there, everyone was getting primed for Solon's annual beef festival: farmers sporting straw boaters with white satin SOLON BEEF DAYS legend. Drinks bought for the house. Fishing stories; off-color jokes. Heard the following, from a hoary farmer in black worsted; suspenders, high-topped work shoes, and boater:

"Young feller and his girl was out for a buggy ride. Pretty day. Pretty day in the summertime. As they neared this stream they seen a little boy fishing. Down by a big log folks used as their footbridge.

"*Catch any fish?* the young feller asked.

"*Yes mister*, the little boy says.

"*How big?*

"*Big as your pecker, mister*, the little boy says.

"Well sir. Young feller and his girl both dropped their heads, embarrassed. After they'd forded the stream and rode on a ways, young feller turned to his girl and smiled.

"*I don't mean to be tossin any bouquets my way*, he said, *but that little boy's got hisself a nice mess of fish.*"

Bud's Tap
Main Street, Cascade (Rt. 151, 22 miles southwest of Dubuque)

Cascade is a bitter cold crossroads town in an ocean of Iowa cornfields, all the more bleak for a stark winter cutting. Cascade is tiny. Two principal streets intersect, with falsefront shops and general stores, forbidding as Kansas cattle-town properties in a grade C western. The wind in Cascade . . . howls. Trucks blat through on their way north or south, and what GMC or International Harvester pickups of farmers and farmers and other farmers about on a cold winter afternoon are lined up in front of Bud's Tap . . . the only island of psychic and physical sanity for many a mile.

Bud's Tap is café as well as saloon; that means restaurant-style food, as well as booze. French ceiling fans hang idle over weathered tables and a remarkable back bar of dark hardwood: two Corinthian columns, medium to heavy entablature, big back mirror. Lovely matching side cabinets and one icebox, primitively hand painted. How this staid old bar and its accouterments came to Cascade no one is certain, but Bud's bartender asserts that they have been here "for about fifty years." Draft beer, Schlitz on tap, is twenty cents a glass and the café food is good.

The Office Tap
Main Street, La Porte City

Another fantastic back bar, late Empire, with Romanesque arches, supported by two fat-footed Corinthian columns. In a middle-of-nowhere town. The bar is mahogany and over one hundred years old—bought during the Depression and installed at The Office Tap in 1933, "when beer come in."

Talked with a congenial fellow, in faded pinstripe coveralls, exquisitely pressed and starched, who was pulling Bud draft (cold, delicious, and thirty cents a glass) for no pay, he being retired from La Porte City's rendering works and "not about to give up my Social Security." The Office Tap was warm, barnlike, smelling vaguely of hay, and dominated by the huge back bar and mirror. Younger men played cards toward the rear of the saloon, laughing and kidding each other when someone lost a big hand. I had a couple of drafts. It was early afternoon. Another old fellow loped in, said it was his birthday, and all three of us stood talking at the bar for over an hour—the old men on the wagon, drinking coffee. All the old men in La Porte City wear pinstripe coveralls and starched blue workshirts. It was a warm summer afternoon and it had been raining. The second old fellow, Jack, was a saw and knife sharpener. I showed him my Randall skinning knife, and he was impressed. We examined it closely together and then passed it around the bar. Jack said that if he was home he could get a real fine edge on it. Jack was missing all the fingers on his right hand.

Jack remembered when The Office had five barber chairs in its front window and there were pool tables in the back. "First haircut I ever got was in this barroom," Jack said. The Jinx Brothers owned it in those days, and barbers cut hair until twelve midnight Fridays and Saturdays, and the chairs were always full. Jack also recalled when you couldn't smoke a cigarette on the streets of La Porte City without being arrested. This was during World War I. It was against the law to smoke cigarettes, but of course you could buy them bootleg. "And we did." Jack chortled. "You know we did."

The two oldtimers were upset about farmers dumping hogs they couldn't sell in the river rather than pay three dollars per head for carting them off to the rendering works. Felt the state should pay for that. Finally, the two old men just drifted off.

I ate a cheeseburger at the Tastee Freeze across Main Street. Spicy and hot, cooked fresh for me with extra mustard pickles and onions, by the smiling Tastee Freeze lady. Had an epiphany about a steaming bread basket of America where even the Tastee Freeze food is good and people smile, talk, and give you what you order without bitterness or sarcasm. I watched La Porte City and its citizens strolling through the summer rain in fine humor, considering the rain not a curse to the afternoon but a blessing.

I spotted the old bartender helping Jack out The Office Tap's door and into a waiting pickup. We waved. *Old dudes just looking out for each other*, somebody had said.

Lourdes Store

Lourdes (off Highway 63, about 50 miles south of Rochester, Minnesota)

An old back-and-front bar combination, also salvaged from Waterloo. Marble columns in the back bar; stained-glass inserts for the windowed section of its arch; a marble counter running the length of the back bar. Strictly farmers, it seems, in this part of the state. Fields bisected by dark, unpaved roads. Highway Sixty-three is the only hardtop. There is a mammoth Our Lady of Lourdes Catholic church in Lourdes, with tall Gothic spire, which you can see for miles over the cornfields. Lourdes is a minuscule town—just the church and two bars, with grocery facilities attached. A thin farmer with a gray, pinched face came into Lourdes Store and sat next to me. He ordered shots and beer. We struck up a conversation. He was worried about his credit at Lourdes' general merchandise counter; he paid some of it off, though, because he'd received cash for a few hogs sold. After he settled his tab he cheered up some. "As long as I got my health, I'm okay." It had been rough the previous year. Monday was payday for the farmers, so Lourdes Store was full. The general merchandise was situated toward the rear of Lourdes' barroom. Plus café tables for homemade country suppers. A tall farmer at the far end of Lourdes' bar was telling stories about a card game, and some heavy equipment operator he'd whipped last weekend. Showed everyone his fists. They were chewed up pretty bad. Another slim fellow in coveralls and a green cap passed around campaign literature. He was running for county office; he offered his hand and introduced himself . . . then backed off coolly when I said I was from out of state. Thin farmer next to me told Lourdes' bartender to shut off the television, which was rolling over a high volume rerun of *Star Trek*. Old bartender grunted and cursed the machine, referring to it as "the radio." Lourdes' church was a big brick job, of cathedral proportions.

Straight across the street from Lourdes Store. And highly visible from the front bar. A cathedral and two saloons: you could tell right off Lourdes was a holy spot.

Anchor Club
Le Claire (off Highway 67)

Right *on* the Mississippi, where Interstate 80 crosses, east of Davenport. A man can squat on Anchor's dock, next to motor boats and Skelly pump, and dangle his feet in Mississippi River water. Ceremoniously. Le Claire is Buffalo Bill Cody's birthplace and an early taste of wide open spaces after Chicago's schizoid cloverleafs and Turnpike Oases. The Anchor Club is one of the first bars where you can get Grain Belt Premium beer, Midwest's finest. The Anchor has a more formal outdoor terrace, but most travelers prefer Anchor's old plank dock on a warm summer day. Wild ducks swim near shore. The view is spectacular: I-80's tall bridge against the sky, stumps and niggerheads in a lazy current, that vibrant expanse of red and orange which is the Mississippi River at sunset.

The Anchor has a vacationland feel to its interior design; nothing impressive, but comfortable. Rock music from live bands on the weekends for a dollar cover. But hit Anchor on a soft summer afternoon. Bartender there on my first visit was a young fellow just out of the Army. Had completed a cross-country motorcycle jaunt the previous week. We compared notes. Sat outside on the dock in broken deck chairs, radio low, and drank ice cold Grain Belt.

Other bars in Le Claire: The Greentree, The Cody Inn, The Viking—are on Cody Road (Highway 67) and right on the Mississippi. They are all old, they are goodtime bars with a modest fear factor, and quite lively. One could do worse than to spend a summer weekend in Le Claire. A paddle-wheel steamboat rests onshore, in the center of town, near Le Claire's free campground. The campground is beautiful, directly overlooking the river and fifty yards or so from bars and restaurants.

The Cody Inn is physically the most impressive Le Claire saloon. It has a handsome wooden front bar with a large photo of Buffalo Bill behind the back counter. It has restaurant facilities with tables overlooking the river. The restaurant area doubles as dance hall on weekends, with its polished hardwood floor. Drinks are reasonable—in the dollar range, beer around fifty cents. A rough, outdoorsman feel to the Cody. Le Claire's finest.

WISCONSIN

Denniston House Bar

Cassville (one block off Rt. 133, the Hiawatha Pioneer Trail, on the Mississippi River—33 miles south of Prairie du Chien)

The Denniston House has been in continuous operation as either hotel or bar, or both, since 1854. It is an imposing, red brick structure of Adamesque design, with a wonderful front porch for drinking and dining, and rooms for rent at three dollars a night. A front dining room overlooks the Mississippi; everything is very old and rickety, and verging upon rundown. But with the eccentricity of some crazy country cousin in an obscure Wisconsin backwood.

The Denniston House was a river hotel in its prosperous days, and its barroom was a riverman's tavern. Now the walls are covered with every sort of intriguing nonsense: matchbook covers from faraway spots, madly colored posters, photographs of forgotten personalities, and letters of appreciation from Wisconsin governors and congressmen. The daily river stage is still faithfully recorded on an old blackboard at the rear of the barroom, however. Don Oelke is proprietor of the Denniston, and he is something of a local character— plays bass drum for the high school band, marches in parades, dresses in costume at the slightest urging, and generally holds things together in Cassville, on the absurdity plane. Cassville is grateful for Oelke; despite a beautiful setting and Cassville's exquisite stretch of Mississippi riverfront, the winters are long and things do get bleak.

Denniston's patrons, saloonwise, are mostly hunting and fishing types—stocky men in layer after layer of quilted underwear, hooded sweatshirts, and red lumberjack jackets. They drink Wisconsin beer on tap, a quarter a glass, and gossip about each other's jobs or brag about game they've shot. About four or five p.m. Denniston's starts getting crowded. In the summertime, tourists stop by; some even stay at the hotel, but mostly it's people who know the old bar or stumble across it. As I did.

Denniston's is highly recommended: a unique nineteenth-century river hotel and saloon. Run in the old tradition.

The Burlington Inn
Alma, Main Street, Route 35 (about 50 miles north of La Crosse)

To know Hamm's beer is to know it in Alma, Wisconsin. In the heated front room of the old Burlington Inn, before a riverboat-style back bar, a mahogany front, a toe on a rubbed brass rail, and an ear cocked to conversation: steaming the Burlington's riverfront window; glacierland beyond, wispy and caked, frozen thick to a distant Minnesota shore where the grandfather of all Hamm's beer was sired. Alma, a riverman's town; quite small (barely on the map small), a Mike Fink raftsman's town—the Burlington Inn since 1891, a fine Federal-style building on Route 35, overlooking the Mississippi River: near its broadest north-country girth, its most picturesque point, with high bluffs, with glacier clean breath, with denizens who can handle an icy afternoon. Hamm's draft and the talk. A shot on the side. Alcoholism here is circumjacent to bliss. The coolness in an overheated room of mahogany and fresh beer.

Outside, on February's wasted stage set, a cape of rare albescence was being violated by dwarfs. The dwarfs twisted under dark cowls, working into the whiteness with curved blades. They hunched against wooden crates. Some stole toward miniature tar-papered houses where the snow was melted in six-foot rings and smoke puffed in globs from the dampers of tin chimneys. Dwarfs slid over the ice in full-sized pickup trucks. A dwarf ducked out of a shack to lay an armful of fish lengthwise in an open tub. Another edged his truck from Highway 35 down the bank, on the *pelisse* and across toward the center of the river. The dwarfs' trucks stood tethered to the doorknobs of tiny wooden houses, houses and trucks drawing a neat semicircle about black holes. I lowered my field glasses. From the Burlington's front window I could watch dwarfs dip into the whiteness with lines, hooks, and blades, but I saw no dwarfs' faces, for they held them averted.

There were two other men at the bar—men dressed in fur-lined polyester and high-topped shoes, who spoke with that strange upper-midwestern delivery which is almost Swedish and nearly German; where every word contains an O, an empty center with edges polished smooth as granite, but with a whine at the perimeter, an embarrassed quickness of phrasing that is the hangman's trapfall to enthusiasm. A barmaid served us. We were talking about the river.

"De Soto found it," one man said, "in fifteen-something. Was a Spanish. Joliet and Marquette, Frenchmen, captained an expedition later in sixteen-something, but they didn't run it all the way. La Salle ran it down to the Gulf; he was the first. La Salle opened the river and claimed it for the French. That was late sixteen-something."

"Started in the dead of winter," I interjected. "Dragging canoes behind them. Dragged all their supplies, right down the ice. Didn't hit open water until Illinois. That was 1681."

"And you're headed—?"

"Upriver."

"All the way?"

"I'm antsy about snow. It's bad enough here. I just don't have the gear. Can't afford the possibility of weathering a blizzard someplace like St. Cloud, at fifteen dollars a night. Some damn Western Inn. I'll make it far as Minneapolis, though: Falls of St. Anthony. The navigable head of the Mississippi. It's the best I can do."

"Where'd you start?"

"Venice, Louisiana: crayfish and Gulf of Mexico sunshine."

"In?"

"A VW." The man snorted.

"Thought you were running her in a goddam boat."

"I went to Lake Itasca on my honeymoon," the barmaid said. "Walked right across the river. On stepping stones."

"Schoolcraft discovered a source there in 1832," I said. "He was heavily financed by the War Department. I got a book. He was supposed to fix things with the Chippewa and Sioux. He fixed things fine. Became an Indian agent; picked up a bundle. Some cartographers claim him wrong. Say the real source is Little Elk Lake."

"Bemidji was hell," the barmaid said. "Some honeymoon. The river was beautiful, so small there."

"I never been that far," one of the men said.

"You ought to."

"Mind?" one of the men asked, picking up my field glasses.

"Of course not." The man studied the dwarfs.

"Harry just pulled in a monster," he said. "Fish big as a dog."

"Let me," the other man said. "Good God. We'll hear about that one. That's a fish." He passed my glasses to the barmaid.

"What they catching?" I asked.

"Walleye," both men said. "A sweet fish."

"Harry's coming in." I reached for the field glasses. A pickup backed out of the circle, swabbing itself in condensed exhaust. It sledded toward us.

"Is that right," one of the men asked, "Marquette starting in mid-winter? Camping on ice, and all?"

"La Salle. Yes. Man didn't know what to expect: Indians, spirits, huge river beasts. They traveled with a bevy of priests in those days. All expeditions carried priests."

"Tough men."

"They knew what they thought they wanted."

"I'm going up there. Bemidji, you say?"

"Lake Itasca," said the barmaid. "You ought to go."

"It might be Little Elk Lake," I said.

"I'm going."

The pickup stopped out front. A dwarf got out.

"Harry," the barmaid said.

"He'll bring it along."

Frosted glass doors parted and a dwarf stepped inside. He had a fish under his arm. It was nearly three feet long. The dwarf was close to six feet himself. He tossed back the hood of his sweatshirt. The fish wriggled.

"God, what a fish, Harry," the men said. The barmaid drew him a beer. Harry held the fish out straight, like a club.

We all had a beer. Harry wrapped the fish in some newspaper; it banged the floor under his stool. Harry put his foot on it. He was grinning. Hamm's draft was very cold at the Burlington, and you could certainly not fault the view.

1894 Palm Garden
422 South Second Street, Milwaukee

Milwaukee proved a bitter disappointment until I located Jack Munsell and the 1894 Palm. Milwaukee—beer's hometown in America—host to three major breweries, with thousands of local "taverns" scattered throughout its metropolitan area, seemed void of nineteenth-century saloons. Downtown Milwaukee had been gutted: one or two German restaurants such as Mader's, Karl Ratzsch's, and the John Ernst Café possessed bars, but they were either high voltage tourist or local burgermeister. John Ernst's (1878) had a long mahogany front bar, fine Andeker, Schlitz and Schlossbraurerei on tap; its walls were paneled in yellow oak; a back bar, reminiscent of Berg-hoff's in Chicago, framed hand-painted murals—but draft beer was a dollar a glass and clientele decidedly upper-middle crust. The "hip" bars downtown, such as Gatsby's and Safe House, were plasticly pretentious. Officials at the Schlitz Brewery were of little help. Even the several executives at the German bar Schlitz maintains for its staff and guests (in the bowels of Schlitz fortress, high above Milwaukee) could not conjure up any old saloons. Ironic, for Schlitz had been one of the leading manufacturers of ornate back bars during the nineteenth century. Today, no one had a clear idea of what I was talking about.

Following a tip on an old saloon out Kinnickinnic, in South Milwaukee, I stumbled across 1894 Palm. Its glass doors were locked, but I could see a beauty of a back bar and various ornate fixtures inside. I beat on the door for a couple of minutes, and Jack Munsell appeared. I introduced myself, told him of *Saloon*, and was invited in. The Palm wasn't open for business. Jack was working hard toward a weekend premier, with the help of an off-duty cop named Pete, and Pete's son. There was junk strewn everywhere. But what junk! The back bar was red mahogany, stripped to bare wood, carved, with a long entablature, handsome cabinets, and a big back mirror. "I cleaned that bar myself," Jack said. "Had paint and wallpaper all over it, was a mess." A mahogany front bar, scarred and brutish, stood before its mate. Paddle fans overhead; wainscoting; bentwood chairs. "We were open for quite a while and you couldn't top the antiques we had," Jack said. "But we closed last year. Owner sold everything out from under us."

The Palm had been operating as a bar since the thirties; it was a long cavernous place, corners stacked with odd junk, ladders and power tools underfoot, chaotic. Jack Munsell seemed concerned about historic preservation in Milwaukee, although he didn't speak of it as such. "Old bars?" He smirked. "Torn practically all of em down. You're in historic Walker's Point, South Milwaukee, a neighborhood famous for its Mexicans, bikers, and redneck factory workers. It's tough, but there's saloons left. No wonder they didn't tell you downtown. Nobody'd know. There's Sail & Rail, there's Terzan's, hell, there's Tony's next door. Our fixtures have been around Milwaukee for some time. The old bar is 1894; cabinets from that same period. This standup mirror came from the Ferber mansion—sure, they tore it down. I got pool tables and one or two pinball machines here because I'm trying to make it as a hip saloon. We'll have bands on weekends, maybe charge a cover then, but at no other time. I'm selling Coors for a dollar a can, Schlitz and Heineken on tap for thirty-five cents. It'll be a decent spot. We keep a good clientele."

Terzan's
Corner of First and Florida, Milwaukee

Terzan's is a Library of Congress saloon photo come to life. It is probably the most original pre-Prohibition saloon I have found in America. A factory worker's spot, it is peopled by whiskery old gents in painter's whites, welders in striped coveralls, and portly foremen in green twill. There are no women at Terzan's. It is a grimy old saloon, though formal as Buckingham Palace. A short beer can be had for twenty cents, a can of Schlitz for fifty, and home-made soups and chilis are forty cents a bowl. There is a scarred front bar at Terzan's, matched by a somber back piece with Corinthian columns, heavy entablature, and wide back mirror. Tile floors are dirty of a weekday afternoon, and Terzan's spittoons are very much in use. I sat at one of the wrought-iron-based tables and sipped a beer, admiring the matched cabinets, tin ceiling, and antique Wur-litzer which comprise the remainder of Terzan's effects.

A grayhaired man in a white apron sauntered out of Terzan's kitchen, wielding a stiff broom. He began sweeping at the old Wur-litzer, working his way doggedly toward the bar. I stopped him at my table and inquired about the saloon. "Terzan's my name," he said. "Been open since 1916. There was a saloon here since 1912, but my family didn't run it. That back bar was old when we got it in 1916. I couldn't say when it was built. We cater to a working crowd, just like always. We don't change. There's no reason to change. The cabinets we've had a long time. Got several others in the kitchen. Old chairs, bentwood, they're original. No, we don't change. Not much. No reason to."

Mr. Terzan had a proprietary air about him that was sobering. No one stiffened as he swept toward the bar, but conversation dropped a decibel and heads nodded in greeting. Mr. Terzan reminded me of Harold Donnelly of Iowa City. The same dignity, same stubborn authority. I felt comfortable at Terzan's saloon, warm and well or-dered. What more?

Jack's Tap
First Street, Walker's Point, Milwaukee

Old Jack was screaming at a Mexican boy seated near the window side of his bar when I walked in. Something about blacks. Something about segregation, something the Mexican kid couldn't handle. He had a short glass of Seagram's and ginger on the bar before him and was having trouble keeping up with Jack's tirade. Jack drew me a short beer, paddled off the foam, and took twenty cents from my change without slowing. Finally the Mexican couldn't stand it any longer and tossed off his drink. Jack was still ranting as the kid hurried out.

Jack's a toothless old geezer with a full belly and two or three strands of gray hair pasted across his scalp. I let him simmer down a couple of minutes before I started in with the questions. Old Jack and I were the only people in his place. I had spotted Jack's Tap from the street, after an abortive visit to Sail & Rail over on National (heavy midafternoon fear factor, ethnic hostility, a bit much). Jack's had looked like a find, and I'd not been disappointed. A huge Exposition-style back bar stood along one side of the old barroom, matched by a long mahogany front bar. They were in fairly good shape and were flanked by several heavy oak card tables—rare ones, with mug-sized slots at the side, to cradle your beers. The rest of the place was austere: no phone, no jukebox, just a portable TV near the back bar. Jack's was in a waterfront/railroad neighborhood, and the old barroom had the look of a clearing house. Jack harrumped around for several minutes more, but I eventually got him talking.

The old saloon had been in Jack's wife's family since 1925, and had served near-beer and bootleg whisky throughout Prohibition. Jack acquired the business in 1935 when he bought the antique back bar from his father, who was putting a new bar in his establishment. The recollection of this prompted a long monologue from Jack about the quality of craftsmanship in bar fixtures, and how everything had deteriorated. "Some of the finest men I knew were wood carvers for breweries," Jack said. "They were craftsmen, artists. Hell, as much an artist as your sculptor or painter. The breweries employed hundreds of em in the old days. Carved all those back bars by hand, put em in for free at a saloon if you bought their beer. Look at that mahogany." Jack spat, reaching up to finger a molding. "That wood will last! Try an buy a piece of mahogany in a lumberyard today, man'll stand there and laugh at you."

Jack wandered off, shaking his head. I sat alone in the old barroom for a time. The fixtures were well worn, some of them shabby, but excellent company. A middle-aged woman, whom I took to be Jack's wife, came out of a back room. She smiled, and I asked about the card tables. "You should see people try and buy them off us," she said. Then we talked for a while about old saloon life. I finished my beer, some other folks wandered in; Jack emerged from the back room, joking started, and I left.

Stewart's

2900 Kinnickinnic Avenue, Milwaukee

"An old people's saloon," according to Stewart's bartender, but on the afternoon of my visit young fellows were crowded up to the bar, one gimpy, carrying a cane and wearing a Harley Davidson jacket. The old saloon is in an 1891 building (Queen Anne style), a brightly lit corner spot with an overdose of cheer. The front and back bar set is original cherry—carved after the English pub fashion, very thin, very light. A short bock beer can be had at Stewart's for fifteen cents. Dab and Pabst are on tap. Comfortable formica tables are spaced about the barroom, and the jukebox is tastefully stocked. Stewart's is *clean*, almost compulsively so. The front bar and matching cigar cases gleam with fresh polish. What metalwork there is at Stewart's shines brightly. The old tile men's room sparkles with German elbow grease.

MINNESOTA

Triangle Bar
1822 Riverside Avenue, Minneapolis

Near the falls of Saint Anthony, on Minneapolis's west bank, the Triangle is a last-stop Mississippi saloon on the navigable inland waterway—an island of insanity in a 1970s, formica shitstorm. The Triangle Bar is *literally* an island: a nineteenth-century, flatiron building on a contemporary traffic triangle, in the heart of Minneapolis's *vieux carré*. The architecture is almost French in this quarter: wrought-iron balconies, a New Orleans closeness to the houses; galleries, bookstores, pottery shops, and the like. Minneapolis's hip community has migrated across river from Fourth Street since the early 1960s when Bob Dylan lived at Sigma Alpha Mu in Dinkytown and performed at the Scholar coffee house. Patrons at the Triangle Bar, however, seem to have regressed back to their 1940s cultural roots, in some very pleasing ways.

The long hair is there; flashy clothes, rock on the box, drugs in the pocket—but entertainment at Triangle, on evenings I attended, was classic 1940s jazz, straight up the river from New Orleans, with modest sidetrips to Chicago, Kansas City, New York, Denver, and San Francisco, via audible osmosis and the pages of Jack Kerouac. A roadhouse tenor man at the Triangle—blind and crippled, white of skin but with soul black as swamp-wet riverbottom—blew Lester Young and Charlie Parker (with hits of Boots Randolph) until Triangle threatened to expire from the dancing disease. Everyone in black motorcycle garb or short sequined skirts; a Neal Cassady punk with gold ring in his ear, waist-length blond hair, screamed about some Cajun woman he'd left three days earlier in New Orleans (at the Seven Seas, I'll wager) and pumped through ultra-weird ballet with a zonked-out, skin-and-bones black chick . . . bumps and grinds, she dipping to the floor until her dress split up the side, jiving to this incredible tenor man, in black lace underwear and stacked heels. Some folks danced alone, some folks snapped their fingers in zoot-suit solemnity; some on the make, some on the nod. Some just physically reacting to the whole scene—*pulsing* like amoebae.

Beer at the Triangle is fifty cents a bottle. Drinks around one dollar. There is no cover charge, and the bands are sometimes rock. Jazz is often played at the Triangle, and it is always a success. Midwest bars are the loosest in America, and Triangle is a great Midwestern bar. An old saloon-style interior to the Triangle: crusty wooden bar, crusty floor, crusty walls, and a ceiling that is dimly lit. A stage to one side. All very pleasant; a modest fear factor . . . just enough to keep things interesting.

Artists, musicians, writers, actors, and hangers-on of the Riverside/Cedar Avenue clique call Triangle home. A group which has mellowed in Minneapolis, having enjoyed an underground reputation for years as a very hip concern. But . . . this forties madness! Everyone free-form lindy hopping, jotting crazy poems in spiral notebooks, scat singing—*great* chaos in this aging Minnesota saloon, an oceanic peace to it, simultaneously ennervating and invigorating.

Viking Bar
Riverside Avenue, Minneapolis (across the street from the Triangle Bar)

A milder version of the Triangle, for conversation and quiet socializing. Drinks are cheap, the aisles crowded with patrons dressed in heavy lumberjackets and fur-lined leathers. Comfortable wooden booths and tables. A counter-top bar. Echo Helstrom first took me to the Viking. She had been around Minneapolis's underground since 1959 and knew what was available. You're liable to see anyone at Viking who might be drinking at the Triangle or sleazy five-corners bars on another evening. On the tour.

Bank's Store
Highway One, Finland (5 miles west of Silver Bay, Lake Superior, and Highway 61)

Bank's is a red frame building on the south shore of the Baptism River, smack dab in the middle of the Finland State Forest, miles from any place civilized, and farther north in Minnesota's fabled north country than the average traveler would care to venture. Which makes Bank's all the more attractive to a connoisseur. Bank's bright red establishment sports a Phillips pump out front, a Budweiser sign on the roof, and a Grain Belt Premium sign over the door. One hundred yards up the hill, ten or so large black bears can be seen lolling about the Finland garbage dump. They tend to ignore a car's headlights and can be safely observed from a sturdy vehicle any evening after closing at Bank's.

Which is not nearly so early (midnight, on the average) as one might think for an establishment which serves only 3.2 beer. A carved wooden plaque outside Bank's reads: "Get Your Burning Permits Here—State Fire Warden." Bank's parking lot is usually full on a Saturday afternoon in summer . . . with four-wheel drive wagons and dusty pickups, lovely hand-fitted, wooden canoes strapped to their roofs. Two terrifying German shepherds, certainly crossbred with timber wolves, stand sentinel at Bank's front door. Strangers are hesitant to venture near these tall gray beasts, but the bartender at Bank's snuffs noncommitally when any question of their viciousness is raised.

Inside, a plain formica counter and tables serve Bank's beer-drinking customers. Beer is cheap—thirty cents a glass, and sandwiches are for sale. Antique axes and other frontier tools adorn Bank's walls; there is polka music on the jukebox. Patrons at Bank's are friendly— friendly as people in northern Minnesota can be. They are largely of Swedish and Finnish ancestry; the men are tall, broad of shoulder and wide of girth; and the women are hawk-nosed or dough-cheeked. Most people in Finland work at the Northern Reserve Taconite Plant in Silver Bay—some do odd jobs at Tettegouche, a 15,000-acre, private estate nearby. Bank's is a rough bar. Not *mean* rough, but rough in the sense of "roughing it." Patrons are customarily taciturn, but Bank's 3.2 beer does get them laughing and dancing to an occasional jukebox polka. Bank's is a sportsman's bar, where sports men and women congregate to drink before, after, or instead of the hunt. Bank's is therefore recommended for maximum liveliness on a Saturday afternoon or evening. And beware of black bears near the parking facilities.

Jack's Place

311 Second Street, International Falls

International Falls is an American border town, a place for getting away with things. The crossing, changing; redistribution of lives.

Jack's is an American bar quite close to the border—railroad yards, a paper mill, and the gloom-drenched Rainy River. Jack's is a spiritual embarkation point and psychic detention center. It smells bad. Indians slouch whine piss in wooden booths toward the jukebox/pinball rear of Jack's Place; a sulfide rot wafts through Jack's front door from the paper mill across Second Street. Sulfide gas, in cahoots with honest piss and old beer, gives Jack's an olfactory distinction.

Still, there is quality to Jack's. A long wooden bar stands to the right as one enters. It is a handsome bar. Minnesota cowboys slug back double shots of port wine with twenty-five cent beer chasers, and music on Jack's jukebox is uptempo border-rock. Loud, and with a Nashville twang. Rosey is Jack's fattish, forty-year-old barmaid who has worked Second Street longer than she cares to recall. To her Jack's is a kind of home, and the regulars are "family."

Indians seem to be treated respectfully at Jack's. Which is not always the case elsewhere in International Falls. One notices Indians outside of liquor stores and bars, nodding off, loaded, black, and desolate as their Eastern counterparts. Younger Indians drink at Jack's Place. Sixteen- or seventeen-year-olds. One supposes they possess IDs. An Indian girl staggered to Jack's front bar as I was drinking with Rosey, and ordered "pigs' feet all around." A cowboy sauntered to purchase a bag of Mail Pouch, recognized the girl and said, "You snockered, kid?" A news item kept flashing across Jack's TV screen about a Minneapolis woman who had been kidnaped by masked abductors, held for a one-million-dollar ransom, and chained to a tree in the woods outside Duluth. Jack's Place is rough; and drunken Indians in the corner babbling, or comatose in the street out front, do not ameliorate Jack's fear factor.

Stupidly enough, Jack's encapsulates some specific essence of International Falls. Jack's Place is not physically unattractive: photographs of Gibson Girls hang in wormy frames behind the bar; the wooden fixtures at Jack's are venerably handsome. Rosey fears Jack's will soon be lost to urban renewal, however. "They can't stamp it *all* out with bulldozers," Rosey reflected. "They can tear it down, but they sure as hell cannot stamp it out."

Outside: Warroad. The mood one enjoys on a satisfying automobile trip (transcendent, hypnotic, tuned-in) is identical to that experienced in a Great Bar. One *wears* the car as one wears the bar. The car is our extra hide; it embraces the most complicated part of our

American soul. We know that. One remains stationary in a car, yet one is in motion—one enjoys the concept of "destination." In a Great Bar one wears the music, the people one is with, the fixtures; even the room.

For Americans there are really just cars, chemicals, sound waves, and geo-historical locations. Geo-historical locations are places where people once were very brave or enjoyed a good time. The essence of bravery or good time lingers—like sound waves in the universe, Caesar's voice. It never dissipates. The soul of bravery or good time hides and sleeps in artifacts, like road signs, Civil War relics, and Great American Bars. Its *métier* is motion.

We ride the turnpike like a conveyor belt of light; above it our tires barely touching, but within it, trapped by our car skins speeding through radio static and rain, until time becomes whole and stops. We are driving *above* the land, and it escapes us. We hurtle through space on/in our conveyor belt of atomated particles, from city to town, from history to history, without locating a past. In this bar? Here? This woman or man? This decayed rock garden of American skyscrapers? Were our mothers ever here? In better times?

NORTH DAKOTA

Andy's Friendly Bar
Third Street, Langdon

Andy's sports a seventy-five-year-old Romanesque back bar, with matching mahogany front—the only such combination I was able to locate in the northeast section of North Dakota (see First Hundred Days). The bar set is worn, and Andy's Friendly is rough. But loneliness/boredom/dread are quickly allayed. Beer is cheap, drinks reasonable, and ancient dirt farmers deal cards at scarred poker tables in the light from Andy's front window. A hint of Van Gogh's "Potato Eaters." North Dakota's settlers are largely of German, Norwegian, and Russian ancestry, and it shows in the old farmers' faces.

Langdon is a kind of modern boomtown, and scores of honkytonks line its two central streets. There is literally a tavern or saloon in every other building. The Safeguard Ballistic Missile Defense System has been under construction at Langdon for several years, and many thirsty workers crowd Langdon's saloons from sunup to way past midnight. Langdon is also host to the International Bonspiel each February, when angry curlers slip and slide up Third Street in search of the perfect North Dakota tequila sunrise.

A stench of black dust and road dirt fills Langdon, the wind bellows against car hoods and falsefronts—so that a traveler is more than ready to get off the street and into Andy's for a comfortable beer. Andy's bartender is happy to debate Great Bars and the lack of such in North Dakota. Stand up to Andy's front bar, use his spittoons, cock your heel on his brass rail. Anxious, distressing, but unique. Highly recommended: a classic American saloon.

Dick's Place
Cavalier (off Highway 5)

A venerable saloon with ragtag pool table, honkytonk jukebox, ducktailed personnel and crusty fixtures—in yet another stultifying ABM town. Dick's is a touch of the nonsynthetic in a bar-drinking region coated with polyurethane. The tentacles of electronic discontent do not extend here. At Dick's one may procure a cheap drink or glass of beer, indulge in friendly banter with regular folks, and lubricate oneself against the fear of surrounding missile sites. In Cavalier, or nearby, Dick's is the place: morning, afternoon, and evening.

McCullough Footnote

Dear Flint:

As to your thoughtful letter concerning humble Great Bar salespitch, I feel inclined to say a couple of things: First, the principal value of a bar as I see it is to escape media time. You're right about Bar as shrine, so far as that goes. But the whole business has little to do with sex, even Mother/Son sex. As I've said, the basic function of every good bar is to relieve L. B. and D. But the *greatness* of an American bar lies in its ability to transcend media time (i.e. make you forget radio, TV, pop music, newsprint, and the rest . . . by being and expressing the epitome of its environs, whether geographical, sociological, aesthetic or what). In other words, a saloon is *so* Iowa City, so Baltimore, so San Francisco, or New York that the essence, the magic, if you will, of that particular spot on this planet is trapped as pure cultural energy. I may be crazy, but I believe the saloon is the only public or maybe private establishment in any given geo-historical area where we can escape media-barrage; whether that means TV or simple fact of suburbia and Interstate Highways. The magic lives, sleeps in physical artifacts of the saloon—which is why I have elaborated so much on interior design—but is transmitted via motion and the narrative tradition. Which, as all us literary historians know, is *the* valid link between essences of civilizations. Think on it: The Great Bar is the last stand of the narrative tradition in this country.

Second, travel. Or "motion" if you insist. I really believe there is this incredible network of energy cross-circuited over and through the United States. This energy being the highway system, the highway system being this energy's transmitter. Get out a road map of the U.S.—which in reality is a composite of various aerial photographs of the continent. Study it. Look at those Interstates: they are arteries. Literally. Look at Indianapolis: examine the fucking veins and ventricles pulsing around that city. It's alive. Of course it's alive; the entire continent is one throbbing organism, and if Indianapolis isn't the physical heart, then I don't know my anatomical geography. Find yourself a highway, not a two-laner like that one that runs through Taos, but a big four-lane job, preferably without a median. A highway like Route One, between College Park and Laurel. Take your shoes off. Walk across it. Feel its pulse, feel it move, feel its slick reptilian curve, the coolness in the center where it's humped like a vertebrate. Watch rain water run off its back. Nestle down and give your ear to the massive rumblings of its belly. You *know* it's alive.

Ever since travel started in this country—and travel was and is what America has been about—there have existed petcocks along the flow (islands in the stream as Ernie put it or might have if he'd been writing about American bars), which were first resting points for the first travelers who got tired, too tripped out or whatever: so that they felt the need to stop, have food or drink, fuck, piss, listen to some music, pray, or do a bit of dancing. Where these people stopped were signs of a campsite once they'd moved on. It was more often than not an excellent place to camp; so somebody else camped there next time around. You can see where I'm going with this. Soon that clearing was a recognized stopping point. Somebody got the idea to create a facility. The first building was raised; it served as meeting house, church, bar, restaurant, hotel and general shelter from all psychic and natural weather. A town grew up around it. The artery was just outside. You could walk across it, you could live beside it, and travelers siphoned off it every day. These are the holy spots in America. They still exist. I have found them, the very spots where the first traveler stopped, prayed, pissed, drank or pulled his pud. . . .

Yours,
T.

MISSOURI

Kelly's Old Westport Inn
500 Westport Road, Kansas City

People have fun in Kansas City. Fun, because Kansas City is a gift: a jumble of flat gray skyscrapers on a bloodshot horizon after two hundred miles of cheerless prairie. Missouri mule teams, Iowa cornfields, and heartbreaking Kansas towns with spotless frame houses dotting sandy streets. Kansas City works: dirty, once decadent, a shotgun marriage between Modernistic commercial architecture and suburban-style city planning; with acres of lush parks, capricious art institutes, gourmet/gourmand eateries and carefree saloons. Kansas City is the "city" in Kansas, the "our" in Missouri; a crossroads where possibilities collide, turn somersault and mate with kaleidoscopic regularity. What's more, people smile. "Kansas City's okay," a transient filling station attendant admitted, "I ain't in no hurry to change the sheets."

Kelly's Old Westport Inn is the oldest building (1837) in Kansas City, and a national historic landmark. It is a two-and-one-half-story brick colossus, directly on the Sante Fe Trail. A nephew of Daniel Boone once owned the structure, employing it as a trading post to outfit westbound wagon trains. Westport was a boomtown on the Sante Fe Trail during the gold rush of 1849. John Sutter, of Sutter's Mill, California (where James Marshall discovered gold in 1848), was a resident of Westport before heading West in 1846 with a loan and one pack horse. Francis Parkman wrote in *The Oregon Trail*, about this time, "Whisky . . . circulates more freely in Westport than is altogether safe in a place where every man carries a loaded pistol. . . ." In Old Westport's dirt cellar there remain heavy timbers with iron stanchions, where slaves are said to have been chained en route to Kansas, and freedom. For a time, Old Westport sported an athletic ring; patrons could drink, bet, and finagle while watching a wrestling bout or a boxing match. The Old Westport Inn is one of those magic geo-historical locations where a first traveler stopped and others kept stopping; no matter where you drink, sooner or later someone who has been around will concur that "Kelly's *is* Kansas City."

Randal Kelly is a Black Irishman in his sixties, who has been as-

40

sociated with Old Westport since the mid-nineteen-forties. An immigrant who worked as longshoreman in New York before being drafted into World War II, Kelly had settled in San Francisco as a bartender. He found himself seeking employment in Kansas City after the War, however, while his wife, a Kansas City native, was having a baby. Kelly tried Old Westport, and the owner, a former Kansas City police lieutenant named Arthur Brock, hired him. The rest is Kansas City history. Kelly became co-owner; then owner. Arthur Brock still retains a piece of the place, and is honored by all those who are familiar with Old Westport's heritage. Randal Kelly does not tend bar as often as he used to—a son, Randal W., manages Old Westport today—but Kelly remains something of a legend. Robert K. Sanford, a regular at Kelly's for many years, has written in *The Midwest Motorist:* "After having known [Kelly] I happened to be in the Mission district of San Francisco, his old haunt. I stopped for a beer and happened to mention Kelly's name. The man whom I was talking to stood up. 'Randal Kelly!' he said, remembering instantly the figure from years before. 'Randal Kelly was a man who would come over the bar.' "

It is difficult to imagine Kelly coming over the bar at Old Westport today. There seems little enough need. At twelve thirty on a sleepy weekday afternoon, Kelly's is comfortably crowded with businessmen wolfing sandwiches from Kelly's backroom deli; freaks killing time with twenty-five-cent Miller draws; and a stable of garrulous old men—full of beer and outrageous stories. In the ninety-degree heat of a Kansas City summer day, Kelly's three cavernous rooms are cool as a warehouse. There is a timeless, breezeway feel to Old Westport; and zero fear factor. A pretty girl at Kelly's well-worn, but otherwise nondescript wooden bar, laughs at her horoscope in the *Star* and says, "I could use a little love today." The captain's chairs which front Kelly's bar as swivel-mounted armstools are all occupied, but this pretty girl rattles her paper and rotates, laughing. Her barmates don't seem to mind. Kelly's is lighted during the daylight hours by a big front window, but brightly colored beer signs from many exotic places add to the illumination. Kelly's is dusty and rumpled, a sprawling three rooms with photographs of early times in Kansas City decorating the walls: photos of former bartenders, photos of ancient cars, photos of sophisticated ladies in evening dress, photos of celebrities. Paintings of Old Westport (interior and exterior) by various artists hang in the front barroom. Some of them are quite good. One in particular, behind Kelly's back bar, shows Old Westport in its heyday as an outfitting post: covered wagons drawn by sullen oxen inch past false front buildings which once endured clouds of Sante Fe wagon dust as Old Westport's neighbors. Now they are recollections in a portrait, and the Sante Fe has been paved with macadam. After sunset Kelly's fills further, as if by magic. There is a Christmas tree mood to Old Westport, even in midsummer. Everyone dressed well, rich and poor alike, in whatever their best rags might be. A chaos of jostle and hustle, the essence of "destination" along American Road, is prevalent at Old Westport after dark. That chaos which is balm to a true American traveler—invigorating; promising; suggestive of intoxication, euphoria and hope—wafts through Old Westport like a tropical hurricane.

S. Jack Odell was a regular at Kelly's in the late fifties/early sixties, "when Ferraris and Jaguars lined up outside every night, and you couldn't get to the bar without elbowing somebody rich, beautiful or famous." Kelly, by this time, had transformed Old Westport into a true characters' saloon; and those wealthy Kansas Cityans, who, Hemingway discovered, "did all the things the British did without their 'bloody snobbery' or the English accents," * were making a strong play for Old Westport. And it was something other than slumming. "Donald Schon, the philosopher, first took me to Kelly's," S. Jack remembers. "I told him, 'This looks like a roughneck joint,' but he says naw. We sat down, and an awful fight erupted—some guy getting his head kicked into the bar, blood every place—I screamed at Schon, 'I *told* you this was a roughneck joint, we shouldn't *be* here!' In all the years I drank at Kelly's, that was the only fight I saw." S. Jack had recently quit Macy's and a career in haberdashery. But before that he was "in the dancing business," as both performer and instructor. "My job took me to night clubs and cocktail lounges all over Kansas. I even performed in Miami, Florida, ballroom dancing in night clubs there for a month. But I had to get out. It was ruining me. I became dissipated, alcoholic, lost weight. I hated those night clubs. They got me out of Sedalia, but I hated them. Kelly's was the first bar which ever meant anything to me."

S. Jack, an articulate member of that strange Korean War generation, so often silent, had been a high school football star who suffered the small town hero's fate of losing status after his senior year triumphs had passed. "All my friends left for college," S. Jack says.

---

* Carlos Baker, *Ernest Hemingway* (New York: Scribners, 1969), p. 194.

"I got a job as a Manor Man—you know, 'Ding-ding, Manor Man!' and then up I'd go door-to-door to deliver bread and hustle pastries. Then I sold Wearever. That nearly killed me. Here I had quarter-backed my high school team less than one year before, a true star, and I was reduced to selling pots and pans. I quit. The dancing business got me out of Sedalia to Wichita—and an Evan Charles studio. Then it was night clubs. All around the Midwest. The night clubs in Kansas were all private clubs, because of Kansas liquor laws. None of them meant anything to me. Not like Kelly's. The first bar I ever patronized was a roadhouse outside Sedalia, called Twin Acres. They say your first bar is supposed to nestle into your heart like a first piece of ass. But I never cared for Twin Acres. I went back there once, after I was a dance instructor, to tango and impress the locals. But Kelly's was my first real affair."

S. Jack had stumbled across a Great American Bar, and it had ensnared him. "I first played the Drinking Song from *The Student Prince* on Kelly's jukebox in 1958." S. Jack recalled. "I can still play it today—when I'm in Kansas City and get the chance." Classical music was *de rigueur* in the late fifties at Old Westport; the jukebox was about half classical, and Kelly employed a bartender who late of an evening was wont to perform popular arias. This bartender subsequently migrated to New York and the Met, according to Kansas City legend, where he enjoyed a successful career in opera. Celebrities of every strain have found a second home at Old Westport. Thomas Hart Benton, the famous Missouri regionalist, lived nearby and was a regular at Kelly's. S. Jack drank with Arthur Kraft, a noted Midwestern muralist and sculptor, "who was the first city guy I ever saw wear bib overalls and a T-shirt in public. This was the fifties, and Kraft was considered very eccentric to dress that way. I used to love talking with him. Schon introduced us. Kraft's passion was Freud and he could talk for hours, very articulately, about Freudian theory." Maston Gregory, a Grand Prix driver of that era, was known to frequent Kelly's. "I never saw him, but I heard he came around," S. Jack says. Sean Moore, lord mayor of Dublin, was once in Kansas City for St. Patrick's Day and visited Kelly's. Moore was unable to get inside, however, because of Kelly's huge crowd. He stood in the street for a time, but left before Kelly could fight his way outside to greet him. One supposes Moore took certain consolation from the fact that Westport Road, the Sante Fe Trail itself, had had its white stripe painted Kelly green.

"Kelly sold dime glasses of beer in those days," S. Jack says, "two of which added up to more beer than you would get from a twenty-five-cent draft. We used to buy em by the tray. Kelly knew why we bought beer like that, but he never said anything. It was tradition. He'd smile and wash all those little glasses, fill em back up and not gripe, because that was how things had always been done. His son—Randal W.—cut out dimeies. He was also the one who annexed the sandwich deli. He's trying to ruin Kelly's. It wasn't the same when I went back in 1973. Still a Great Bar, but things had slipped. I told old Kelly about *Saloon,* and he was excited; thought it a *great* idea. Gave me this article for you. Wished you well with your search. You've got to have a man in charge who respects tradition."

Regulars like Jay Nichols, the Kansas City entrepreneur whose grandfather built Country Club Plaza; Tom Devine, Kansas City architect and concert pianist; his partner in architecture, Fred Myers—all still frequent Kelly's; but not with the dedication once displayed. Kelly's today is one of the finest bars in America; tough to imagine what it must have been like fifteen years ago. Beer is universally cheap, in all varieties, and Kelly's sells brands from around the world. Drinks are reasonable, below one dollar, and a Jack Daniels on ice I ordered was generous. There is an other-world, thirties gangsterland atmosphere to Kansas City, which Kelly's translates well. One can almost hear the K.C. sound of Lester Young, Bill Basie, Coon-Sanders, Ted Weems, Alphonse Trent, and Billy Moten echoing through the canyons of downtown Kansas City . . . and flashbacks jostle a jazz fan's memory even in an Irish saloon like Kelly's. Old Kansas City has been chopped up by freeway overpasses; Kelly's operates a delicatessen and dimeies are lost to the wayward wind; but travel is still what Kansas City represents to most Americans and Old Westport is the spot to soothe wandering pains.

DRINKING in a skid row bar off Twelfth Street, downtown Kansas City, I asked a black hotel captain if any jazz spots of the thirties and forties remained. The captain smirked. He patted down his pompadour and straightened his short red captain's jacket. "No such luck," he said. "This town *dead.* Only thing she need to wrap it up is an oldtime honkytonk funeral.

"You heard the song," he said. "I know you done heard it f'you know about Lester an the Count. *Standin on the corner,*" he scatted, slapping a knee of his tight black britches, *"Twelfth Street 'n Vine . . .*

my Kansas City baby and a bottle Kansas City wine. I know you heard that one." He tugged at his cuffs and grimly sipped a watery Seven and Seven. "But ain't nothing left there but a couple raggedy blocks."

Twenty feet of unidentified concrete mushroomed from Twelfth where Vine Street should have been. It disappeared into a vacant lot, backed by rubble and an already decaying housing project. A black woman about seventy years old got off the bus and I started for her.

She tried to hurry away. "Wait a minute," I called. "Excuse me. Can . . . can you tell me if this is Vine Street, where all the great jazz clubs were? In the thirties?"

She stopped, shifting a bag of groceries to her free arm. "Sho," she said, surprised. "Why you askin?"

"I, uh, read about those places. I listened to records of the bands. It always meant something to me, that history of Kansas City music. Especially the nightspots."

"They gone now," she said. We stood quietly, surveying. "They sho *been* gone."

"Place must have swung," I said finally.

"Young man," the black woman said, almost flirting, "it *jumped.*"

The Bismarck Café
410 North Twelfth Street, St. Louis

Eero Saarinen's six-hundred-thirty-foot, stainless steel arch hunkers over St. Louis's historic riverfront, and Anheuser-Busch brewery, like a twisted aluminum poptop. Saarinen's arch is keystone to something called the Jefferson National Expansion Memorial—a three-hundred-million-dollar project to "revitalize" St. Louis's downtown river area through devastating urban renewal and minimal historic preservation. Gateway Arch and the Jefferson project are to commemorate St. Louis as America's nineteenth-century "gateway to the West." What Jefferson project has succeeded in doing is to have rid nineteenth-century St. Louis of all but two or three of its legendary Gaslight saloons. In true to form, twentieth-century style.

The Bismarck Café possesses the Number One liquor license in the state of Missouri. It was issued in January of 1934, when Bismarck reopened after Prohibition, as both restaurant and saloon. Bismarck was founded in 1903 as pure saloon. It has been neither refurbished nor reconstructed. It has survived. Across Twelfth Street, a Gashouse Lounge in the bowels of the Sheraton Jefferson Hotel has Billie Holiday on the jukebox and fake Gaslight plush everywhere else. The Bismarck Café is austere, like one of Harry Truman's suits, or St. Louis itself. Indeed, Harry Truman was one of Bismarck's favorite customers. An autographed photo of the old Missouri barnstormer hangs on a wall, to right rear. There is also a token of appreciation from Edward G. Robinson. It is said that both men heartily approved of Bismarck's famous catfish dinner, a speciality of the house still available, at three dollars and ninety-five cents a platter. Clippings from restaurant sections of national magazines, including *The New Yorker*, hang along Bismarck's walls. Each gives Bismarck's Mississippi catfish highest marks.

The Bismarck is like an old man's hat: formal without being stiff, dark and durable, with an air of shaky disdain. There is no measurable fear factor at Bismarck, unless one counts a nonspecific uneasiness that all this might soon go under to urban renewal. A quiet dining area is situated on one side of Bismarck's L-shaped room, with wooden booths and wainscoting, fresh damask cloths on the table tops and polite waiters of the old school, who take orders with patient indulgence toward a new customer, cordial efficiency toward the regular. But the highlight of Bismarck's interior design is the old mahogany front bar, joined by Bismarck's striking back bar arrangement—with its Baroque cupola, Ionic columns, and bright back mirror. A Michelob draft at the bar was sixty cents for a large glass; and in the home town of Michelob one must admit that the beer takes on an added nuttiness, which may have something to do with freshness. Regulars at Bismarck stand quietly before the old back bar, reminiscing with a mustached bartender or commenting dryly on whatever tourists are on hand from Sheraton Jefferson across the street. The Bismarck Café is the last Great Bar in St. Louis, and in a sense it *is* old St. Louis, in the way that Kelly's is old Kansas City.

Phil's Ye Ole Bar

708 South Washington, St. Louis

Phil's Ye Ole is a continent of nineteenth-century decadence in a crosscurrent of freeways and riotous urban renewal. Phil's is the first-floor saloon in an ancient river front hotel, on a tiny block of rubble—the last bastion of ratty disrepair on the banks of St. Louis's Mississippi. Phil's is a workingman's saloon, with rough oldsters lined up before an old front and back bar set, joking and slapping their legs to keep away the cold. Phil's is sporadically heated, and every so often an oldtimer will excuse himself from his comrades and shuffle to a hot air register. Shots of bar whisky are fifty cents a glass, so that is another alternative. Cold Bud and Michelob are on tap, twenty-five cents a glass, and the old men kid each other about beer runs and whether so-and-so can make it out the saloon door and down the hotel corridor to Phil's crapper. At eleven o'clock on a weekday evening, Phil's is empty but for five or six regulars in coveralls and thick wool lumberjackets. They stand at Phil's handsome oak bar like stuffed bears; waiting quietly for bedtime upstairs, and a cold Missouri wind rattling broken window frames; or the sound of wrecking balls, a crash of heavy machinery, and dust in the throat which no quantity of Anheuser beer from fancy Mansion House bars or Stouffer's Riverfront Inns in the Jefferson project will ever wash away.

Broadway Tavern
Main Street (Rt. 79), Elsberry

Eero Saarinen's stainless steel arch is a high-style variant of a Midwest standard—the falsefront building. Falsefront is the *true* gateway to the West; towns don't really start to look Western until that twenty feet of two-by-four planking rises over the stores and restaurants, and one is propelled down Main Street like a good idea, with the notion of progress toward some specific Western goal.

Elsberry, Missouri, is such a town. Near the Mississippi River, north of St. Louis, Elsberry has kept its frontier architecture and atmosphere, and urban renewal has not proved necessary. At Broadway Tavern, workingmen argue over stages of the river; whether the moon affects Mississippi tides, and whether the center of the river is higher than water at its banks. Like a highway. Beer is free flowing at Broadway and inexpensive. There is café service; the food is respectable country fare. Draft beer is ice cold. One can partake, comfortably ensconced on antique ice-cream shoppe barstools. Primitive hand-painted murals adorn the walls. Near the cash register, floral arrangements and toys from Elsberry's Old Folks Home are for sale. Old men sit at sunlit tables, drinking beer and reminiscing about life on the river. Or rough Missouri farms. Broadway is a fine old saloon, perfect for lunch and a midafternoon draft on that long run north of St. Louis.

J. K. Mills Tavern
224 North Main Street, Hannibal

Larger cities by the Mississippi River are dying, like ghost towns along a deserted highway. The Mississippi, of course, was America's first superhighway—its steamboat traffic supplanted in mid-nineteenth century by railroads, and in mid-twentieth by the Interstate Highway system. Hundreds of tiny river villages have disappeared completely, as have many railroad centers. A town like Hannibal, Missouri, would not have stood a chance, but for industrial tourism. Mammoth Interstate Highway projects are under construction, to run the length of the Mississippi—they will fatten tourism—but today, narrow blacktops skirt the river and a few small towns which have survived the past in a small way.

Mark Twain left Hannibal, Missouri, when he was eighteen years old; a boyish departure, as was Huck Finn's, for "the territories" of experience. Despite maintenance and restoration of Twain-related memorabilia, Hannibal still seems best suited for leaving. A bustling steamboat town at mid-nineteenth century, Hannibal today is a sleepy tourist spot—and only small time tourist at that. There is the Tom Sawyer Drive-In, the Becky Thatcher House, Mark Twain Cave, Mark Twain Boyhood Home, Grant's Antique Drugstore, and an Excursion Boat touring Hannibal's river front. All in sleepy fashion.

Near the foot of Hill Street, and the white clapboard house where Twain grew up, is J. K. Mills—a Missouri saloon which doesn't seem to have noticed change, at least not since Twain last bent his elbow at its scarred mahogany bar. J. K. Mills is dark. It is not exactly dingy—but neglected, with the dust of unconcern. There are standard Missouri oldtimers, snuff-stained and chaw-dribbled, who nurse their beers in Mills's midsummer coolness, with the patience and dedication of monks in a Bavarian snowstorm. The old men remain unruffled by an occasional tourist father who stumbles in, sweaty, mussed, and up to there with kiddies and campers and general fidgetiness of American Family on the Road. Mills's patrons ebb and swell about the stranger, making room, then enclosing him in the comfort of Dark Cool Saloon.

J. K. Mills is at the site of the oldest cabin (1818) in Hannibal, Missouri. It has a matched front and back bar set which is a handsome, if not outstanding, tribute to nineteenth-century saloonmanship. The wood is dark veneer on the back bar, of some undetermined hardwood. A large Bud draft at Mills Tavern is twenty-five cents. Food is available, stews and sandwiches for the hungry traveler, to accompany that welcome draft. Oldtimers play at shuffleboard, and there is an air of friendship at Mills which makes outrageous tales come easy. The citizens of Hannibal do not seem to have changed much since Mark Twain's day—old men especially—and it is difficult to disengage oneself from Mills Tavern without experiencing at least one shaggy dog extravaganza, after the Twain manner. J. K. Mills Tavern is still in the grips of a narrative tradition which industrial tourism, Winnebago campers and future Mississippi River Interstates are not likely to dislodge. The river fostered this tradition, and the river still flows, imperturbably, a block away.

ILLINOIS

Cairo, Illinois, the goal of Nigger Jim and hustling Huckleberry Finn—and an important nineteenth-century river port at the conflux of two mighty rivers—today was just another Mississippi ghost town. Downtown Cairo consisted of row after row of deserted brick buildings, with not so much as a diner open, let alone a saloon. Cairo was having racial problems and was likened to an armed camp by a filling station attendant I met. There was heavy unemployment, and the railroad, which had prospered after Cairo's river traffic had slacked off, was shutting down the majority of its operation. Cottonseed oil plants had folded, as had several cotton gins. Unemployment was staggeringly high and Cairo's population was shrinking every year. There was no such thing as a good bar in Cairo. I ate a catfish dinner at the Mark Twain Restaurant and hit some downtown bars before retiring. Cairo's fear factor was awesome. Several bars I was afraid to enter. I called a motel from one bar, mentioning the bar's name as landmark for directions, and the clerk said, "Forget it, Jim, we got no room for you."

In 1842, Charles Dickens had characterized Cairo as "dismal . . . a breeding place of fever, ague, and death." Herman Melville had observed in *The Confidence Man* that "at Cairo the old firm of Fever & Ague is still setting up its unfinished business . . . in the dank twilight fanned with mosquitoes and sparkling with fireflies, the boat now lies before Cairo—that swamp and squalid domain."

Still, Huck and Jim had sought salvation there. I sought the Great American Bar. For each there was disappointment.

Mae's Red Bud Café
128 West Market Street (Rt. 3), Red Bud

There is a redness to Mae's which belies discontent—that discontent being the urge to drink, wherever it may surface—a minor concern, one hopes, this side of diagnosed alcoholism. But Mae's redness absolves guilt and relaxes a Mississippi traveler in mid-jaunt, so that he may move his tortured body a little closer to destiny or Destination, and lube his ravaged traveler's bowels on Mae's comfortable hopper, without terror of disrepute or interruption. Mae's fear factor is that low.

Mae's redness is nonspecific. It is not *just* the tint of her table-cloths, formica, and barstools. Red hovers in the air like a memory of mommy's womb. Or pink bosom. Or a traveler's first cat house. Though Mae's is none of these. Photographs of Mae's sons—one a Marine, one a Sailor—are stationed toward the rear of the saloon. Mae's is a big airy place on a main street corner of a last-century Illinois farm town, and the spaciousness of Mae's reflects that easy come and go. Patrons at Mae's are on the move, for Red Bud is a busy little town. A beer here, a sandwich, soup, then back to chores. Mae has been in business since 1955, but the building she occupies is old and her front-and-back bar set pure nineteenth century. The front bar is mid-century mahogany, the back a light hardwood, possibly cherry, with a heavy digited entablature and four Ionic columns. Farmers take their beers before Mae's lovely bar set at midafternoon; they line up in pinstriped coveralls and blue denim engineer caps, trading news and tall stories. There is plenty of light in Mae's, but not so much that it interferes with the desire to drink. Both Falstaff and Bud are on tap—thirty cents for a large glass. Mae sells café food, and it is hearty homecooked. I sat in Mae's for a couple of hours, nursing a draft and reading, and no one bothered me. Mae's was so red and warm I felt like a slab of roast beef in an infrared oven. My bowels moved, my heart overflowed, and I was ready to head downriver.

The Wittenbrink Saloon
995 State Street (Rt. 3), Chester

Just up from the Mississippi river front, Wittenbrink's sports a mid-nineteenth century mahogany front bar and a modest, locally crafted back bar, constructed in 1937. Chester is another of those drowsy Illinois river towns, more Southern than Midwestern, which has survived the twentieth century. Wittenbrink's saloon occupies a slim building in the center of town, about two blocks from the river. Wittenbrink's doubles as both saloon and ice-cream parlor (not that strange a combination, as many saloons became ice-cream shops during Prohibition) and food is available at comfortable café tables. Younger patrons may enjoy tall dishes of fresh ice cream while oldtimers decorously sip stronger fare. Wittenbrink's is so clean and well ordered it is more like a pharmacy than a barroom. The barkeep on duty the afternoon of my visit could not say exactly how long Wittenbrink's had been in business, "except for fifty years I know of, personal." A card room is located toward the rear of Wittenbrink's, with a friendly riverboat atmosphere. Old men drink beer in Wittenbrink's brightly lit back room, while their nursery age counterparts nag for ice cream and sodas at the front.

Deluxe Lunch
Green Street, Champaign

Deluxe Lunch may be the classiest college saloon in America. Deluxe is college, in that a majority of its clientele is associated with the University of Illinois; Deluxe is classy because it is old, clean, orderly, and run by gentlefolk. Six pool tables, count them, *six*, are situated at the rear of Deluxe Lunch, but shooters play quietly, and there is rarely anything bordering on poolroom ruckus. The forward area of Deluxe Lunch is peopled by diners and drinkers lured there by Deluxe's reputation for fine food—or the simple prospect of ice cold Stroh's Bohemian at thirty-five cents a bottle. Deluxe's beautifully japanned front bar is also an attraction: sturdy oak counter with a hand-painted landscape on its top, protected by a thin coat of lacquer. Deluxe's cabineted back bar is nothing to scoff at: it is glass and oak, a delicate piece of cabinetwork; both back and front bars were handcrafted in 1936.

Deluxe's lunches are famous in Champaign–Urbana. Homemade soups are excellent; I had the bean, sprinkled generously with fresh onions ("Cuts the gas," Deluxe's chef asserted) and it was good as any I've encountered. But Deluxe's specialty is its fish sandwich, served on Friday and Saturday. Champaign lines up four deep at the bar for its weekly shot at those fish sandwiches: generous hunks of cod, deep fried in a secret Deluxe batter. "You get people here at eleven o'clock on a Friday night, in bluejeans, furs, or tuxedos," Deluxe's bartender told me, "all of em swilling large draws and dripping fish sauce down their fronts." Bartender had been working at Deluxe Lunch "since the thirties," and was exuberant when I told him about *Saloon* and my search for Great Bars. For a moment, I thought his eyes would mist over. He summoned his two helpmates and introduced me; they stood together, a sodden triptych, proud to be a part of Deluxe Lunch, and grateful to be documented. My tip was refused with customary Midwest humility, so I bought a sack of Red Man, pretending the change was for that. A sign behind the bar at Deluxe read, WE DON'T WANT ALL THE BUSINESS, JUST YOURS.

Other college bars near the corner of Sixth and Green, Champaign, are depressingly typical. Champaign was a heavy bardrinking town in the late fifties, many sophisticated university clubs with well-dressed Midwesterners in attendance. Murphy's Pub, at 604 Green Street, used to be called the Capitol, and was one of S. Jack's favorite bars. S. Jack had been a graduate philosophy student at Illinois and did a good bit of palling around with a mad philosopher named Jim Zartman—who drank with S. Jack at the Capitol, and built crystal sets in his spare time which could pick up Radio Moscow. The old Kams Bar, now closed, held the American record for most Budweiser draft sold in a month. The Wigwam on Sixth Street, still open, has metamorphosed into a college beer hall of the old Varsity Grill genre, with cheap beer, cheap sandwiches, loud music, dancing, and the like. Murphy's Pub is more of a sandwich spot—tacos and Michelob draft at fifty cents. None of these bars has an ounce of the style and tradition of Deluxe Lunch.

Chicago

"Neighborhood bars are your story in Chicago," Studs Terkel * had advised. And he was right. They are ubiquitous; shiny as copper quarters, dingy as buffalo nickels—and they are nearly all taverns: post-Prohibition fare steeped in chromium, glass, and leatherette. I had nurtured great hopes for Chicago. A 1919 Library of Congress volume, entitled *Substitutes for the Saloon*, had bragged that turn-of-the-century saloon life in Chicago was unsurpassed. That the best free lunches in America could be found at Chicago saloons. That on a typical day in 1901, from 150 to 200 pounds of meat, one and one-half to two bushels of potatoes, fifty loaves of bread, thirty-

---

* Chicago radio personality and author of *Hard Times, Division Street: America,* and *Working*.

five pounds of beans, forty-five dozen eggs, ten dozen ears of sweet corn, and assorted vegetables would be handed out. Brewers furnished beer and food at wholesale prices to the saloons, in competition, to attract beer-swilling customers. They also supplied expensive bars, plate glass mirrors, paintings and other fixtures. Chicago's legacy today, and America's, is the dry-roasted peanut, bulb-lit beer sign and the bouncing neon ball . . . still readily supplied by ad-conscious American brewers. Chicago's neighborhood bars, though ethnically beguiling, are ninety percent plastic. And fearful: "Check the Daley bars in Bridgeport," Terkel has suggested, "where, like Royko says, *heads turn when a stranger comes in*—and he is looked upon with suspicion." I have called Mike Royko * at the *Chicago Daily News;* he's supplemented Terkel's list with several pighangers of his own. But the best bar in Chicago, neither Royko nor Terkel has thought to mention—perhaps because it's so staid. That's Berghoff Men's Bar, at 17 West Adams, in the heart of the Loop. Chicagoans are obsessed by the brutality of their city; Royko has published a column since I've been in Chicago advocating weighted canes as weapons against street crime: one of the most violent essays I have read in a daily paper. Perhaps Royko and Terkel, inveterate Chicagoans, dismiss Berghoff for its peacefulness. Perhaps it no longer epitomizes "Chicago" for them.

Berghoff Men's Bar
17 West Adams Street (the Loop), Chicago

There is a photograph in the foyer of Berghoff that shows founder Herman Berghoff holding the Number One liquor license in the city of Chicago. As photos go, it is fairly recent, for it was snapped in 1933. The Berghoff has been open since 1898 and is the last of Chicago's traditional *brauhaus* restaurants. In the men's bar can be found the closest link to Chicago's famous free lunches of the nineteenth century. Berghoff's sandwiches are not free, but they are so inexpensive as to be nearly gratuitous. A smoked thüringer sandwich may be had for one dollar, and Berghoff's own draft beers are on tap for fifty-five cents a stein.

---

* Newspaper columnist and author of *Boss: Richard J. Daley of Chicago.*

It was Bock Beer time when I visited Berghoff, and the tall brown glasses of double dark were being raised the length of the men's bar. Berghoff celebrates four festivals yearly: Bock Beer in early spring, May Wine, Octoberfest, and Christmas. Each is graced with distinctive additions to the Berghoff menu: dark beer for Bock, spring wine steeped in woodruff for May, special lager beer for Octoberfest, and a gourmet's wonder world of delights for Christmas—roast goose, hassenpfeffer, rehpfeffer and rehbraten. Berghoff's bock was so strong that one stein took off the March chill, and two steins had me reeling. Bartenders at Berghoff are stiff but not unfriendly; they tap and draw Berghoff's bock expertly and are right on target when your stein grows empty. Waiters at Berghoff wear white aprons and are formal, hurrying from bar to restaurant with derby dispatch. There must be twenty waiters on duty at Berghoff, and although the prices are bargain, service has not been sacrificed to trim the budget.

But interior design is what Berghoff's really about. The moment I stepped through the Men's Bar door I knew I had found my Chicago saloon. A sixty-foot mahogany bar stretched the length of the barroom and mahogany wainscoting was omnipresent. It was like drinking inside a mahogany closet. A mahogany back bar, mock-fashioned, framed hand-painted murals of Old World minstrels. A mahogany clock stood at the center of the back bar; stained-glass windows faced the street, and heavy chandeliers loomed overhead. The place was very much a man's bar; although women were legally allowed to drink there, I saw only one or two at a very crowded lunch hour. Berghoff's clientele is largely businessmen, cops, downtowners in the financial district, who want a quick sandwich and an excellent draft. The Wisconsin beer cheese sandwich goes for eighty-five cents, Berghoff's private stock bourbon for ninety cents, so that a man can get away with some change in his pocket. Lunch is the most interesting time at Berghoff; a chef and sandwich lady are on duty behind a makeshift lunch counter, and stand-up wooden tables are spread out around the barroom. Full-fledged luncheons are in progress next door at the restaurant, but the Men's Bar customer usually wants nothing of that and is comforted by the old saloon smell of damp mahogany and strong cheese. At cocktail hour, men hurry up to the bar, shake snow from their hats and begin swilling the famous Berghoff double dark. One or two steins find them quiet, but at a third, conversation ripples out and the bar takes on a cheerier air. Men in heavy overcoats hunch over glasses of beer the length of the old mahogany bar, like cowled monks at evening prayer. Berghoff is a warm place in downtown Chicago, nearly blessed; and Chicagoans are less bitter for its existence.

Billy Goat Tavern

430 North Michigan Avenue (entrance on Hubbard), Chicago

Billy Goat's is a river front saloon near Michigan Avenue Bridge, in the shadow of the great *Tribune* Tower and a stone's throw from *Sun Times* and the *Chicago Daily News*. It is almost directly beneath the Wrigley Building. Studs Terkel had recommended the Wrigley Bar to me, for its journalistic clientele and four-ounce martinis, but Wrigley cannot hold a candle to the Billy Goat. Billy Goat Sianis—a Greek immigrant and 1909 newsboy—founded his saloon in 1934 as a haven for the Fourth Estate. The old saloon has kept its newsman's character and is kind of a cross between the New York Lounge in Washington, D.C., and the Stage Delicatessen in New York City. It is a late night joint, open twenty-four hours a day, with good sandwiches and a boisterous clientele. Hell, it is boisterous almost any hour of the day. But if you want to see Billy Goat's at its best go after eleven o'clock when all four Chicago dailies are shutting down, and everybody's either heading home or lubing up for a midnight shift. Columnists, editors, printers, truckers . . . eventually they all wind up at Billy Goat's. Chicago newsmen use Billy Goat's saloon the way others rely on automated canteens. Mike Royko recommended the spot to me. "Billy Goat was a friend of mine," Royko said with emotion. "He's dead now but the place is pretty much the same. Yeah, Billy Goat's a good one."

The tablecloths are red and white checked, and a thirties-style formica bar angles rectangularly to the right as you enter. There's a small grill and food counter straight ahead, where a variety of standard sandwiches, doughnuts and coffee are sold. To the left is a large dining area, but the heart of Billy Goat's is the old barroom, with its blown-up columns along the molding, its star columnists' by-lines, and pictures of Billy Goat Sianis from almost every era. There is a "VIP" room at the rear, and one wonders if any semblance of hierarchy is observed there. Wise-ass signs and aphorisms cover the walls, plus a few practical notices such as:

PRESSMEN

DO NOT SIT ON CHAIRS
OR STOOLS WITH GREASY OR
DIRTY CLOTHES OR YOU
WILL BE RESPONSIBLE
FOR DAMAGE.

Characters wander in and out of Billy Goat's like you would not believe. One fellow, whom Billy Goat Sianis claimed to have drunk 150 shots of whisky—eighty dollars' worth in an afternoon's sitting—is the basis of local legend. Mike Royko wrote a column about this phantom drinker after he telephoned Rutgers University's Department of Alcoholic Research and discovered the feat to be impossible. When he told Billy Goat his man had died, the Goat replied "No! When?"

"He was dead before he left here," Royko said, and then reported his scientific findings. Billy Goat stuck to his guns, however, and never admitted to himself that the drinker had been a figment. Or Superman.

Everything at Billy Goat's is cheap to eat or drink, but the atmosphere is rare as peacock's tongues. There is an awful lot of chatter, and most of it does not come from any mouth so delicate as a peacock's; but if you can stand the heat come in from the cold and wrap your fist around a glass of the Billy Goat's finest.

Schaller's Pump

3714 South Halsted Street (Bridgeport), Chicago

It was a community that drank out of the beer pail and ate out of the lunch bucket. The men worked hard in the stockyards, nearby factories, breweries, and construction sites. It was a union neighborhood. They bought small frame homes or rented flats. It had as many Catholic schools as public schools, and the enrollment at the parochial schools was bigger. . . .

This was Bridgeport, Chicago's "great and powerful South Side," as Mike Royko so deftly describes it in *Boss.** Bridgeport, into which Richard Daley was born in 1902, a few hundred feet from the

---

* Royko, *Boss* (New York: New American Library, Signet Books, 1971), p. 33.

house where he currently resides as mayor, and only blocks from venerable Schaller's Pump. Schaller's is over eighty years old, but it blends the feel of a pre-Prohibition saloon with that of a thirties tavern. The atmosphere is decidedly small town, for as Royko notes, Chicago was and is a city of small town neighborhoods. Halsted is the main street of Bridgeport, and Schaller's Pump is that local which has served the most Irishmen the longest.

It's a Daley Bar, as Chicagoans say, with clientele and management apparently one hundred percent behind the old South Sider; Daley's photograph hangs behind the back mirror and campaign posters are pasted in the window and along the walls. Schaller's bartender is a smug little Irishman with the radio up full blast, a hockey game washing over Schaller's patronage *en masse*. No one seems to mind. There is good home-cooked food at Schaller's, cheap and plentiful. An old man sits before a spotless white tablecloth enjoying his supper, listening to the game and petting a tiny mutt who sleeps on the chair beside him.

There is a high mahogany front bar at Schaller's, which has survived (remarkably) eighty years of Irish wrath and heavy Bridgeport drinking. Delicate cabinet fixtures at the back bar support a marble counter with a variety of the world's whiskies on display. There is a godawful lot of formica about Schaller's, though; plus leatherette barstools, padded chairs, and photos of the owner's family behind the bar. A tall draft and a Jack Daniels on the rocks came to one dollar seventy-five. Not bad. For Schaller's is clearly the "nice" pub along Halsted, where a Bridgeport family ventures together for an evening out, as special treat. Which is not to suggest Schaller's has no bevy of hard-boozing regulars.

Although I found the old tavern quiet and a bit cold for my taste, I could envisage its hot points. A modest fear factor prevailed, but nothing so dramatic as Mike Royko had suggested. Well worth a stop on any South Side tour.

Vernon Park Tap

1073 West Vernon Park Place, Chicago

Vernon Park Tap is an Italian joint, the pride of Sammy Tefano and his father before him—reputedly Al Capone's favorite cook. "I never asked Sammy about this," Royko confided, "but they say Al Capone set old Tefano up in business."

"It ain't so," Sammy says, "that's been the story but it just ain't the truth." In any case, Vernon Park Tap retains an Italian clientele which, on certain evenings, might have stepped from old reels of *The Untouchables*. Students from the University of Illinois campus at Chicago, whose expansion forced Vernon Tap's move from across the street (where the old saloon had served residents since before Prohibition), are encouraged to do their drinking in an interior room. Oldtimers stand up to the formica bar, cupping glasses of Chianti or knocking back tall mugs of beer. Tables in the main barroom are filled of a cold March night, with rough workingmen, one or two wives, stray truckers and night laborers in for a quick nip or a lasagna to go. There is no sign outside Vernon Park Tap, and if one did not know the place, he would never locate it. Sammy's is that much of a neighborhood club. But when a stranger with balls enough to stand up to Sammy's front bar does enter—orders a meal or demands a drink—he is treated with respect.

Sammy's crowd is boisterous, to say the least. Of the Great Bars I found in Chicago, Sammy's possesses the most attractively rowdy clientele. They're screaming at each other, pounding each other on the back, cursing over that omnipresent Big Game, or screaming at you from the moment you walk through the door. All in mock hostility; mostly all in fun. The food at Sammy's can't be beat for its price. Most dinners are between a dollar and a half and two twenty-five. A glass of Chianti is thirty-five cents and a bourbon on the rocks seventy-five. The food is good workingman's fare, nothing fancy. All the Italian bread you can eat, and that's fresh baked; excellent. There is a fake back bar at Sammy's to match the unobtrusive formica front. Nothing exotic design-wise at Vernon Tap, everything functional and sturdy. Still, the atmosphere of pre-Prohibition Chicago siphons through. Sammy is a tall, goggle-eyed Italian in his forties, who proved cordial, even sympathetic when I told him of *Saloon*. He had a hard time taking his attention totally off that game, though. Damn thing never did stop blaring, patrons never ceased screaming, but that's Vernon Tap. That's a great Italian bar in Chicago.

O'Rourke's

319 West North Street, Chicago

God save us, another writer's bar. Studs Terkel suggested this one and he was smack dab on the money. A coven of Chicago-based artists, working writers, homosexuals, and hangers-on comprises the majority of O'Rourke's clientele. That's what's so strange about Chicago: one notices so few workaday homosexuals. Well, if gay's your action, Old Town's your quarter. Not that the gay population there is any larger than in Greenwich Village, North Beach, or Georgetown. It's just that one doesn't stumble across gays so often in other Chicago neighborhoods.

O'Rourke's is *not* a gay bar. It's Chicago's Admiral Benbow, Donnelly's, Kelly's, and Varsity Grill wrapped into one. A lot of vomit-scented wood for interior decor; an old mahogany front bar, well worn but not original (O'Rourke's was founded in the early sixties, has been at its present location since 1967); posters of famous writers (Bernard Shaw, James Joyce) and other intellectual garbage pasted across the walls; dartboard enclave; articles about the place from local publications; and a community bulletin board.

"Darling, I'll buy the whole bar Irish Coffee next *week,* just as soon as my trust fund comes through," a slim Negrito whines to O'Rourke's bartender—who sets him up to a free beer. Stroh's draft at O'Rourke's is sixty cents a stein; Guinness on tap, eighty cents; Watney's, seventy; Black and Tan, eighty; a bottle of Bud is seventy cents; Heineken, one dollar. There is good hip music on the juke, some traditional Irish ballads, a few South Side blues. The atmosphere at O'Rourke's is slightly frenetic, but not to the point of discomfort. Jesus, it's one of those goddam intellectual bars, with the usual smattering of motorcycle types and frustrated aesthetes. It can get rough. If there is a spot in Old Town which reflects the neighborhood's positive side—a carnival, offbeat self-consciousness—it is O'Rourke's. The room is conducive to conversation and leisurely drinking. One can imagine many afternoons at O'Rourke's finishing as early mornings. I wouldn't fight my way off Kennedy Expressway to get there, but if I were staying in Chicago, O'Rourke's is where I'd probably wind up. Particularly if I were making a late evening of it. A lot of good looking, female bohos; a large opportunity to connect. Cheap beer. Good music. Negative ethnic fear factor. Hip sensibility. Terkel was right. The place is a dump, but you can't pass it up.

Queen Bee
Corner East 74th Street and Chicago Avenue (South Side), Chicago

When the Second World War broke out, everybody left the cotton fields for the assembly lines. The people from the Carolinas and Georgia went to Harlem and Bed-Stuy. The people from Mississippi and Alabama went to Chicago. And the people from Texas and Oklahoma moved to L.A. That's why there were three different sounds in the beginning of commercial R&B. New York had a pop, jazz, nightclubby thing to it, Chicago had the Delta blues and California R&B was a Texas transplant.*

This Delta migration was aided and abetted by Illinois Central Railroad, which charts a straight course from New Orleans, via Mississippi and Alabama, to the Sixty-third and Twelfth Street stations in Chicago. Such blues greats as Junior Wells, Buddy Guy, Jimmy Cotton, Otis Rush, Otis Spann, Hounddog Taylor, Howlin' Wolf, and the immortal Muddy Waters stepped off trains at Twelfth Street station and started picking their way through Chicago's South Side. A similar Black migration can still be seen any evening around midnight, according to Chicago critic Jory Graham, when passenger traffic at Twelfth Street is so heavy it is routed one-way through a separate entrance, rather than into the station proper.

Chicago blues bars are legendary—for their brutality, as well as excellent music. Imagine my chagrin at emerging unscathed from Queen Bee. Cocky little white boy, blond as a Swede, blue-eyed as Eichmann. An afternoon visit to case the spot had proved unnerving: Queen Bee was dark as a barrel at midday; Detroit juke bouncing heavy bass riffs off the walls and ceiling; hog-fat barmaid responding to my inquiries reluctantly; drunken patrons monitoring my every move with hooded eyes. But the sign out front—JUNIOR WELLS, TUESDAY THROUGH THURSDAY—had drawn me back. At eleven p.m. on Tuesday night Junior Wells was not to be found—but Muddy Waters, Jr. instead, with an assemblage of sidemen from the Howlin' Wolf, Muddy Waters, and Junior Wells bands. The sound was un-

---

* Jerry Wexler of Atlantic Records, in an obituary for T-Bone Walker, *Rolling Stone*, April 24, 1975.

believable. There was a lot of black light, a smeerage of dayglo paint and soul sister love-fuck decals, but the atmosphere was . . . oddly neighborhood. Here in Chicago's vicious South Side ghetto, bars were as informal as those of an Irish or Italian neighborhood. The sign out front might have read "Queen Bee Tap—Home to Friendly Folks, Come In." Beers at Queen Bee were eighty cents a bottle. There was a small rectangular bar. The band was situated at the rear of Queen Bee, on a small stage. Perhaps thirty people were in attendance; most of them sitting quietly, nursing their drinks, digging the music intently, or falling asleep. It was a working-class clientele, several of the men in filling station jackets or coveralls. I had two beers at the bar and no one paid me the least mind. One other white man came in about one o'clock.

Other Chicago blues bars (where there may or may not be a cover charge on any given night, and the crowd may or may not be as friendly as Queen Bee's) are: Pepper's Lounge, "The Home of R&B," at 2335 South Cottage Grove; Turner's Blue Lounge, at 4012 South Indiana; Theresa's, at 4801 South Indiana; Silvio's, at Lake and Kedzie; plus Smoot's and Kansas City Red's, in the same neighborhood, under the El.

Fear factors vary with each spot, so exercise caution. Remember, you are there for the music—which cannot be topped. Chicago blues is the scratch and whine at the foot of the industrial ladder; Chicago blues bars are post-Pro taverns which have succeeded in transporting a feel of turn-of-the-century Memphis/New Orleans barrelhouses to the North.

Respect the tradition, as one which has long included violence.

The Midget's Club
4016 West 63rd Street, Chicago

The bar at Midget is less than three feet high. Parnell St.-Aubin does not top that mark by much, and he likes to keep his counter low. A little person can walk up to the bar at Midget, rest his elbows on the formica and say "Gimme a beer," just like a Normal. The pay phone is a couple of feet off the ground, and all the toilets are low. Chairs at Midget's bar are standard width, but the legs have been trimmed to compensate for the shift in bar height. Consequently, seats are only a foot off the floor and Normals have a tendency to sit with their knees up about their chins. Tables around the barroom are lowered; as are the chairs which surround them. The dropped bar, tables, and other fixtures are largely for the convenience of Parnell St.-Aubin and his wife—Midget's owners. The majority of their customers are regulation-size people. "If I had to depend on midgets for business," Parnell confesses, "I'd starve to death."

Parnell St.-Aubin is an old show business trouper, and working stage-front does not bother him in the least. He hustles up and down the bar, mixing drinks, serving "short" bottles of Bud or Schlitz to his regulars, and cradling fifths of whisky in both arms to refill a customer's glass. He has operated Midget at its present location for seventeen years, and has been in the bar business for thirty-two. Before that, he toured with Singer's Midgets: a legendary troupe of diminutives who were on every circus, carnival, and vaudeville card throughout the thirties. Singer's Midgets played the terrible Munchkins in *Wizard of Oz*, and Parnell himself was "the first Munchkin to greet Judy Garland, you know, as she come down the Yellow Brick Road."

"Been in show business since I was nine," Parnell says. "They used to book me as the shortest man in the world, said I was twenty-two years old when I was nine, stood me up in the palm of a ring master's hand. I was Scrubby the Pig from fifty-three to fifty-four on *Scrub Club*, a kid's TV show you probably saw and don't remember. I did a lot of things on tour: sang, played sax, danced, fronted a band. There wasn't much for a little person to do in those days but show business. Now they're all educated. You can't get one near the big top, can't hire one to work in a bar. I had a scholarship to college when I was a kid but I went with the circuit because that's where the money was. My wife, too. We met on tour. Running a bar was the alternative. When Las Vegas was just getting good, after the War, a fellow offered to set me up in a bar there. As a gimmick. But I couldn't stand Vegas's altitude. Chicago's my hometown. The club's a good life. I work hard at it, twelve hours, fourteen hours a day. I got a good investment here. Only handicap, with the counter set up short like it is, I can't unload the place once I retire. And little people won't work a bar now. So it's business for today and today only. What the hell."

Parnell has a habit of shaking his head and *tchh*ing philosophically, with loud suckings of his teeth. He is a fiftyish little man, balding, paunched, with the studied air of a professional barkeep. The

Midget's Club is unobtrusive: a good bit of plastic and formica, everything functional, clean and simple. It's a neighborhood spot, and it is not very long before you forget you are being served by midgets. Normal-size oldtimers line the bar, scrunched down in their seats, knees up around their ears, drinking quietly or joking with Parnell. "Jeez," Parnell will laugh, with enthusiastic suckings, at a story which tickles him. "Ain't it the truth?" Mrs. St.-Aubin is a pretty, dark-haired woman with delicate features and a lilting, high-pitched voice. She is less outspoken than her husband, but friendly. And courteous. No one seems to think it odd that everything is scaled so small at Midget. Personally, the place reminded me of the Thorne Rooms at Chicago Art Institute: a series of miniature interiors which are viewed through glass partitions by Normals, with a mixture of childlike fascination and Brobdingnagian detachment. Other patrons at Midget did not seem distracted by such thoughts; they felt no discomfort at appearing gigantic in a little person's world, and the dollhouse effect did not strangle them. Perhaps the contrast made them feel good. "Little people stop in here," Parnell said, "particularly the show business crowd when they're in town. But my heavy trade is Normal. That's my living. That's the business."

Prices at Midget were neighborhood—eighty cents for a Bud *and* a Coke—and why not, the club is no speciality house. Parnell and his wife are "just folks" to Midget's regulars, their only attraction being their good humor and competence as saloon keepers. There is a jukebox at Midget which plays all the hits, and is itself competent and unremarkable. Zero fear factor at Midget; on the contrary, one is encouraged and departs the little club less afraid.

Helen's Olde Lantern

13301 South Western Avenue, Blue Island (Chicago)

The midgets told me about Helen's, but when I got there next afternoon the place was closed. It was a Victorian brick structure with "1890" etched across a pediment, topping a sturdy neo-classic cornice. Some polished wood and fake lanterns on the façade. Disconcerting. Blue Island was a Lithuanian neighborhood on Chicago's dreary southwest side: miles of industrial swamp, pools of foul water, earth where no grass could grow, empty lots. Blue Island existed as a frontier community on the border of a wilderness more terrible than any in Gothic fiction. Two main streets intersected, the Calumet River sludged nearby and Interstate 57, the George Brennan Expressway, passed overhead with a horrific clang and clatter.

Helen's looked good though, so I banged on the door for several minutes hoping somebody was in. Finally I walked around to a service entrance and snuck in through the kitchen. Helen's back bar was a beauty. Most ornate I'd found in Chicago, a turn-of-the-century (1890) monster, surprisingly Baroque, with Corinthian capitals, columns, Romanesque arches, and an Empire entablature over three large back mirrors. The front bar was mahogany, lined with bright copper coal scuttles, handsome pumps and brass spittoons. There was a beautiful brass icebox behind the bar, likewise polished to a high sheen. Antiques were everywhere. An old potbelly stove stood in one corner. There was an extra Empire arch at the side of the back bar, where a woman with a typewriter and several stacks of receipts sat fast at work.

I told her the midgets had sent me but she didn't respond. I asked if she were Helen . . . no, no, she was the manager. Helen was out and wouldn't be in all day. I explained about *Saloon* and tried with the midgets again. Nothing clicked. She said I could look around but I could tell she was keeping her eye on me. I asked about the back bar. Schlitz Brewery had built and installed it for Helen's grandfather when the old saloon opened in 1890. The business had been in Helen Sadunas's family from the start. Helen was Lithuanian, about fifty years old, and tended bar herself. She was famous for her mixed drinks, particularly fancy coffee drinks. The phone was ringing and it kept ringing; people were phoning for reservations. It was Wednesday, three thirty in the afternoon, and already Helen was booked full for dinner. "The food here is outstanding," Manager said. "People come from all over Chicago. We get awards. Dick Butkus is a regular, claims it's his favorite restaurant in the world. Food's simple—roast duck, steak, chicken Kiev, barbecue—but it's how the cook fixes it. We're primarily a restaurant. But people do come in for drinks. We have an early crowd at the bar. And a late one, too. But mainly it's the food."

I snatched a menu and checked Helen's prices: between six and nine dollars for entrées. The Irish Coffee was two twenty-five; most drinks about one twenty-five. German light and dark draft was available, including bock. Also straight Schlitz draft. Less than a dollar a glass, although Manager could not remember the exact price.

There was a pressed tin ceiling at Helen's, plus antique paddle fans, swinging doors, and authentic Tiffany lamps. The bar stools, though plastic, had filigreed wrought-iron bases. There were Victorian statues on pedestals at the back bar; but the counter over the brass ice chest was imitation marble—plastic. The entire room, despite its antique fixtures had a plastic air; that sleazy Chicago atmosphere so prevalent in neighborhood places trying to look fancy. It was tough to tell what the crowd would be like after dark. I couldn't stick around. Too much to do, too many bars to hit. Already I had given up on two Royko taverns I simply could not locate: Club Cello, a Serbian spot at Ninety-fifth and Ewing, and Tamburitza Café, "a *great* place," Royko had said, at 13530 South Brandon. The entire West Coast was out there and I had a few hundred saloons between Chicago and Seattle I wanted to check. But not before summer. Florida beckoned. My ass was freezing and I longed to warm it on some rattan barstool south of Miami. So long to Helen's, so long to Chicago. Back to the Godformica-saken, empty-noggin freeway.

SOUTH

FLORIDA

Captain Tony's occupies the ground floor of a yellow frame building at 428 Greene Street in Key West, Florida, two blocks from the end of the American Road. The bar was opened legally in 1933 and is the oldest licensed saloon in Key West. It may be *the* Great American Bar. Sloppy Joe Russell held the lease as early as 1930 when the place was a speakeasy called the Blind Pig. It specialized in gambling, girls, and Hoover Gold, the Conchs's nickname for bootleg hootch. Joe Russell was a man about town. He was also known to have done his share of rumrunning during Prohibition. Like most Key West Conchs he believed in eliminating an unnecessary middleman. Joe had a charter-boat business on the side, and he ran a tiny speakeasy at the foot of Duval Street which capitalized on Cuban booze and the dice. This was the original Sloppy Joe's. It was a fisherman's joint, rough and tumble and open 24 hours a day. Ernest Hemingway discovered it in April of 1928 during his first visit to Key West, and became fast friends with Joe when he cashed a $1,000 check from Scribners which the Florida First National Bank had refused.

By 1933 and the end of Prohibition, Joe Russell had made more than 150 successful rum runs between Havana and Key West. He made these runs in a 34-foot cabin cruiser, the *Anita*, generally credited with the first load of Cuban liquor ever brought into Key West. Joe had sacked away some dough. The decision to move Sloppy Joe's up to 428 Greene Street with three times the space seemed only natural. But the Depression was grinding through its fourth tough year in Key West; people were starving. Joe bought his liquor license and business boomed. Ernest Hemingway could not understand it. When he blew into the new place in July 1934 looking to coax pal Josie into one of their extended Cuban fishing trips, Joe actually declined. Grinning over customers packed four deep at the bar, Joe said, "Times might be hard Cap, but ole Mr. Hoover done put a helluva thirst on all the *honest* folks." *

The new location had the space and it possessed a sort of local his-

---

* See James McLendon, *Papa: Hemingway in Key West* (Miami: E. A. Seeman Publishing, 1972), pp. 115–16.

tory. The building had housed a wireless telegraph station during the 1890s where, in 1898, first reports of the sinking of the *Maine* were picked up and relayed. Before that it had been an ice plant, which doubled as a city morgue in the days before electric refrigeration. It was a cigar factory in 1912. Then it was a whorehouse, popular with the Navy and finally forced out of business by an admiral who was anti-girls. Then it had been a series of speakeasies. When Joe Russell moved in, the long wooden front bar was off to the left, a deep dimly lit room with booths stretched toward the rear; a large side room served any spillover. Except for daylight from two huge French doors, the place was dark as a closet. Hemingway described the interior in *To Have and Have Not*. He called the spot Freddy's, and accurately depicted fist fights, skullcracking bouncers, gambling, "the loud-speaking nickle-in-the-slot phonograph playing 'Isle of Capri,' " Navy and Merchant Marine boozers and the discouraged, morally wrecked Bonus Marcher Vets who had been herded into Civilian Conservation Corps camps all down the Keys, to "work the new road" from Miami to Key West:

> They were opposite the brightly lighted open front of Freddy's place and it was jammed to the sidewalk. Men in dungarees, some bareheaded, others in caps, old service hats and in cardboard helmets. . . . As they pulled up a man came hurtling out of the open door, another man on top of him. They fell and rolled on the sidewalk, and the man on top, holding the other's hair in both hands, banged his head up and down on the cement, making a sickening noise. No one at the bar was paying any attention.
>
> —*To Have and Have Not*

At that time, and until 1938, Key West had no direct approach by highway. Key West was a nine-square-mile island, 120 miles off the U.S. mainland, accessible by railroad, ferry boat or steamer. "Our Southernmost City, the Gibraltar of America, 375 miles south of Cairo, Egypt," the tour books bragged. Key West had been a tourist stopover on the way to Havana, but during the thirties that trade inevitably slacked off. Even the Navy was cutting back. Key Westers chartered, fished, or otherwise employed their boats to run guns, rum, Cubans, or Chinese back and forth from Havana. And they ate grits. They worked on the Relief, doing repair jobs around town such as tearing up trolley tracks in Duval Street or fixing lamplights, and at that they made maybe eight bucks a week. Loose skin was slapping on the bone. A businessman like Josie Russell was to be respected.

The Conchs had earned their nickname from a characteristically hardshelled attitude of self-reliance; and because their ancestors had sworn they would survive on conch meat before buckling under to any man, dog, or system that interfered with their independent lifestyle. On a good day in winter Sloppy Joe's would average $1,500 pure profit. Joe Russell wasn't digging ditches for the goddam government. He was living proof of the Old Way.

Joe was a sport all right, a man who enjoyed the completely adventurous life. Pictures that remain show a jaunty little guy with a face like beat mullet, usually decked out in bloodstained ducks, usually beside Hemingway usually with a drink in his hand, usually near a fish. Such a photograph can be found after page 334 in Carlos Baker's *Ernest Hemingway: A Life Story* (Scribners, 1969). It was snapped on the San Francisco Wharf, Havana, in 1932. At that time Joe Russell and Hemingway were learning the new Gulf Stream sport of stalking, hooking, fighting and landing large billfish from the stern of a powerful twin-engine launch. They would disappear from Key West two months at a stretch, holing up nights in the Ambos Mundos Hotel in Havana. Joe would charge Ernie ten bucks a day charter fee for the *Anita*, and he would write the whole trip off as a fishing expense. Hemingway had met a grizzled Cuban fisherman in the Dry Tortugas by the name of Carlos Gutierrez, who knew as much about hunting marlin as any man around the Havana wharves. They hired him on as mate. Carlos had been taking marlin for nearly 40 years—with handlines from a skiff. He was the total Gulf Stream fisherman and a fine storyteller. Carlos Gutierrez later served Hemingway in another capacity, as prototype for Santiago in *The Old Man and the Sea*.

Business eventually would beckon both Key Westers home, Ernie to his writing and Joe to an iron grating he had installed over the cement floor behind the bar, to keep his legs from aching. The Sloppy Joe's mob had transferred intact from Joe's hole-in-the-wall speak on Duval Street, and they seemed to be mixing with a majority of the newer rowdies. Besides Key West fishermen and other boat people, some of the regulars who occupied stools around Sloppy Joe's front bar, with their names painted across the varnished seats, were Charles Thompson, who ran a local hardware business and whom Hemingway later portrayed as Karl in *Green Hills of Africa;* Bra Saunders, who had a charter-boat business, told Hemingway the story for "After the Storm" as he had lived it, and taught him a good deal of what he knew about fishing the Gulf; George

Brooks, who was a Key West lawyer and politician, and who later was characterized as Bee-Lips in *To Have and Have Not;* Toby Bruce, Hemingway's longtime friend, secretary and chauffeur; Jewfish-Earl Adams, a Key West newspaperman; and Sully Sullivan, who owned a local machine shop and who would later share the dedication of *Green Hills* with Charles Thompson and big game hunter Philip Percival. Hemingway's out-of-town mob, who would assemble annually for several weeks of fishing the Dry Tortugas and lounging around Key West,* included Scribners editor Max Perkins, painters Henry Strater and Waldo Pierce, wanderer John Dos Passos, who had first told Hemingway of Key West; and Bill Smith, a boyhood pal from Horton Bay, portrayed as Bill in many of Hemingway's Nick Adams stories. Ernie would meet them around three thirty every afternoon when he was writing, and the fun would start. Other saloons around Key West were certain to be hit—Raul's Club, which sported a tank of trained grouper behind the bar and a live rhumba band; Pena's Garden of Roses; the Tropical Club "Where Good Fellows Get Together," and Baby's Place for "Foreign and Domestic Beer, Anything You Want"—but the Hemingway mob always finished at Sloppy Joe's. There was something about it. As Ernie would later write, remembering Joe Russell and Manhattan's Toots Shor: "Mr. Joe Russell, popularly known as Sloppy Joe . . . ran a saloon which was the counterpart in Key West of the saloon and restaurant run by Mr. Shor." The place had style.

You could get bar gin for ten cents a shot, blended whisky for fifteen, and a draw of beer was five cents the glass. At thirty-five cents, Scotch and soda was top of the line, and no matter what your call you got Teacher's, the cheapest Scotch Josie could stock. Hemingway usually drank the Scotch and soda at a special house price of twenty-five cents. Once in a while Skinner, Joe's 300-lb. black bartender and bouncer, would mix up a batch of *Papa Dobles* for Ernie in the rusted electric blender at his end of the bar. They consisted of two and a half jiggers of white Bacardi, juice of two fresh limes, juice of half a grapefruit, and six drops of maraschino.† Skinner thought Hemingway one of the noblest men he had met, and he enjoyed preparing the *Dobles*, taking pride in each step of the bartender's art. But by all accounts, and contrary to myth, Hemingway preferred a simple Scotch and soda.

---

* See McLendon, pp. 34–44.
† McLendon, p. 164.

You could stand at the bar in Sloppy Joe's under slowly revolving ceiling fans, your bare feet in the sawdust and your fist wrapped around a cold bottle of Dog's Head ale, and watch customers dally at roulette, blackjack, craps, one-armed bandits, faro, or celo—three dice—which the Navy would be tossing on the barroom floor. You could dance to a rhumba band, pick up a girl, a sailor, or stuff your last nickel in the nickelodeon. You could watch former State's Attorney Georgie Brooks "deviling Papa," as bartender Bill Cates would later remember, by sicking homosexuals on him, announcing that, sure, old man Hemingway is queer as a double-assed buffalo, just go up to him, throw your arms around his neck, and give him a big kiss. You could then watch Hemingway beat up on a homosexual. If you stuck near Bill Cates—Joe Russell's baseball playing son-in-law, whom Hemingway once got invited to try out at a Brooklyn Dodger training camp—you might have overheard the plots of *To Have and Have Not*, *The Fifth Column*, and *For Whom the Bell Tolls*, and you could observe Bill Cates, by no means a literary man, occasionally bridle. If you had been at the bar one afternoon in December 1936, you might have seen tourist Martha Gellhorn, fated to become the third Mrs. Hemingway, latch on to Ernie and share a run of *Dobles* with him into early evening, herself dressed to kill in a one-piece black dress, blond hair flowing and delicate white legs shored up in high heels, himself burned black by the sun, barefoot, and funky in canvas shorts and a bloody T-shirt, the two as Skinner later recalled, looking for all the world "like Beauty and the Beast." * And if you had been on hand one mad spring evening in May 1938 you might have bent your back and lent Josie Russell a hand in moving his entire establishment half a block up Greene Street to Sloppy Joe's third location.†

Joe Russell, Jr., remembers that the move took place over an argument concerning a four-dollar-hike in rent. Joe Senior didn't like the idea of the hike, and he didn't like landlord Isaac Wolkowsky pointing out fine print in his lease to the effect that none of Sloppy Joe's fixtures could be removed if Joe should ever decide to leave. Joe had another location already picked out, a breezy corner building at Greene and Duval, which was even larger than the second spot. It had been most recently the failed Columbian Cuban restaurant, and

---

* See McLendon, pp. 164–167.
† Dates on this move are in conflict. McLendon says summer of 1937 but Joe Russell, Jr., who bartended at both second and third Sloppy Joe's, says May 1938. Captain Tony's manager, who has researched the leases, agrees with the 1938 date.

it had the longest bar in town. The place was airy with high shuttered Spanish archways that could be opened on warm evenings for complete ventilation. The night Joe's lease ran out on the old saloon it seemed like every oldtimer in town showed up, and as Bill Cates remembered, "They carried the whole damn place down the street where they got set up to a night of free drinks." Isaac Wolkowsky did not return from a business trip for several days, but when he did he fell into a rage. There was little Wolkowsky could do but fume. Apparently he decided against pressing the legal matter further, for there is no recollection of a reprisal.

So Josie had his third and final location. The operation staggered on in pretty much the same fashion—though Hemingway was off at the Spanish front, and he was never to spend as many hours in the new joint. The Overseas Highway had been completed, and a new brand of shutter-clicking tourist descended on the island, lurching through Sloppy Joe's, intent on a glimpse of its most famous tippler. Old trade was dying off, and Hemingway became fond of quoting Joe: "People dying this year that never died before." * Joe would run the new place until his own death in 1941, due to complications from emergency surgery in Havana.

Tony Tarracino was on the lam when he hit Key West in 1948, in trouble with our other law. Tarracino, a short cocky New Jersey Italian, had figured a way to beat the bookies to out-of-state handicap results by a full seven minutes. He would place his bets at what was considered the very last second and then he would clean up. At least he was cleaning up for a while. One evening he decided to leave New Jersey on the late flight. Actually, he hitchhiked. A girl friend talked him into touring farther south than Hialeah—she had been to Key West and liked it—so he said what the hell. He had some cash, and he was having a fine time with this girl. A huge odd man by the name of Morgan was proprietor of a saloon called the Duval at 428 Greene Street, and Tony Tarracino and his girl started going there, Tony blowing $300 a week, Tony and the girl having rhumba fun, doing Key West right.

Morgan was "gay as gay could be," Tony remembers, "and looked exactly like Charles Laughton." Morgan had decorated the old saloon with late-Victorian trappings and English drawings of the Beardsley school. He was quite the aesthete, a weighty sylph, worthy in his

* Carlos Baker, *Ernest Hemingway*, p. 366.

decadence of an Oscar Wilde or a Joris-Karl Huysmans. Which is to say the Navy took a dim view of his establishment. Morgan would throw large, wonderful parties in the Duval Club, where the Navy claimed sailors were blatantly harassed by his guests. Morgan persisted with his famous parties, ignoring all warning, until the Navy put him off limits. Oddly enough this cut away 80 percent of the Duval Club's business. Tony went before the Navy board with Morgan to lend an air of heterosexuality to the proceedings, but it was no go. "They turned him down cold," Tony says. "His business was gone, his best friends had deserted him, so he closed up and went to Pennsylvania where he committed suicide."

The old place at 428 Greene Street was again vacant. It had remained empty for a time after Joe Russell's move in 1938, but it was eventually filled in the same style by landlord Isaac Wolkowsky, and leased to a tenant who renamed it the Osceola Bar. Then it was the Silver Slipper for a while. Then it had become the Duval Club in 1940. The building was condemned in the late fifties, to be saved through the intervention of David Wolkowsky, son of Isaac and proprietor of the present-day Pier House Motel. He had been a Philadelphia contractor specializing in restoration before his return to Key West, where he quickly took a hand to save numerous architectural deadmen from the ball and bar. In 1958 he offered Tony Tarracino the chance to reopen the old saloon, thereby resurrecting the building, for $1,000 down and $300 a month. Tony accepted. As he later told writer Lawrence Mahoney, "All I knew about running a bar was that twenty-four cans came in a case of beer." But Tony had been in Key West for a few years, and he had been around.

Tony's mother and father were show people, of sorts. They had run a traveling puppet show out of Elizabeth, New Jersey, which they would set up on street corners in Italian neighborhoods around Manhattan. Tony and his brother Sal would help with the costumes and with setting up the stage, and sometimes they were allowed to pull strings. During the Depression Tony worked a number of jobs: he hustled pretzels, apples, and peanuts around New York, he was a gravedigger who would wait until a funeral procession had packed up and left before he snatched plastic frames off flowers to sell back to the florist, and he peddled a "Miracle Powder Carburetion Cure" on one cross-country stint, the cure consisting of crushed mothballs in a little white envelope which when poured directly into a carburetor actually opened it up nicely for a time, but in a day or so froze the bugger tight. He went through 2,000 boxes of mothballs on that venture. "Had eleven dollars when we started, eighteen dollars when we got back, but we traveled all over the place." He was a merchant seaman during World War II. Then he was a professional gambler in Seattle, running a Casino when wartime Puget Sound roared with twice its normal shipping, and big bucks were to be gleaned off every shoreleave sailor, off-duty aircraft engineer, or shipbuilder, from his shoeshine to his shave.

When the cash ran out after those first few weeks in Key West, Tony took to heading shrimp for a local seafood processing plant. He got out of there and onto a shrimp boat as soon as possible. He was mate aboard the *Mary Ann* of Brunswick, Georgia, but the work was backbreaking, hauling shrimp all night, bad weather and the bugs eating him as they fished the Dry Tortugas. Tony claims the *Mary Ann* was haunted, and that her captain, one Bernie Mc-Cracken, habitually set a third place at mealtime for the boat's ghost. Tony laughed at this "until about three o'clock one morning off Dry Tortugas, stormy and rough as hell, there he was, the third man big as life. Standing there in a slicker braced against the wind. That's when I gave up working other people's shrimp boats."

Tony filled his belly thereafter by deep sea diving, salvaging cannon off old Spanish wrecks, working as a movie extra, and making nineteen (give or take a few) gun runs to Cuba. "I run guns into Castro before he took over and went Communist, and I run guns into the refugees afterwards." Tony bought his own shrimp boat sometime before Wolkowsky's offer to reopen Josie's old saloon, but he admits that the shrimper's life drove him crazy. "I finally ran my goddam shrimp boat into the dock at Garrison Bight, sinking her like a pop bottle. She had the right insurance."

Tony no sooner had started his first watch at the old saloon when the Navy began dishing out trouble. He was called before the Navy board, like old friend Morgan, over incidents concerning sailors and homosexuals in his saloon. There were two alleged incidents, and as Tony later told the *Miami Herald*, "There was this board, all officers and one really big shot, all dressed up and sitting at a long table. It was obvious that they were all knuckleheads. Here I am, just a little wop, but they called me captain." The board claimed that two sailors had reported being approached by homosexuals in Tony's saloon. Tony asked the sailor's names, but the board would not say. So Tony told them to station two shore patrols at the front door, and he would hang a sign ten feet long and two feet high, reading NAVAL

PERSONNEL NOT ALLOWED. "I had 'em," Tony says. "Nothing they could do."

Tony was determined to start his saloon venture on a diplomatic note. "I respect a human being in my bar," he says. "Homosexuals are beautiful people, and we've got a lot of them in Key West. They have their little ins and outs. They're bitchy, but mentally they're usually way ahead. At the same time they're tragic; like Jesus Christ hanging on a cross. It's a rough trip. A relative of mine is one of the biggest queens in New York City. They used to call him Anna Magnani and I'd get the hell kicked out of me at school for defending him."

The first thing a beer drinker notices at Captain Tony's is that he serves neither Budweiser nor Busch Bavarian. Time and again a new customer will wander into the coolness, arrange himself on a stool at the long rectangular bar and say, "Gimme a Bud." The barmaid will answer patiently that they don't sell Bud.

"Well, gimme a Busch."

"We don't sell Busch. I can give you Miller's, Schlitz . . ." and she names them off.

This is unnerving to a new customer, particularly if he is a Floridian. "No *Bud?* No *Busch?* What kind of a joint is this? For chrissake, I never *heard* of a joint that didn't . . ."

When pressed, Tony will explain. "I used to serve exclusively Bud and Busch; it was the only beer I'd stock. We've always had a lot of gays come in here, not a majority of my customers, but a percentage. They know how I feel. Anyhow, a son of the local Bud and Busch distributor is gay. He used to come in here. Few years back he took over Delmonico's restaurant and bar. Sonuvabitch told all his pals that I didn't want no more of their business. Said I was throwing gays out in the street. Bullshit, totally. A goddam lie. So I told him and his old man to go screw, go screw your attitude and your goddam Anheuser beer. I ain't had a Bud or Busch in my place since."

Life is like a penis.
When it's hard
You get fucked,
When it's soft
You can't beat it.

The men's room at Captain Tony's is a bamboo-screened affair, back toward the garden and behind Tennessee Williams's monkey cage. The monkey belongs to Tennessee Williams, who lent it to Tony ten years ago. He and Tony have been close friends for a long time. Tennessee doesn't come in as much as he used to, but he will drop by occasionally to visit the monkey, whom he named Creature, and to sip a rum and tea. To get to Captain Tony's men's room you pass by Creature's cage. There is a WE BITE sign and Creature delights in rattling his bars ferociously when booze-heavy patrons lumber through. The old saloon has always been a favorite with literary people but no one seems certain who is responsible for the men's room's unique graffiti:

> A man without a god
> Is like a fish
> Without a bicycle.

"Tony practically *raised* Herlihy," Linda was saying. "He took him in like an orphan, gave him a place to stay and time to write like he was his own son." Linda refers to novelist James Leo Herlihy, author of *Midnight Cowboy, All Fall Down, Blue Denim,* among others, who is a longtime resident of Key West. "Herlihy still thinks of Tony as a father. He'll come in on a busy night, jump behind the bar and mix drinks for hours. He says it's because he likes to observe people but I think it's usually for Tony. Herlihy's a strange man. Silent; sits by himself when he's drinking."

Linda is Tony's 28-year-old, lovely, redhaired manager, who like Herlihy, came to the end of the American road, found Captain Tony's Saloon, found Tony, and hired on. She is seated at the far end of the bar near the cash register. She is on break. Her skin is exquisitely light and it must be sore, for she is burned from a day's fishing aboard Captain Tony's boat. It is Saturday night in the old saloon. Linda appears unruffled. People press close, people stop and throw their arms around her. She doesn't seem to mind. Somebody buys a drink leaving a sizable tip for the barmaid, and she reaches up to clang a ship's bell, yanking a large sculptured banana suspended from a chain to do so. A black limbo band called the Junkanoos is beating on congas, an ancient upright piano, and is singing *"Down by the seashore siftin' sands"* just as loud as they possibly can and nobody ever hears the bell.

"Captain Tony's boat," Linda says. "He'd go crazy if it wasn't for that thing. Out every day until four, with too few fishermen to make gas and bait. No wonder, with people he takes from the saloon. People going out for free, like me."

Tony owns and captains a 55-foot drift and bottom head-boat, the *Greyhound IV*, which he coaxes into the Gulf Stream every morning for fishing, sleep, sun, and the delight of however many tourists he has aboard. The boat is named *Greyhound IV* for at least two reasons: Tony's intense love of gambling, and the fact that dogs *I*, *II* and *III* have met various memorable ends along the line.

"Who can say what Tony's up to?" Linda groans. "He lost one boat off the coast of Haiti . . . during his second Haitian revolution, trying to overthrow Papa Doc. They blew the stern off that *Greyhound*, Tony lost twelve men and the U.S. Coast Guard picked him up swimming in the Caribbean. Another time, in 1965, he took six newsmen to Camarioca, Cuba, without a State Department permit. Camarioca was a refugee embarkation point where thousands of Cubans were waiting for relatives to take them out of there with just small boats. He says he saw kids in militia uniforms, 13 and 14, carrying .45s. A sad tremendous propaganda show. When he got his boat back to Key West the Coast Guard impounded it.

"Tony was in Bay of Pigs, you probably heard. God knows what else, half the time I never know what he's up to. For a 60-year-old he gets around. When we go to Haiti now for vacation and so he can gamble, these strange characters are always watching him. He laughs about it and sometimes he explains. But mostly he can't." Linda smiles. Tony has emerged from a closet at one corner of the bar. He has showered and is wearing a starched shirt open at the throat, and clean slacks. The closet hides a ladder which leads to Tony's apartment above the saloon. He shuffles across the floor in rubber shower shoes. He is quite changed in appearance from the old khakis and T-shirt worn on *Greyhound IV*, and he has his teeth in. Tony comes over next to Linda, glances across the bar and asks her something about business.

He looks at the same instant thirty years older and ten years younger. His face is lined and he affects a kind of posture here in the saloon, where at sea he had joked and slouched like a kid. A kid with no teeth. The bridge he is wearing improves his face, but it makes him look hard. Like a real person. Before, he had seemed just a beautiful idea.

Linda goes back on duty. She slips under the bar, brushing aside several of Tony's sailor's hats from navies all over the world, and gets fifty cents out of the register. "Cigarettes?" she asks Tony. He shrugs and turns to me. "How about running up to Sloppy Joe's and getting Linda cigarettes? Our machine is on the fritz. You know, I don't like to go in there."

I say okay and head out, past couples swaying to a tinny "Jamaican Farewell," tan-faced boozers crowded to the bar and into the aisles, past one well-dressed group huddled around Tony's open fireplace where a long spar is burning, out the big French doors and under Tony's huge stuffed jewfish which swings creakily over his sign in the sixty-degree breeze. A cat flushes from the innards of a rusted-out World War II anti-ship mine which Tony keeps chained to an anchor and lamppost in front of his saloon. I follow the stray up Greene Street to Duval, where he ducks into an alleyway. I duck into Sloppy Joe's.

There's a sizable crowd on hand tonight. Much older and more down at the heels than Captain Tony's, but having a fine time. Sloppy Joe's III is a Great Bar almost in spite of itself. I bump into Stan Smith at the cigarette machine, proprietor since 1962 and a tall tough-looking ex-paratrooper. He smiles and says hello. Stan and Tony get along, but there have been differences between them concerning the Hemingway myth: its manipulation and actual fact. Tony says he has no interest in exploiting a dead man and that he would rather go on his own name. Stan Smith has hung his bar with Personality Posters of Hemingway, a hundred Hemingway mementos, and has gone so far as to pose for photographs with the oldest man in Key West—a white-bearded Hemingway look-alike—and hang them in conspicuous spots among Sloppy Joe's memorabilia. There is a large painting behind the bar in a style that might be described as Bahamian-Marc Chagall, depicting garishly and in sur-realistic multi-color: bartending Joe Russell, black Skinner the 300-lb. bouncer, and Ernest the writer, all toiling mightily at their various trades. Hemingway is sitting down inside the bar, typing. The painting is quite extraordinary. Stan Smith has further embellished Sloppy Joe's interior by hanging large parachutes from the ceiling, which billow out dramatically over the horseshoe bar. There are other autographed photos around the room from the likes of Frank Sinatra and Tennessee Williams, but practically everything else is Hemingway. It is even rumored that Stan Smith posted large photographs of Ernie on the *out*side of his bar, until the family heard about it and made him take them off.

The help at Sloppy Joe's plays down Captain Tony's almost to extinction. An obese woman behind the bar had told me with a straight face that Josie Russell kept his business in Greene Street exactly one month.

"He was waiting to get in here," she said.

I chew the fat with Stan Smith for a few seconds at the cigarette machine and get out of there.

Back at Captain Tony's the Junkanoos are inflamed. The whole bar is rocking with the limbo beat, one subtropical organism bilboed to drink, glassily slopping, one against the other, sweat, perfume and pink rum. I spot our crowd from Captain Tony's boat, but before I can reach them two powerful hands grip my biceps, spin me about—and crush me to the chest of a short stocky figure in a navy blue slicker.

"You sleep with women?" it says. "I don't sleep with women, I ain't slept with a goddam woman except my mother, bless her, in my whole goddam life. Captain Katie don't sleep with dykes and she's no bull dyke herself. You wanta see the monkey? I gave Captain Tony this goddam monkey. Come over, come on, come *bam*, that's right, *bam* go on and bust your bars you sonuvabitch. He loves me, see? You see that? Goddam I guess so I raised the bastard and give him to Captain Tony. You got a girl friend, sailor? You sleep with women? How about a drink for Captain Katie? You got a bottle of beer for an old girl don't you? You're talking to a *Captain*, sailor. You see, you see, come . . ."

"Hey Katie," someone screams, "get your leather ass over here. I got a drink of whisky for the first leather-assed crazy comes sit with me. *Hey Katie*." The figure's platinum wig has slipped from one eye to both, and as it turns to the music, still ranting, it releases me with broad gestures, moving off toward the loudness.

I hustle back to the bar.

"You met Captain Katie," Linda says. "Poor Katie. Such a mess. She's riddled with cancer. Lost both breasts. Wears that navy blue slicker zipped to the chin. Drinks all day, hits every bar in Key West. You never heard anyone talk like Katie."

"What the hell is she?"

"A retired Army nurse. She was on Corregidor in a Japanese prison camp nearly the whole war. I've heard she was the only woman on the island. Saw some pretty bad things. Went through an awfully bad time."

"She said she raised the monkey!"

Linda laughs. "Tomorrow she might tell you she raised Captain Tony."

I toss off my drink and ease down the bar away from Captain Katie. Tony's brother Sal is sitting with a table of gays near the band, so I shuffle over that way looking for an inconspicuous spot against the wall.

Sal Tarracino is a character among characters. He is a sculptor and a professional photographer from New York, who shoots stills for motion pictures like *The Godfather*, but spends his winters every year with Captain Tony in Key West. Several nights a week he plays organ in the old saloon and sings. He also shows slides of famous people, which he puts together six at a clip with a CAN YOU NAME THEM? caption at the bottom of the screen. "Sal's back!" is the cry among gays when he shows up every winter, and they barrel into Tony's saloon to see the show. Sal sings all the old songs for them, gets everybody to sing along or try and name that tune, picks at famous opera themes, or entertains with his slides which nobody ever scores 100 percent on. The gays love Sal. Occasionally he titillates them with lewd shots of some boy in leather or a group of naked queens prancing in the buff. "Oh Sal!" they scream. He is always a hit.

But tonight it is the Junkanoos, and the whole city of Key West is on the dance floor. Tony shoulders his way to my side, shakes his head, and hands me a fresh drink. "Ain't it a shame?" he says. "Bunch of crazies. They love it. Saturday night and the natives is restless. It's almost like Key West in the old days; but then nothing's ever gonna be like that. Town's changed. Excuse me being sentimental, but I hope it don't change too much. Kids care about a lot but they don't notice historical things like we did when we was young. Me with all my carrying on, I run for Mayor twice. I want a say in what's going to happen in this town. First time I ran I was just like the kids though, didn't give a damn what people thought, I campaigned barefoot and lost by eighty-six votes. The second time I shaved and bought a pair of shoes, since I was running to split the vote. Helped a friend of mine get in. He got in. What the hell I want to be Mayor for? I got too much fun here and on the boat."

Two Junkanoos have a limbo stick on the floor now, and the crazies have lined up shuffling *boom shucka boom shuck* to the heavy limbo beat. "Watch this," Tony says. "These goddam Junkanoos— they're local boys you know, they worked a wedding this afternoon and there ain't one of em sober—they get so drunk half the time they don't know what the other's playing. On Saturday everybody was dancing and having a great party like tonight, when I notice the band is playing two different songs at two different beats. Half of em was singing 'Yellow Bird' so slow and romatic it made you cry and the other half was off and running to 'Uncle John's Mule.' Nobody but me even noticed."

A striking black woman with short gray hair, elegantly attired in a floor-length silk gown and silk slippers, is dancing under the limbo stick, and the crowd applauds madly, urging her back again and again. She does very well for her age. The stick descends and the crazies scream for more. I lean over and ask someone at Sal's table who she is: I'm told she's a famous madam from West Palm Beach. I relate this to Tony, and he just laughs.

"I never seen her before but then it don't surprise me none. See this guy: that's Patty from the boat." I recognize a tanned little man with long brown hair, spiffily dressed in a flowered silk shirt, silk suit and imitation patent leather shoes. Quite a transformation from the fish-slimy mate I had met that afternoon on *Greyhound IV*. Patty is dancing with a girl about 22 years old, holding her close against the limbo beat; his wife Maria glaring from an adjacent table.

"Patty thinks he's king-cocksman of Key West." Tony laughs. "That dude is ten years older than *me*. Cuban Conch, came over years ago. Best man I ever knew. He ain't got any teeth either. He lost em—it was kinda funny—we was out on the *Greyhound* and in those days I used mostly handlines for the tourists, it was easier. A guy hooked a little yellowtail and Pat was helping him with it, the line tangled or something, so he leans down to cut it with his teeth. Just then a big kingfish hits the yellowtail and wham, there went the fish, the line and about eight of Pat's teeth. I call him *Te-Te* ever since. Vain old bastard. Dyes his hair."

Captain Katie busts by en route to the bandstand with a brown-haired woman in tow, both of them bellowing at the top of their voices. Something about a car in the way of a wall, which they want the band to announce over the P.A. Katie crushes the woman to her shoulder with a sisterly hug. "Oops"—Tony mugs—"somebody gonna get laid tonight."

The Junkanoos are fighting openly among themselves now, and their music is suffering. Somebody screams that Tony should plug in the jukebox. Katie and her pal have accepted drinks from two sailors on the condition that they join a game of mixed doubles in the deep cistern room where Captain Tony keeps his pool table. Linda is mixing drinks so fast the foam is flying into people's hair; a matronly woman of some decorum is trying on Tony's antique Spanish chastity belt, and a drunk with a perfectly red bald head is begging to dance with a skeleton lashed to a beam at the steet end of the bar. Victor, Tony's second mate on *Greyhound*, hobbles to our side. His right foot is puffed up like a muskmelon. Tony examines it, sits Victor down and frowns.

"Better get him to the hospital," Tony says. "Nothing serious I don't think, but he stepped on a hook this afternoon. Got some fish slime in the cut."

Tony slaps me on the back, tells me to enjoy myself and come back anytime—even sleep upstairs in his apartment, "If you can stand all the naked women."

Tony gets Victor to his feet but turns back to me, something odd wrapped across his face. "Did I tell you they're making a movie of my life?" he grins. "No bullshit. Guy named Peter Barton is producing it. They're trying to get Dusty Hoffman for the lead."

Tony looks amused. The idea obviously tickles him. "What the hell would Joe Russell think of that? And old Morgan? Shit, they shoulda made movies of *those* men's lives. But I done a lot of things. Lot of things the average guy would be interested in, too. They're even talking about a TV deal coming out of this picture. Spending a lot of dough, they got Woody Strode, Tiffany Bollins, and Sheree North signed up. *Sheree* North, you remember her? Jesus Christ. Some guy named Philip Leacock is directing it. Reason I know is because I just got off the phone with Barton. He wants me to play myself in the picture—the hell with Dusty Hoffman."

Tony eyeballs the room, staggers a second under Victor's weight, and laughs out loud. All the lines have dissolved from Tony's face and it's like he hasn't got his teeth in.

"You know, three years ago somebody offered me eighty thousand dollars for this joint and I turned him down. I wouldn't sell it tonight for a hundred. Shit, I ain't bragging. Who'd look out for all these crazies? Where in hell would we all go?"

Duval Street at eight a.m. on a weekday morning is hangover lane. A double *café con leche* at Two Brothers Restaurant may help, and if white tropical sunlight does not stream too thickly through the open door, you will find comfort in a brightly painted fisherman's mural on Brothers' back wall, and chatter from black laborers or Cuban taxicab drivers, most of whom have been up all night. The sidewalk outside is already hot. Not enough to burn your feet, but to

warm them comfortably, massaging the soles as they pick their way
through last night's debris. Across Duval from Two Brothers, Big
Mama's Lounge, a black topless club of some repute, is already open
for business, the bartender sweeping out broken glass and other
wreckage. The Shipwreck has been closed for several years now, but
one can remember raucous nights there with fine local bands and
think of a Jimmy Buffett tune which recalls Shipwreck in its fondest
era. White topless clubs down Duval are closed at this hour, and all
you can see is chipped paint about their doors that black light some-
how disguises. The Bull, formerly Lou's Club, is sweeping out but
not yet open, and big shutters of the Spanish-style house which
hosts this freaky hangout are raised, allowing huge gusts of morning
air to dispel the stench of last night's indulgences. West Key Saloon
is fast at business, its down-at-the-heel winos and Conch early
drinkers lined up at the bar. Delmonico's, a gay saloon and steak-
house, which used to be a favorite eating spot of Ernest Hemingway,
is closed tight—aghast at the possibility of opening so early. A
breakfast crowd is waiting on seats at Shorty's, impatient for waffles
or French toast or fresh orange juice from Shorty's big blender.
Sloppy Joe's will not open its doors until eleven o'clock. So if an
early beer is needed, one should sidetrack down Caroline past the
defunct Red Doors (which was so violent a spot in its heyday that a
man was reputedly hanged over the bar one evening) to Mascot, a
shrimper's tavern in the fisherman's tradition, where a cold draft
with tomato juice bracer is a distinct possibility. The Big Fleet,
another shrimper's joint which had been rocking the night before to
live country music, is closed and will remain so until late afternoon.
Back at the foot of Duval Street, Chart Room's movie moguls and
literary notables have not stirred yet, and there will be no noticeable
movement at Chart until early afternoon. Other bars around Key
West will not open until evening or have been open for several
hours. Key West *is* a bar drinker's town in the old manner, and one
can find a saloon there to fit one's taste.

The saloons had changed though, since my first visit to Key West.
Captain Tony's in particular. No structural alteration, except a new
sign out front, an expanded dance floor toward the rear and four new
pool tables in a side room. But Tony had hired a DJ to spin disco-
style records after nine thirty—for a largely gay crowd. About sixty
percent. This improved the action after dark at Captain Tony's
perceptibly. A younger crowd seemed to hold sway, though oldtimers were always present, bumping and grinding along with the

gays. A quieter crowd congregated in Tony's garden during afternoon hours (the old saloon opens at noon, often stays open until four
in the morning), where Creature's cage had been moved to isolate
him from the drunks. Several headliners were no longer in attendance: The Junkanoos made only rare appearances; Captain Katie
had been arrested in Fort Lauderdale for hitting a cop over the head
with a beer bottle—"It ain't funny," Tony laughed. "She almost
murdered the poor sonuvabitch"—Katie was subsequently incarcer-
ated in a state mental institution; Victor, Tony's second mate and
part-time bartender, had made a lot of money bartending in Prov-
incetown the previous summer, and was hunting elk in Canada.
Tony's movie had fallen through, though a film *Key West* with Barton's described cast had been completed and aired on TV. "We still
got a film cooking," Tony assured me. "Burt Lancaster's gonna play
me. I met him this fall, helluva guy. Should be a much better deal."

Tom McGuane recently had finished directing a movie version of
his novel, *Ninety-Two in the Shade*—starring Peter Fonda, Warren
Oates, and Burgess Meredith. "They was in here every night,"
Tony confirmed. "Fonda, all of em. And you know what? They
wanted *my* autograph." Not much action for Tony, CIA–wise, since
Nixon's resignation. "Whole damn business fell through right after
he quit," Tony said. "Funniest thing. We had this deal worked out
in Panama—was going to overthrow the government, get that fucking canal cleared up. I had a piece of it. But soon as Nixon croaked,
damn thing fell through. Then I heard they made some other kind of
deal. So the revolution was off." The Watergate cast was not unfamiliar to Tony: "Howard Hunt handed me five thousand dollars in a
Cuban cigar box after Bay of Pigs," Tony said. "I didn't know Hunt
by his real name. But when I saw his face in the papers—sonuvabitch
if it wasn't the same guy."

Bud and Busch were back on sale at Captain Tony's ("We finally
come to an understanding"), along with other American brands, for
seventy-five cents a can; Heineken's and several other foreign labels
were going for a buck twenty-five. Drinks at Tony's hovered around
the dollar-fifty mark, and Alan, Tony's new barboy, mixed an excellent margarita. Tony, in the tradition of hysterical entertainment
long enjoyed at the old saloon, had hired Staunton, a black dancer
from the original cast of *Hair*, who performed Saturday nights, at
twelve and two—in a G string; body greased with oil, chiffon scarf
for a tail, sequined top hat, ruffles around his neck, ruffles at his
wrists and ankles, and a smile. The crowd loved Staunton. His act

consisted of nothing more than mimicking a few old Beatles tunes, speeded slightly for an effeminate touch, and strutting to the beat. Tony just shook his head. "I think the guy's good," he argued. "The saloon has changed. If we had Sal or the Junkanoos here every night, we'd fold in a week. Look at other Key West bars. Business terrible. And it's going to get worse. Was very tough down here during the Depression. People want disco music in 1976, fine. That's what I'm in business for. To please my customers. This saloon ain't gonna change any. The physical saloon, I mean. It's been here a long time and it'll be here long after I'm gone."

A certain irony to the fact that Captain Tony's, Hemingway's favorite bar in its earlier incarnation as Sloppy Joe's, was now sixty percent gay. A bar, which Hemingway is rumored to have co-owned, often bragging that he was Josie Russell's "silent partner."

Sloppy Joe's III was so middle of the road now that it was nearly uncomfortable to drink there. The fear factor was high and a money-grubbing atmosphere prevailed, which kept the customer constantly checking his wallet. Stan Smith had gone so far as to have pasted Hemingway's birth certificate on Sloppy Joe's wall—along with several hand-scripted Hemingway checks that were discovered thirteen years ago in a Sloppy Joe's storage room. Draft beer was no longer available at Sloppy Joe's, the lunch counter had been closed, cocktails were overpriced, and an elderly organist entertained the troops after dark. Still quite an experience to hear Belafonte's "Jamaican Farewell" on the juke at Sloppy Joe's, though—that first drink of the day toasting a lavender sunset from one of Sloppy Joe's wide Cuban doors.

The Birdcage

Casa Marina Hotel, corner Seminole Avenue and Reynolds Street, Key West

A thirties-style lounge in a deserted resort hotel worthy of Jay Gatsby, Cornelius Vanderbilt, or Henry Flagler—the Florida empire-builder who financed Casa Marina as a stopover for tourists en route from Palm Beach's riches to the pleasures of Havana. The Birdcage is elegant, but Casa Marina is something else: A Spanish Renaissance villa in the Beaux Arts tradition, envisaged by Flagler in 1912 when his trans-Keys railroad was completed and he arrived in

Key West on the first train, walking into town on a solid path of roses. The trans-Keys railroad cost Flagler thirty-five million dollars, and Casa Marina a mere three hundred and fifty thousand more by 1922. The hotel has been closed since 1959 but the grounds are kept, the pool filled, the grass cut . . . as if by some anonymous benefactor who cannot bear to see the place go under.

The Birdcage was reopened in August of 1974, but the rest of Casa Marina remains vacant. To drink at Birdcage is to have an entire resort hotel to oneself; solitary patrons stroll at will around the old grounds, sipping drinks in deserted lawn chairs by Casa's private beachfront, under an outrageous Key West moon. There is no bar sign outside Casa Marina to indicate the presence of Birdcage, so few redhots have wind of the spot. Birdcage is an "In" Key West bar, exclusive, perhaps the only such establishment . . . with well-dressed locals in attendance, mostly quiet, reserved, and rarely numbering more than twenty at a time. The cast of *Ninety-Two in the Shade* were regulars at Birdcage, and one of two bartenders had a part in the film. As a bartender, naturally.

Birdcage was not added at Casa Marina until the early thirties, and it reflects the sophisticated tone of that era. The barroom is small, perhaps thirty feet wide and octagonally shaped—like a Victorian birdcage. Everything is white inside: chairs, tables, walls, the ceiling. A delicate birdcage chandelier, also white, hangs at the center of the room. A high Art Deco bar cuts the floor at a slant, with a polished hardwood top for drinks and the obligatory strip of chrome across its face. A brass rail and comfortable leather stools complete the set. Hand-painted murals of tropical garden scenes decorate one wall, and tall, finely cut mirrors hang at intervals. During daylight hours, Birdcage vibrates with white—tropical sunlight, white furnishings, gossamer curtains, and a bucketful of motes which play about the border of green murals. After dark there is a Bogart/Bacall feel to the room. Almost haunted. As if a drinker had been shanghaied to some dangerous saloon midway between Key Largo and Casablanca.

Drinks at Birdcage are reasonably priced—around a dollar twenty-five—and they are generously mixed. Rumors circulate that Casa Marina may not be vacant long . . . rumors of a sale, rumors of the old hotel being cut up into condominiums . . . but they are unsubstantiated. It is hard to imagine so beautiful a resort not remaining a hotel, but as one Birdcage bartender observed, "People don't want to pay for style anymore." Celebrities too numerous to list have vacationed at Casa Marina, including Presidents Harding, Roosevelt, and Truman. Because of its solid construction, Casa Marina has served as shelter during many storms and hurricanes. One can imagine Birdcage put to hard use then. Casa Marina was requisitioned by the Navy during World War II for officers' housing, and by the Army during 1963's Cuban Missile Crisis for commando barracks. Casa Marina has long been a stopover for out-of-towners, and an anomaly to Key Westers, whose life style has proved so antipodal. But one hopes Birdcage will integrate Big Buck sophistication with low budget, Conch liveliness once and for all, and an historic bar will continue to serve an end of the road community.

Alabama Jack's
Card Sound Road, at Key Largo

Alabama Jack's is a fishing camp for the complete Florida fisherman; that means food, boats, beer, and bait. Whisky is not served, but anything else a saltwater angler might require is on sale at Alabama's, including stone crabs as sweet as any you'll eat between Key West and Miami Beach. A formica counter runs the length of Alabama's, with beer, soda pop and homemade suppers for sale. Homemade sandwiches are all under a dollar (try Alabama's pork barbecue for seventy-five cents), and beer about fifty cents. The crowd varies from commercial fishermen to weekend tourists . . . but architecture and setting are really what Alabama Jack's is about.

Alabama's is a yellow frame building, rectangular in shape with an extra rectangle on top—the whole resembling a large houseboat more than a bar. At first glance Alabama's seems afloat; but it is perched on a pier at the very edge of Barnes Sound, so close to water, sea birds, and grotesque mangrove hammocks that one feels part of the exquisite seascape and Everglades topography. Scattered down Card Sound Road are ramshackle houses and fishing camps—more shacks on stilts than anything else—and Alabama's is luxurious by comparison. A tall flagpole with American flag affixed and antennae whipping in the wind intensify the impression of Alabama's as some stranded seagoing vessel.

Across a fifty-cent toll bridge from Alabama's is the nineteen-mile mystery of northern Key Largo: a jumble of dense vegetation, Australian pine and swampish backwater. Not forty miles south of Miami, Alabama's is a beer drinker's outpost in a subtropical wilderness. A pet raccoon washes his food and devours it on Alabama's outside terrace. Fishermen come and go in rented skiffs, slapping huge catches on the dock at a beer drinker's feet, or cursing their fate at being skunked. The wind howls off Card Sound with a modicum of mercy and an Everglades sun frenchfries the unwary. Alabama Jack's is protection from the elements and an assurance that availability will endure. You can get there from Alabama Jack's, or you can come in from the storm.

The Playhouse Bar is a brassy old tart. She keeps herself company. At Twenty-Eight Ocean Drive, South Miami Beach—a half block from the Miami Beach Kennel Club (dog track) and across the street from the South Beach pier—with Turf Club next door and Joe's Stone Crabs around the corner, where waiters still know about black dinner jackets and what you hear in their voices is pre-War New York, she is an MIA rose of the Bowery. That's okay by her. All retireds might not like it: ones on the fishing pier, in apricot knickers and Mexican straw hats; with big Browning surf-casters, Penn reels and 30-gallon styrofoam coolers, they could not approve. . . . Might raise an eyebrow at that fortyish hustler with lanky gray hair and the loping stride, who paces in front of Playhouse, inextricably nervous, the same path every afternoon. Money retireds will scoff, but that's all right. They are not trade. Little old men barely five feet tall, scanning jai alai sheets and the racing forms, a hitch in their step from twenty years of jockeying respectable nags around the exercise track at Hialeah, they could care. They could care less. Ex-pugs and South Beach widows, the working trainers from Chris Dundee's, Ratso transients . . . to them the old girl's swell. She's been swell. Playhouse Bar has always drawn a sporting crowd. When Ice Cream Joe was a kid peddling popsicles and Good Humors along Miami Beach, the Playhouse drew the sports. Everybody on South Beach knows that; to them it means something.

One gusty Sunday evening, Playhouse Bar is overfull. A stocky barmaid serves the crowd, a big woman, nearly six feet. "May, you gained weight," she says to an old woman buying a pint of wine. "That ain't weight," says May, "that's bloat." May laughs with a rippling cackle, like a shotglass of BBs pouring down the bar. The big woman frowns. But not for long; everyone's in a good mood tonight. Tonight Ice Cream Joe plays his movies.

Sunday's the night. "It's always the night, so long as I got some-body to run the projector," Joe says.

Ice Cream Joe Savino migrated to Miami Beach from Pennsylvania in 1949. He bought Playhouse in 1965. From '49 to '65 he sold ice cream on the Beach. Playhouse has been in business since the thir-ties. Its walls are hung with photographs of many obscure sports fig-ures, some famous—including every championship fighter who ever stood still long enough for a shot. There are photos of obscure show business personalities with the usual scrawl; photos of busty women in black silk and ermine, hawk-laughing at the camera. There is a clipping next to the bar, from the *Miami News:* a story about Play-house by sportswriter Jack Crittenden. Crittenden mentions Joe's Sunday night movies.

"Every Sunday at nine," Joe says. "Used to be we'd never miss, but lately the projector's screwed up." Joe bought his movies for $300 right after he took over Playhouse, and they were an immediate hit. The films are of old fights mostly, but also of great World Series games: of Bobby Thompson hitting against the Dodgers, Willy Mays's fabulous over-the-shoulder catch, the classic swings of Ted Williams and DiMaggio. The Floyd Patterson/Willie Troy fight (Pat-terson at 19), Bobo Olson/Gene Hansen, Louis/Schmeling, Louis/Marciano, Louis/Ezzard Charles. . . .

"Louis always breaks their hearts," Joe says. A tan little man with a pencil-thin Boston Blacky and a Dolphins visor cap is trying to operate the projector. "Some nights Dundee stops by," Joe says. "He sits at this end of the bar and tells everybody who's dead."

The man in the Dolphins cap is having problems. "*C'mon,*" pa-trons jibe. They elbow each other as the little guy sweats; they laugh and order more beer. Playhouse is full to the flycatchers. People stalk about the room. Outside, retireds pause, glaring. It is prome-nade hour on Ocean Drive. Cadillacs ease by en route to Joe's Stone Crabs. Passengers turn a quick glance. On other evenings, a bar-tender at Joe's Stone Crabs has told them: "Stop into the Playhouse, but I'm warning you—that's the honest-to-Christ Wild West."

A portable screen has been set up on a table and Joe's fights have started. Floyd Patterson, a skinny brown rabbit at 19, is working the TKO on Willie Troy. Doesn't take long. Many comments from the Playhouse home squad. "Sonuvabitch could hit then," says one old-timer . . . He has a paper plate full of stone crabs spread out on the bar, and he grimaces through draft beer and the crab slime. Ted

Williams is explaining how to hit a fast ball. The camera zooms in tight for a slow motion shot; Williams's wrists snapturn like *bolas*. A moment later he is crossing home plate with a spit for the Boston fans. The Playhouse crowd loves it; they consider Williams a Floridian, one of their own. Ezzard Charles dances across the screen, sultry and multi-racial, like a stocky Sugar Ray or a young Ali; like Miles Davis in a three-piece suit. Everyone remembers what Charles did to Joe Louis on the comeback trail. They curse quietly. Bobo Olson, Hurricane Jackson . . . the pace lightens, there is snickering at these fighters, no patience for their minimal grace. Someone starts an argument about Tinker to Evers to Chance. "Who the hell was the *third baseman?*" The whole lower half of the bar winces.

Joe Louis is on the screen: first Schmeling, second Schmeling. Playhouse goes wild. But Joe Louis is old. He has fought seventy bouts and lost just two, one to Schmeling, one to Ezzard Charles. A wiry Italian bounces in the corner opposite Louis. A wiry Italian *boy*. Joe Louis is thirty-seven years old. The Playhouse crowd simmers down. Someone slaps thirty cents on the bar and demands a fresh beer. He is ignored. Louis and the Italian are circling now. Uptown and the lower West Side; it's a neighborhood brawl; it's in everyone's eyes. For big turf. Takes eight rounds—Louis staggers, is knocked sprawling through the ropes. Most perfect fighting machine ever bred . . . finished, an old man. Playhouse takes it poorly. There is an absolute silence as the film runs out. Old jockeys and touts, ex-pugs, the trainers from Chris Dundee's who have worked America's best, the man in the Dolphins cap, even burned-out frazzled whores . . Marciano is some other era.

"That's the show," Joe says. "Next Sunday at nine, if we got a man to run the projector."

There are things in Florida called Big Daddy's Lounges. They are not bars and they are not night clubs; they are attempts by a conglomerate to do for the booze business what McDonald's did for hamburgers. Each Big Daddy's is the same, and there is a Big Daddy's in every Florida town of any size. Inside is a bar, usually rectangular and formica, plus a bunch of formica furniture, formica waitresses costumed like stewardesses, formica combos after dark, and drinks which are cheaper than any in the state. The drinks, like McDonald's hamburgers, are not bad for the money: beer about fifty cents, whisky hovering around the sixty-five-cent mark. Happy

Hour drops prices even lower. These Big Daddy's sell so much booze in so short a time that they can afford to give most of their drinks away.

There are no windows in a Big Daddy's. They are rectangular buildings into which no daylight is ever permitted. At three o'clock in the afternoon, a Big Daddy's is as dark as it will be by three in the morning. A package store is usually attached, and booze to-go is reasonably priced. Big Daddy's Lounges are just terrible. They are the essence of what a Great American Bar *is not*, and they are doing for Florida saloons what supermarkets did for the corner grocery, and what fast food spots did for the neighborhood café. Fear factor is incredibly high inside a Big Daddy's; dread is overwhelming. Nobody likes drinking there, but greed cannot help itself.

Big Daddy, whoever he is, understands the American character. Give em a price they cannot refuse. It is whispered that Mafia money is behind Big Daddy's, and that "Big Daddy" is itself a euphemism for "Mafioso." Captain Tony says he was approached several years ago, when Big Daddy's opened, to act as some kind of front man for the organization. Tony refused; but before the representatives left, they picked up one of Tony's illustrated napkins with the drawing of Tony and his beard, and asked if they could keep it. "Next thing I knew," Tony says, "they got a caricature of a guy with a beard on their Big Daddy's sign. I ain't saying it's me, but seemed funny at the time." The bearded visage is out front of every Big Daddy's in the state. A long article about a Big Daddy who was supposed to have started the chain appeared in the *Miami Herald* some time ago, but it was unconvincing. Big Daddy's Lounges are contemptible and unworthy of comment . . . except as examples of how far we've gone in the wrong direction.

The Palace Saloon

117 Atlantic Avenue, Fernandina Beach

I drove all day to reach the Palace. It was eleven thirty on a Monday night when I found her. I could hear music playing, laughter and hoots, even before I pushed through Palace's cut-glass doors and faced the most beautiful front-and-back bar set I had seen since Boise, Idaho. North Florida crackers swayed to George Jones and Tammy Wynette, their shabby deck shoes shuffling across a white tile floor, beehive hairdos seeming just to miss Palace's low paddle fans. By-golly locals with dark tans and open sport shirts swigged draft beer at Palace's forty-foot bar, picking at baskets of spiced shrimp, their feet on a polished brass rail fat as a Louisville Slugger. A barmaid served mine and I relaxed against one of Palace's high-backed Captain's stools, gazing into the eight-foot back mirror at an exhausted yet happy traveler, content in the knowledge that he had discovered another Great American Bar.

Chance mention in the *Miami Herald* had provided the tip. A column about touring historic Florida had mentioned Palace as an ideal kickoff point. Located on Amelia Island, ten miles northeast of Jacksonville, Palace is the oldest bar in Florida (1903) and a cultural landmark in the small Victorian town of Fernandina Beach, a city nearly forgotten by tourists (AAA's guidebook does not list it) and an anachronism in a New South obsessed with urban renewal. Fernandina has a modest renewal plan on the books: its goal to reconstruct downtown Atlantic Avenue as accurately as possible. This will require little more than the re-creation of several Atlantic Avenue façades, as Fernandina's Victoriana is largely intact.

During the eighteen-seventies and eighties, Fernandina was a major East Coast shipping port and the richest city in Florida. It had a railroad and a steamship line; posh Jekyll and Cumberland Islanders to the north: Carnegies, Rockefellers, Bakers, Goodyears, Fergusons, Goulds, Pulitzers, and Morgans, all of whom stopped regularly at Fernandina; and it had Louis G. Hirth, a German immigrant and Florida entrepreneur, who had been saving to open a saloon in Fernandina for twenty years. Hirth had his eye on a haberdashery at Center and Second Streets, a stout brick building constructed in 1878 upon a six-foot bed of crushed oyster shells, with brick walls three feet thick and enough first floor space for a regal barroom. As soon as the building became available Hirth snagged it up, and in March of 1903 he opened Palace for business. Hirth had his competition cut out for him. Twenty-two saloons already crowded Fernandina, most of them lining waterfront side streets in easy access of seagoing vessels and the sailors who ran them. These were usual seamen's dives, rife with prostitution and random violence; anything a sailor might want for an easy price. What Fernandina lacked was an elegant gentleman's saloon, an establishment worthy of ship's officers and railroad tycoons, old guard yachtsmen, and squeamish industrialists who were traveling to Florida in ever-increasing numbers, for the enjoyment of that oddity, the "winter vacation."

Not just any bar fixtures would do. Louis Hirth called upon his old friend and fellow countryman Adolphus Busch of the Anheuser-Busch Brewery in St. Louis, a man with bravado. Under Busch's expert guidance, Hirth selected the Claes & Lehnbeuter Manufacturing Company to outfit Palace with fourteen hundred dollars' worth of English oak bar fixtures, in the St. Louis "Exposition" style. The single arched back bar, with two caryatids (undraped female figures) supporting the twenty-foot entablature and mirror, was fashioned of black mahogany and oak by German-born craftsmen and hand-carved to the last detail: medallions, dentils, scrollwork. Hirth went whole hog, ordering cigar cases, partitions, "Pioneer" wall cases, a cigar counter, a lunch counter, a front bar with mahogany top and half-round Doric columns, and an English oak door for the toilet room. Fourteen-pound brass cuspidors were situated around Palace's geometrically inlaid floor, and polished oak tables with wrought iron bases were at the service of any patron wishing to sit down. A jeweled lantern hung before Palace's beveled-glass swinging doors, a marble and brass cash register settled accounts behind the bar. Despite all this luxury, a large draft could be had for five cents and Palace's free lunch was often paté de foie gras with truffles.

Busch himself traveled from St. Louis to oversee the installation of Palace's furnishings. Hirth had embossed the old haberdashery's ceiling in tin, and wainscoted his barroom in Italian marble with a handsome granite border. He was later (1907) to commission Fernandina artist Roy Kennard to paint a series of four murals: action scenes copied from frontispieces of timeless works of literature in an N. C. Wyeth/Maxfield Parrish style, quite remarkable for its verisimilitude. Kennard's murals were bordered for perspective and positioned around Palace's walls like windows, so that one might gaze upon the lifelike figures of Falstaff, Shylock and Portia, English barristers, and Mr. Pickwick with the sense that they were just outside. The murals are so like portraits that a Carnegie boy in his cups one evening paid some anonymous rascal a good bit of money for the privilege of owning one, only to discover next morning that his purchase had been painted on the wall rather than hung.

Palace was a money-making concern from the start, and Louis Hirth pulled no punches to attract the big Fernandina buck. He bottled his own whisky (Cumberland was a favorite brand name, to appease the Carnegies of Cumberland Island), crocked his own beer, and even minted his own aluminum money to be offered as change, good only at the Palace. He sold iron slugs, six for a quarter, to be used in Palace's slot machines, and kept roulette wheels spinning throughout Prohibition. An interesting side story attached to Prohibition: the last day liquor was legally sold at Palace, Hirth rang up over sixty thousand dollars in sales. Liquor was dispensed directly from railroad cars, and every store in Fernandina sold out of suitcases to cart the stuff away. A monumental traffic jam resulted, cars said to have been stopped all the way from Yulee, twelve miles west. During Prohibition, Hirth is said to have operated Palace as a combination speakeasy and gambling casino, with the first floor converted to a genteel ice-cream parlor. A close examination of Palace's back bar mirror will show shadows of price and flavor listings, handpainted on the glass surface.

Hirth's son, Albert Hirth, took over Palace after Louis Hirth's death in 1938. Young Hirth managed the old saloon until 1957, when D. C. Land and H. E. Williams acquired the business. They initiated a painstaking process of restoration which resulted in Palace today, listed on the register of National Historic Buildings and virtually the same saloon Louis Hirth opened in March of 1903. Gone are Hirth's potbelly stoves and block ice shipped in from northern lakes, but his ceiling fans still turn, his gem-studded brass lamp hangs over Claes & Lehnbeuter's front bar, the old cash register works, a player piano tinkles amiably in a far corner, oak tables stand up to heavy elbows and bushel after bushel of spiced shrimp, Roy Kennard's murals have been retouched by Mr. Kennard himself (with a new one added, a disarming pirate scene) and the front-and-back bar set is in mint shape, appraised recently at fifty thousand dollars . . . though, as Aubrey Williams, H.E.'s son and Palace's current boss conjectures, "Who can tell what it's really worth."

Heavy velvet curtains drape Palace's arched windows, so that there is never more than a sliver of daylight allowed inside. Palace opens at eight a.m., closes at one a.m., so that it serves a panoply of patrons from fishermen to laborers to shopkeepers to tourists to businessmen-from-Jacksonville, to bar folk in for a good time no matter why. A Michelob draft can be had for sixty cents and a basket of shrimp for one ninety-five. There is homegrown entertainment on weekends or whenever somebody feels like playing Palace's old piano. A museum display case is situated against Palace's front wall, full of fascinating objects for passing the time: giant shrimp pickled in alcohol, antique pistols, thousand-year-old shark's teeth, current shark jaws, Palace money with Hirth's "H" engraved on the back, daggers, diaries, and other memorabilia. The eight flags of Amelia Island (French, Spanish, British, Patriots, Green Cross of Florida, Mexican, United States, and Confederate) hang along a side wall below thousands of tiny hooks, said to have supported fly catching lengths of string which protected Palace's elegantly embossed ceiling. A miniature still, built and presented to Palace in 1903 by a Russian coppersmith, sits atop the old player piano. The most exciting event all year in Fernandina is the annual shrimp boat race, first weekend in May—same weekend as Kentucky Derby and Virginia Gold Cup—when town fathers, including Aubrey Williams, deck out in pirate costumes and take over Fernandina's waterfront. Patronage at Palace is largely devoid of Carnegies and Vanderbilts these days, but Samuel Goldwyn once stopped in, as has Richard Boone, who lives in St. Augustine. Fernandina is on the intracoastal waterway, so many vessels, large and small, discharge passengers into Atlantic Avenue and ultimately the Palace. But the cream of Palace's clientele are Fernandina's locals, who respect Palace's historic dignity and zero fear factor, continuing to employ her as their downtown club and home away from home.

The Tavern Bar
Commerce Street, Apalachicola

A Gulf Coast oysterman's saloon, at the tip of Florida's elbow, Tavern boasts an old oak counter with polished brass rail, a clientele as salty as the local catch, well-chilled beer, and nothing plastic about the decor. Gulf shrimp are a big industry in Apalachicola, and shrimp nets hang from the ceiling at Tavern, with dried shrimp and horseshoe crab strung throughout the netting. Conch-type frame houses dot the streets of Apalachicola, and the feel of the village is Cape Cod or Key West before the overseas highway. Tavern Bar is clean and respectable, with oldtimers, off-duty fishermen, and one or two travelers in attendance, all trying desperately to get warm in the thirty-degree blow. Everybody was very excited about the possibility of snow the day I visited. Beer was cheap, about forty cents a can, whisky and wine were available to the hearty. Very quiet, very restrained sort of village, a quiet and restrained saloon. Zero fear factor. But obviously capable of getting very funky.

Hunt's Oyster Bar
Route 98, Panama City

You can rave about Gordon's in Baltimore or Felix's in New Orleans, but for pure oyster satisfaction I'll take Hunt's of Panama City any old time. A ramshackle, flyblown, sweaty workshirt sort of place, Hunt's nevertheless will shuck a dozen oysters for seventy-five cents, and more or less lose count after the first two orders. Beer is from the can as fast as you can drink it, hot sauce is homemade, hot as you like it, and clientele is slap-em-on-the-back, slurp-em-down, honest country.

The first thing I noticed, upon wandering into Hunt's, was a hand-printed sign behind the bar which read:

> Our record—
> nineteen dozen
> set by a woman
> 5' 10", 160 lbs.
> just passin thru.

Hunt's bartender was a wizened little man, tan as a football, who'd been on shucking duty the day Hunt's record was set. "She ate them oysters in two hours," he said, "with five bags of chips, six beers, and only went to the toilet twiced."

The exact identity of Hunt's record holder is unknown, but her feat is not forgotten. "I seen it," said a teen-aged boy, lounging in front of Hunt's TV. "She took it real slow and steadied herself with chips. Don't reckon she required that beer, but anyhow, she done it."

I ate three and a half dozen oysters at Hunt's myself—which came to one dollar and eighty cents, after appropriate deductions and miscalculations. The oysters were excellent: fresh, firm, and with a hint of salt water. Beer was cheap, thirty cents a can, and crackers were free. Hunt's bartender shucked at least a half dozen oysters for me gratis, but three and a half dozen was about my limit. I wished I could have done better by him, but a record just wasn't in me.

SOUTH CAROLINA

Wagon Wheel Saloon
336 King Street, Charleston

The Wagon Wheel Saloon, on downtown King Street, is the oldest saloon in Charleston and an anachronism in a town which prides itself on historic accuracy. Charleston is a seaport, its reputation founded on easy access to a safe harbor. Thus, the typical spate of nautical beer joints along Route 52 in North Charleston, unremarkable for their similarity to others of the genre—visible on City Hall Street in Norfolk, Royal Street in Mobile, Decatur Street in New Orleans, and to a degree, East Baltimore Street in Baltimore. Neon is the atmospheric bath; plasticoated the drinks; loud the Nashville music and the military people obnoxious; bar girls, go-goes, whores are consistent in texture and scent. Charleston is an eighteenth-century city with an air of formal decadence not moderated by the situation of honky-tonks north of town. One would do well to remember that Charleston's famous plantations, with their paradisiac formal gardens and ordered grounds, are likewise located north of the city. Or the city south of plantations, depending upon point of view. In any case, Wagon Wheel has been serving aristocrats and lowly sailors, Northerners and Southerners, since 1865.

Wagon Wheel is a modest saloon, in an Italianate row house at King Street center, which is dark as a closet at night and dimly lit from a large front window during the day. Whisky is not regularly served at bars in South Carolina, "but you can get it if you know where and are willing to pay," Wagon Wheel's bartender affirmed. Beer at Wagon Wheel is plentiful and cold—a large draft for sixty cents. Wine drinks are available. An old front bar stands to the left as one enters Wagon Wheel's narrow barroom, scarred and mug worn, and a jukebox with contemporary sounds, verging on art-rock, is situated to the right. A lovely Art Deco back bar graces rear left. Interesting posters and junk memorabilia from everywhere cover Wagon Wheel's walls. The bartender is a serious, mustached fellow of an intellectual bent who does not mind discussing problems of the contemporary South. Such as a lack of good drinking spots. The crowd at Wagon Wheel is neighborhood hip, nautical, business, professional; and only an occasional tourist stops by. Wagon Wheel's most intriguing physical characteristic is its beamed trapezoidal ceiling, shaped like a mansard, or the bulkhead of some antique sailing vessel. The feel of Wagon Wheel is the forecastle of a wooden ship; that dark and secure. The fear factor at Wagon Wheel is negligible, and if you're looking for a bit of nineteenth-century saloon life in eighteenth-century Charleston, Wagon Wheel's the spot to hit.

Henry's Seafood
North Market Street, Charleston

Henry's is not a saloon *per se,* but a fine old seafood restaurant with a thirties-style Art Deco bar, and black waiters who serve clean damask napkins and cheese dip with your draft—your waiter graciously unfolding a napkin and draping it across your lap, taking your order grandly and hurrying to Henry's kitchen where marvelous dishes such as crabmeat omelettes and traditional clams on the halfshell are being prepared. There are high-backed wooden booths in Henry's barroom, and the feel of the place is post-Prohibition, pre-World War II, deep South. Penn Warren stuff. Beers are sixty cents for the large draw and Charlestonians do come in just for beer and cheese. Service at Henry's is elegant but not stuffy; the decor musty and reminiscent of old Charleston Market, across the street: a market which still sells fresh produce during the day, in the old way . . . open air and bustling. Pictures of famous ships and other nautical scenes adorn the walls at Henry's. There are the customary overhead fans. A large dining area is off to one side, but the bar is recommended for colorful dining and drinking. A must on any Charleston bar tour.

GEORGIA

Crystal Beer Parlor

301 West Jones Street, Savannah

When Blocko Manning founded the Crystal in 1933, hamburgers went for ten cents apiece and beers for twelve. Forty years later, the prices have risen proportionally, but Crystal remains an inexpensive spot to eat or drink. A large Michelob draft can be had for sixty cents, and Crystal's luncheon special on the day I visited read:

> *Fried Flounder*
> *Cole Slaw or*
> *Tossed Salad*
> *Green Beans Pimento*
> *Macaroni and Cheese*
> *Grecian Bread*
> *Iced Tea or Coffee*
> *$1.90*

Crystal's menu was hand-printed on white cards placed strategically across the bar—a thirties-style walnut counter which at one time was the longest bar in Savannah. An Art Deco back bar, in lighter wood with wide bands of chromium, is also in attendance at Crystal. A café counter angles off toward the left of the bar, and a spare dining room to one side. Crystal's chef, Henry, has worked for the management over forty years. The three waiters have a combined total service of nearly seventy-five years. Appointments at Crystal are venerable, as befits a post-Prohibition saloon in a marginally seedy neighborhood. Padded booths with antique coatracks are situated to the rear of Crystal's barroom, and a row of formica tables runs down the center. Old photos cover Crystal's walls, dispersed by maps, and one or two neon beer signs. Crystal's well-worn wooden floor is swept and the feel of Crystal is that of a clean, midafternoon saloon. Crystal closes early (nine p.m.) so in a sense Crystal *is* midafternoon: the midafternoon essence of sleepy Savannah. Oldtimers line up at Crystal's walnut front bar, around three thirty; one foot cocked on Crystal's polished brass rail, they reminisce in soft Savannah drawls, munching Crystal Burgers and swilling cold draft beer, under slowly revolving ceiling fans.

Macon to the hurried bar traveler is pretty much a bust, with the exception of Len Berg's Restaurant (established 1908) in Old Post Office Alley, where a platter of filet mignon, collard greens and black-eyed peas can be had for two ninety-five, and the service is Old South with a smile. Len Berg's is by no means a bar, but beer is served with dinner, at old wooden booths by ancient black waiters. A world apart—and as much "New South" as Len Berg's is "Old"—is Nashville South at 2020 Riverside Drive, a cover charge dancehall in a miracle mile section of New Macon, with cops at the door, a dress code for men (no jeans, no tanktops, no work clothes . . . no freaks) and brutal bouncers everywhere. There is good country music in and around Macon, and a lot of it passes through Nashville South. On almost any night, creditable bands can be heard; there is an acre of dance floor surrounded by at least two acres of tables and a small army of waitresses. Nashville South is purported to pack them in on weekends, but on the Tuesday eve of Elvis Presley's fortieth birthday, about one hundred patrons were present and very few of them danced to a long-haired country band which blared mimicky renditions of the Nashville top forty over an ear-splitting sound system. Still, Nashville South conveyed a definite energy. A modest bar was located toward the rear of the huge ballroom, and Schlitz draft could be had for sixty-five cents a glass. Cover charge at the door was one dollar. The monstrous building occupied by Nashville South had at one time belonged to the American Legion. Which added a certain cultural leverage. Fear factor at Nashville South was not exceptional, however. Older bars in Macon are located in the downtown area, near Broadway and Third, but they are black clubs in a black neighborhood, very wino and rundown. Macon has a proud history of black music . . . Little Richard washed dishes at the Greyhound Bus station in Macon, writing songs and gigging clubs on the side. Otis Redding was from Macon; there is a bridge named in his honor. James Brown got his start in Macon saloons like the Two-Spot on Fifth Street, downtown. And of course Macon is hometown to the Allman Brothers' Band, avatars of New South rock, and Macon-based Capricorn Records' hottest property. The Brothers' band has been known to jam at Grant's Lounge, downtown; or at Uncle Sam's out on Gray's Highway, where the redoubtable Cher Bono has been seen in company of Brother Gregg. Are they worth the trip?

At Flovilla, a small town between Macon and Atlanta, a teenage waitress in a Main Street café asked where I was headed. She shivered when I told her.

"I wouldn't go t'Atlanta," she said, "for nearly nothing. All em niggers. All em cutting each other and you too."

Skyscraper Atlanta may be the murder capital of the nation, but in *Underground Atlanta* there is a surfeit of police, and the worst that can happen to you is being hit over the head by a portable Hurricane, or having your pocket picked. Underground Atlanta is the real thing . . . a two and one-half block area of restored Victoriana, complete with gas lamps, stained-glass windows and cobblestoned streets—extending from Central Avenue to Whitehall, beneath Hunter and Alabama. Underground Atlanta was the commercial center of the city at the turn of the century, before streets were raised one level to connect with bridges and viaducts which had, in turn, covered railroad tracks. The neighborhood is enclosed by streets or parking buildings overhead, and a musty, evening-in-Atlanta atmosphere prevails at midafternoon. Though located near the current financial center, Underground Atlanta is primarily a tourist attraction—peopled by tourists, catering to tourists, and reminiscent of touristy Bourbon Street. Most of Underground's "saloons" have nice fixtures and many of these fixtures are authentic; but no saloons are. Each has been cut out of an old warehouse, designed and refurbished to salve the seventies' Gay Nineties itch. Muhlenbrink's Saloon possesses the most impressive front and back bar set, but the old mirror is painted with multi-colored advertisements for exotic drinks, and the atmosphere after dark is cloyingly tourist. The Burning of Atlanta has a piano bar, Sgt. Pepper's live rock, the Blarney Stone, the Bank Note, the Planters Exchange, the Apothecary Lounge, P. J. Kenney's Saloon and the Bucket Shop are all insufferably tourist. Examples of saloons which could have been done tastefully, but succumbed to the temptation of Big Tourist Buck.

WEST VIRGINIA

Strand Pool
Main Street (Center), Grafton

When stranded in Grafton, Strand is the solution. If your pleasure is hard rock with a country twang, Hickory Inn on Parkview Road is a must on weekends, but on a daily basis Strand is tough to beat for beer and eight ball in downtown Grafton. It's a small place, with only two pool tables and one rack boy . . . comfortable. There is no such word as pressure at Strand; white-haired men line the back wall, sitting straight as fence posts in wobbly cane chairs, watching the action, grinning feebly or nodding off. Hotshots stride around the tables, sighting carefully along a stick or busting the rack with violent jabs at the cue ball. Country music plays from a nearby juke and someone always seems to be screaming into the phone at a girl friend or angry wife. "I ain't here," is the commonest word to Strand's bartender when ducking incoming calls. West Virginia freaks and salty old men crowd Strand's Art Deco front bar on a slow Saturday in the old B & O town of Grafton: a grim, mountainous spot, cold and craggy, with a hint of the millennium to its features. Strand is the beer drinker's warmth.

A longhaired fireman for B & O waxed friendly and bought a beer. "Might I ast yr name?" he inquired politely. He was a forty-nine-dollar-a-day man, had been working for B & O on the Grafton-to-Parkersburg run for some years, and was bored. We talked for a while. He wanted me to stick around, hear this band from Morgantown "who sound just like Led Zep, they are the best in W Vee A." I ordered another Stroh's at forty cents a can and stared into Strand's back mirror, at old men who sat motionless toward the rear of the room. Strand had been open for business since 1949, could very well be open in 2009. Grafton hadn't changed much since its founding in 1865. I could see my fireman in the big back mirror with white hair and un-hip coveralls. Still killing his Saturdays with a cold Stroh's and the warmth of Strand. It was not an unpleasant thought. Strand's bartender was about the same age as my fireman. He would remain too—under Strand's dusty photos of Major League ballplayers. Nothing would change. The rack boy, himself an oldtimer, checked Pro scores on the big blackboard behind the pool tables and cleared off empty beer cans. The Art Deco back bar which had seen service in Grafton since the thirties, stood quietly about its mirror. We drank, there was variety, motion, yet all remained the same.

Welcome Corner
Route 50, Parkersburg

Parkersburg is Mothman Country. Home turf of what noted UFO-logist John A. Keel, in *Strange Creatures from Time and Space* and his extraordinary book about the 1966 West Virginia UFO flap, *The Mothman Prophecies,* has called "that infamous feathery Garuda." Keel spent a year in the Parkersburg/Point Pleasant area, investigating Mothman . . . a giant batlike "bird" with gleaming red eyes, who had been terrorizing locals for some time. Parkersburg is a cold, dirty industrial town where people shuffle from work to barroom, barroom to work, with the weight of the world on their shoulders. The last thing they need is Mothman, but apparently he's around; and people are reluctant to speak of him.

Welcome Corner sits on the southwest side of a soot-flecked intersection, where the wind blows, traffic whines, and the sun goes down early. It is a lonesome corner, but the old saloon has been comforting patrons and shooing Mothmen since Prohibition. A bottle of Bud is fifty cents, a short Iron City light or dark draft is twenty cents, and your companions at Welcome will be cordial if not overly vocal. There is a formality to the old saloon which belies its décor—though that is customary post-Prohibition saloon: old wooden booths, to which Welcome's bartender is happy to carry your drink, crowd a back wall; country music selections people the jukebox, and a wooden front bar "over seventy years old" serves standup customers. There is a false back bar at Welcome, like wainscoting, which frames a casual display of Hav-a-Hanks, Hot Shot Disposable Lighters, Chip-ets, Cheez'n Crackers, and Red Man Chewing Tobacco. Welcome's bartender is a pleasant, gray-haired fellow, who diligently mops both front bar and tables before serving a beer. West Virginia working types sip their Iron City, away from wind, industrial filth and Mothman, with the poise of Eskimos in a snowstorm. Food is available at Welcome, inexpensive sandwiches, shrimp or fried oysters, so that one needn't take a step outside. Beer is served in larger mugs for thirty cents, but whisky is not on the bill.

Welcome is open early and closes late. There are honkytonk country music bars all up and down this same stretch of Route 50 in Parkersburg, but Welcome is the spot: zero fear factor and mothballs in every salt shaker.

Quiet Knight
Route 2 (Center), Parkersburg

Quiet Knight is Parkersburg's hip saloon, reminiscent of the Varsity Grill at its finest hour, but with a more sober design and something of a post-Indochina aimlessness to the clientele, which cuts Knight's fear factor to near zero. Still, there is Mothman outside and the terrible Men in Black: deeply tanned "census takers" wearing black business suits, who harassed West Virginians during the 1966 flap, stopping citizens along deserted roads and ushering them into spanking new, black 1938 Buick sedans so new they *smelled* new; issuing vague threats, asking questions . . . Where else but in a Varsity Grill bar to recall the words of Dr. T. Peter Park, College Park's most infamous UFOlogist and student of Library Psychosis, who authored the now legendary UFO poem, *MIB:*

> The Men in Black came up to my door
> A squeaking mouse blasphemed my floor
> Orange brilliance specked hourly my ceiling
> Blue-lit cities crushed all feeling
> A black-haired daughter of the father of nations
> Screaming at the immolations
> Of spider-crucified men and women
> Mocked at by the cross-armed checkered demon
> And the con-desecrated oakbranch hanged swine
> Obeying them like lowing faithful kine
> Saw helicopters burning bright
> Saw tigers glowing in the night
> Tearing tearing tearing, hunger past all tears
> Baring, baring, baring, coldness past all fears
> In blue-lit lusting virgin lands
> Traversed by midnight-stepping bands.

Yes, T. Peter possessed a mind which could fathom the despair of Parkersburg, West Virginia. But the Quiet Knight had a certain active peace. There is an excitement to rural hipster bars which is no longer prevalent in more cosmopolitan taverns. Patrons and proprietors remain small town folk under long hair and spangled bells, and a rural cordiality tends to surface. Quiet Knight's music was superb: taped Dylan, Lightfoot, Blues Project, all selected with timeless good taste. A draft beer was thirty-five cents for an honest twelve ounce portion, light or dark. The customary weathered booths, dim photos, Gibson Girl prints, pool table, pinball machines and assorted Victoriana filled the room, but not to overflowing. The kids were healthy looking and attractive. Knight's atmosphere was just fine, so much so that I nearly forgot the grisly West Virginia monsters hunkering in the shadows outside.

LOUISIANA
New Orleans

At Congo Square, where jazz was born, I bought a Billy Strayhorn album from a black trombonist who said: *"Need* a drink, brother. So dry I's spittin dust." Billy Strayhorn turned out to be Oscar Peterson undercover, and Congo Square—where slaves had danced the Bamboula and Calinda, practiced zombiism and *vodun*, rattled gourds, plucked marimbas, and shuffled barefoot through the dust—now hosted a municipal auditorium and was called Beauregard. "Where can I hear some good jazz?" I asked the retreating trombonist. "None of this tourist shit, some New Orleans *jazz."* The trombonist tried to focus, dropped his pupils to the sidewalk, then pointed to a plastic lounge across Rampart Street. "Good sound there," he said. "Dyn'mite juke." Then he hurried away.

Jukebox for jazz? In New Orleans? No. I had driven all night for *live music* with breakfast. But . . . well. I hustled across Orleans to Burgundy, and Buster Holmes—where every all-night crusade should expire in a plate of red beans and rice—and they know about jukeboxes, soulish and loud.

Buster Holmes
721 Burgundy Street (French Quarter), New Orleans

Photographs of black musicians line the walls at Buster's: the Olympia Band, Louis Armstrong, all of New Orleans's favorites. Paintings by local blacks, in a New Orleans street style—lots of color, acres of wide expressionistic faces—hang here and there in the way of black workingmen crowded into Buster's for a quick lunch and a leisurely shot of whatever; black workingmen packed in among the freaks, artists, and odd tourists who make Buster's a regular noontime stop. Buster's is a daylight spot, open every day from nine a.m. to seven thirty p.m. It is a soul food restaurant as well as a bar, and it is New Orleans black folks to the core.

You can get a plate of beans and bread at Buster's for thirty-five cents. All you can eat. Fried chicken, beans and rice is seventy-five cents, and no meal at Buster's ever runs more than a dollar. Beer and whisky are similarly priced. Table water for Buster's eating customers is served in old whisky bottles, labels still attached. *Very* loud soul music blasts intermittently from Buster's jukebox, and during slower hours, young blacks can be seen dancing quietly toward the rear of the dining area. Buster is a tough little man in his fifties or sixties, with barrel chest and thick forearms, who affects a long white apron and rarely shows emotion. Buster's is a rough place but there is seldom trouble, due to the patrician air Buster evinces. Big pots of beans and rice are situated behind Buster's heavily scarred oak bar, and he slides plates piled high down its surface the way another bartender might serve beer. There is an oak back bar at Buster's with a domed arch and four Doric columns, but it is not in very good shape and pretty much matches the rest of Buster's decor. Buster's is like a miniature New Orleans in tone: seedy, poor-boy, chaotic, nearly violent, funky, falling apart, but with great élan and an overdose of soul.

Seven Seas

5I5 St. Philip Street (French Quarter), New Orleans

The Seven Seas is a comfortable freak/seamen's bar with a big front room, cheap drinks, and a ping-pong table in the garden. The Seven Seas is the only bar I have ever patronized with a ping-pong table, and that struck me as a good way to get a light workout while drinking, and an obvious choice for recreation. I had long fantasized about a bar with gym equipment and a steamroom where patrons could exercise, sweat out last night's indulgences, and relax with a good bit of controlled physical activity. Seven Seas' ping-pong table was headed in the right direction; I enjoyed several games before the bottom-feeders showed up and *hey man*'ed me off the table.

Seven Seas has a modest fear factor at midafternoon, less modest after dark, but it is a good place to start the day. Draft beer is thirty cents a glass and popcorn is for sale behind the bar, for about fifteen cents. I met a down-and-outer named Joanna at Seven Seas, who latched right onto me, riding me for free beers, but I didn't care. She had her story to tell, and I was into a drunk, exhausted from twenty-seven-hours-on-the-road and no sleep. I asked Joanna politely about the needle tracks covering the backs of her hands.

"You play a lot of ping-pong?" I said.

"Nah, I always get stuck with the bill."

Joanna was a light-hooker when feeling better—and looking a little better than she did today—but hadn't turned a trick for six months. She said. She had a kid somewhere and an old man. The usual story, which I absorbed through a cheap beer haze, burps, and trips to the john—because Seven Seas was lonesome, and chess players who lined the far wall every evening after ten were not yet in attendance, and the place had an empty feel to it, a coldness in the subtropical afternoon which was unsettling. You can *smell* twilight in New Orleans like no other city in America. The air grows tan and warm as a loaf of French bread, and a thin line of salmon pink can be seen across the rooftops. Joanna said she wanted to try another bar, so we paid up at Seven Seas and hit the street.

Johnny Matassas
909 St. Philip Street (French Quarter), New Orleans

Johnny's is a little no-name bar, more like a carpenter's shop or a Parisian wine cellar than a neighborhood saloon: Joanna knew some people there and we elbowed up to the raw wood bar for a couple more beers. Drafts were twenty-five cents at Johnny's, cold and carefully tapped. I had read a long interview with August Luchow in a 1934 edition of *The Outfitter* during my research at the Library of Congress, having to do with the proper tapping of beer, cleaning of lines and refrigeration. Barkeep at Johnny Matassas must have read the same article, for the beer was perfect. And for a quarter. Joanna and I played pinball for a while and danced to the jukebox. Johnny's was matchbook size and patrons were crowded one against the other, spilling drinks, dropping paperbacks out of hip pockets, sketching damply on artist's pads. The fear factor at Johnny's was near zero, you could not beat the price and clientele was motley and gracious.

One block over, Bourbon Street was cascading with its usual flotsam of homosexuals, whores, johns, tourists, panhandlers and nonspecific degenerates. Bourbon Street is closed to cars after dark, so we strolled down its center; past hot dog vendors with their hot dog shaped wagons, black paper boys hustling early editions, old black women dancing for change, barkers hawking nude attractions both male and female—pulling back heavy curtains for a moment, then demanding two or three dollars cover for a longer look; past stalls where beer and Hurricanes were being sold for street consumption, past small folky places, big tourist joints like Your Father's Mustache, Al Hirt's, Pete Fountain's, The Blue Angel, Paddock Lounge, Famous Door, Old Court Tavern, Maison Bourbon, Chez Frank, The Old Absinthe House, and twenty or thirty others, some with nudes swinging from upper windows out over the sidewalk, some quiet and sedate, most jumping with three-thirty a.m. folks partying and generally making a fuss.

Felix's

739 Iberville Street (French Quarter), New Orleans

Felix's is an oyster bar open from ten a.m. until four a.m. every day except Sunday. I have never been to New Orleans when I did not finish an evening or start a day at Felix's. You can get a dozen oysters for two dollars, fresh, firm, as good as you'll taste in the South, and a draft beer for thirty-five cents. Felix's is a restaurant-bar; that translates: food as important as booze—often a hazy distinction in New Orleans, where everyone partakes so much of both. It is inconceivable to think of oysters without beer, so what the hell, Felix's is an oyster bar.

We crowded up to the marble countertop and ordered dozens all around. Great cups full of ketchup, horseradish, Tabasco and lemon slurped onto tin trays; we shoveled it up with crackers. A black counterman named Wade served us, shouting "How 'bout it Doc, one more? F'you friends? Three here on the house, Doc. Comin up." And there would be another magical dozen on the bar, instantly dunked into sauce and devoured, the salty mess dripping over our shirt fronts, across faces, licked off each other's hands.

The place was full at three thirty in the morning: drunks, night workers, cops, musicians, *eaters*. Toward the rear, couples sat at plain formica tables, drinking and dining on fried oysters, Bienvilles, Rockefellers, oyster loaves, fried shrimp, boiled crawfish and pompano. Others inhaled gumbo and crawfish bisque, great gobs of the stuff oozing from the corners of satisfied smiles. I stood at Felix's plain marble bar, my foot on the brass rail, glass of beer in my right hand, and felt a whole lot better.

In 1897, Storyville was designated as New Orleans's official redlight district, and by 1910 over two hundred houses of prostitution were running full bore, with innumerable honkytonks, barrelhouses, cabarets and gambling joints. This meant music, jazz: piano players in every cathouse and a brass band in every dancehall. Jelly Roll Morton could earn fifteen to eighteen dollars a night at Lulu White's fabulous Mahogany Hall, a legend in its time, celebrated for a stable of delicate octoroons and the solid white piano on which Morton worked his hypnotic rags each evening. Today Lulu White's, at the corner of Basin and Bienville, is a lawyer's office and the rear half of the building has been demolished. Anderson's, at Basin and Iberville, where Louis Armstrong played as did many other seminal jazzmen, has been torn down. Ray Owens' Star Mansion, at 1517 Iberville, is gone, and Joe Victor's Saloon, at 1534 St. Louis, is the T & J Food Store.

All this realized deep in the cemetery district on a hangover stomach, Sunday evening coming down, nothing but trash in the streets and a stench of stale cooking from black housing developments blanketing old Storyville. I cut back to Bourbon Street, past Paddock Lounge, 309 Bourbon, where the cover charge was out of my league and they served you seven-ounce bottles of beer for "bargain" prices to hear imitation Dukes of Dixieland jazz: past Famous Door, 339 Bourbon, another old jazz spot which I had visited on my first trip to New Orleans twelve years earlier, with one of the guys from my ship—where I had been ripped off by the same seven-ounce beers and the same cover charge. People who are supposed to know say that occasionally a first-rate band will gig at Paddock or Famous Door, but I have not seen one. Traffic was easing slowly down Bourbon so I stuck to the sidewalk, kicking an empty Hurricane beaker out of the way, past Your Father's Mustache, 426 Bourbon, and the plaque on the brick wall there which read:

> JACK TEAGARDEN
> Played his last stand here
>   One year ago today
>   on 14 January 1964
> This plaque is placed in this spot
> By YFMNOLA in deepest respect for
> His enduring contribution to jazz

and pausing . . . before Crazy Shirley's at the corner of Bourbon and St. Peter, where the kind of jazz I'd been dreaming about sifted through the shutters and into Bourbon Street. A woman at Shirley's front door demanded a dollar contribution, and I hurried inside.

It was an oldtime New Orleans benefit, and every musician in town was jammed into the bar. The dollar cover went to pay some sick musician's hospital bill (I never discovered which one) and the rest to Crazy Shirley. The band was half black, half white, changing every minute as musicians stood to solo, left the bandstand, and were replaced by members of the audience. A tingle started at my coccyx and worked itself up to my first thoracic vertebra. Outside it was grim, overcast, coming up on twilight. Inside Crazy Shirley's it was a new day breaking: trombone, sax, trumpet, coronet, bass, drums and piano, all of them working with and against the grain, filling Shirley's big barroom with joyful hot licks. The group broke into "Royal Garden Blues," an old Red Nichols number, and I didn't think I was going to be able to stand it. Everyone in Crazy Shirley's was on his feet, clapping, dancing, kicking over chairs. The band did a promenade around Crazy Shirley's twice and finished fortissimo, not a dry eye in the house. The applause was frightening. People were not accustomed to feeling this good. The band sensed violence and segued promptly into "Closer Walk with Thee" which took the edge off considerably. This was no Preservation Hall band, shaky and rachitic; these were young musicians with Buddy Bolden lungs who had been hiding—where? What part of town? "They play in bands all *over* town, each working for somebody else," the door lady explained. "But when they get together it's sure's shit like old times."

Crazy Shirley's was okay. Drinks were overpriced, and during the week it was strictly from Tourist. But if Sunday afternoon could see jazz like this, why quibble; she goes on the list.

The Pearl

119 St. Charles Avenue, New Orleans

One block across Canal Street from the French Quarter, Pearl is a great New Orleans oyster bar and a comfortable spot for Sunday brunch. Huge roast beefs, turkeys, hams, and pastramis crowd Pearl's front window, tempting one to slide in and partake of cold

Falstaff on tap, and a variety of Pearl's legendary sandwiches. Oysters at Pearl run about a quarter less than her French Quarter competition, and they are about three quarters as good. A draft is thirty-five cents at Pearl, and there is a standup oyster bar. It's kind of a seedy spot, very bright and dinerish despite an iron-balconied exterior. Pearl is open twenty-four hours a day, seven days a week, and its schedule shows in wear and tear.

Acme Oyster House

724 Iberville Street (French Quarter), New Orleans

The Acme's greatness lies in its Löwenbräu light and dark beer on tap, its Jax Beer for a quarter a glass, and its creditable selection of bottled brew from all around the world. Acme is more of a bar than the Pearl or Felix's, a bit older in design and sometimes more shoddy, but its oysters are first rate—one dozen for approximately two dollars—and its clientele both broken-toothed and ragged, dinner-jacketed and gowned. There is an old standup bar at Acme where you mix your own hot sauce, there is a funky wooden floor, and there are tables toward Acme's rear for the squeamish. Acme opens early, at seven, and closes early, around eight thirty, so it is strictly a daytimer's bar. Some of the best poor boy sandwiches in town are sold at Acme, and they are as reasonably priced as the beer.

Dick's Bar

1732 St. Charles Avenue, New Orleans

Dick's is a seamen's bar out the St. Charles trolley line, with a great semicircular sign reading DICK'S BAR, which is tough to miss and even tougher to by-pass, if you're a bar person with an adventurous spirit. It's a shabby spot, typically New Orleans, with peeling paint, wrought-iron balcony, ratty green shutters and a one-step-up front door. But . . . Dick's is situated on the hem of New Orleans' Garden District, the "American" sector, jammed with antebellum mansions, romantic gardens, and Greek Revival architecture of the first order. So Dick's is something of an anomaly, more suited to the likes of Magazine or Tchoupitoulas Streets. How in the world did it get there, at 1732 St. Charles Avenue, in full view of the trolley line and whatever quality might be aboard.

There is a sign behind the old wooden bar at Dick's which reads:

S.I.U.
WELCOME

That is about the only decoration, excepting usual beer signs, tobacco canisters, cough drops, Red Man chaws, chewing gum, cigarettes, and headache nostrums. There are some stiff barstools and two or three old tables, but that is about it. Dick's pool table is in a back room, and you have to pass by it to get to the men's room; the table is usually full, with rough neighborhood types or heavily tanned seamen shooting for beers. Old women wander into Dick's, purchase half pints, stop to drink a beer, and wander out. Beer is cheap at Dick's, as are most drinks. There are no fancy drinks at Dick's, for there are no fancy customers. It is a lazy kind of joint, with nothing specific going for it except an attitude. Dick's attitude is irresistible, and whenever I'm in New Orleans, almost against my will, I find myself on the St. Charles trolley headed for Dick's.

The Old Absinthe Bar

400 Bourbon Street (French Quarter), New Orleans

The Old Absinthe Bar possesses the oldest front bar in New Orleans (1806) and quite possibly the oldest in America. The bar is from the original Absinthe House, at 240 Bourbon Street, and was installed in 1806 when that establishment was founded. A fire effected Absinthe bar's removal in 1920 to its current location. The 1806 counter with its crusty face and marble absinthe founts stands at the heart of the present-day saloon and is a wonder to behold.

French coffee houses of the seventeenth century are said to have initiated the custom of perpendicular drinking. A standup counter, ancestor to our nineteenth-century bar, was fashioned in France for the rapid consumption of lemonade and cider. Old Absinthe's bar was undoubtedly constructed for the efficient distribution and easy enjoyment of Absinthe Drip, the house specialty and notorious concoction of absinthe, opium, and water. Absinthe is a green liqueur, containing oils of wormwood and anise, which because of its addictive properties, was outlawed in France in 1915. The closest to absinthe you'll get at Old Absinthe today is Pernod. The Absinthe Drip was served until 1918 however, and fauceted fountains which concocted the mess are still prominently attached to the old bar.

"If it could talk, what stories this bar would tell of a thousand and one nights crowded into history," owner Dan Levy has jotted on his matchbook covers. Advertising copy or not, it's a shame Levy does not keep the bar in better shape. Paint is peeling off its face, the counter is not oiled, and brass on the fountains could use polish. Drinking at Old Absinthe is like being inside an old trunk—an antique one with a cardboard liner, shredded and peeling with age. The walls of Old Absinthe are papered with calling cards and greenbacks bearing the names of famous visitors. One doesn't have to be famous to leave one's card, just industrious enough to find a spot of free wall. Cards are piled upon cards, some so old the lettering is faded and the paper crumbling. Five- ten- and twenty-dollar bills are tacked high up behind the bar, with their former owners' names penned across the faces. A guestbook is available for the signatures of less ostentatious visitors, and so diverse a clientele as Bonnie Parker and Clyde Barrow, Lee Harvey Oswald, Jack Dempsey, Ernest and Patrick Hemingway, Gene Tierney, and Mark Twain have signed Absinthe's register. Old Absinthe House was a particular favorite of Mark Twain's, and it is said he spent countless hours at the old bar, drinking bourbon and spinning his indefatigable yarns. Andrew Jackson was another favored patron, as were privateersmen Jean and Pierre LaFitte. Jackson is said to have met with the LaFittes at Old Absinthe to help plan the battle of New Orleans.

Old Absinthe "closed" during Prohibition, but was in fact a speakeasy from 1920 until 1933. Today, it is a tourist bar, but what tourists: the best dressed, most glamorous of the French Quarter lot. A stable of French Quarter regulars makes Old Absinthe a nightly stop, but the clientele is more transient than fixed. People who have not been to Old Absinthe for twenty years return to drink under the photographs of Jack Dempsey and Diamond Jim Brady. Old Absinthe is not so reasonable as other French Quarter saloons—drinks around the dollar and a half mark, draft beer seventy-five cents. But to sit at the 1806 bar encased by thousands of calling cards and wicker-covered absinthe bottles from another era, is to suffer a unique Great Bar experience.

Marti's

1041 Dumaine Street (French Quarter), New Orleans

Marti's is more restaurant than saloon, but it has a barroom with a beautiful copper front bar, an oyster bar actually, with a handsome wooden back bar and lovely antique furnishings. The place is old, as are most establishments of its ilk in the French Quarter, and the bar section is gay. The entire place is a theater hangout—the Municipal Auditorium and cultural center nearby—so that there is an air of feigned sophistication and casual glamour. Oysters are good, very good in fact, at about two dollars a dozen. The omelettes are excellent, as are the desserts.

LaFitte's Blacksmith Shop

941 Bourbon Street (French Quarter)

LaFitte's is another tourist bar, largely gay, which is remarkable only for its history—pirates Jean and Pierre LaFitte are said to have employed it as headquarters for a variety of shenanigans—and its architecture, that of a humble nineteenth-century tradesman's shop in the medieval Southern manner. Drinks are overpriced, the atmosphere is cloying, but it is a lovely old spot worthy of at least one drink on any French Quarter tour.

Tujague's

823 Decatur Street (French Quarter), New Orleans

Tujague's is a French Market saloon which has served New Orleans politicians, sportsmen, hucksters, butchers, businessmen, and entertainers longer than anyone cares to remember. Over 150 years, actually. The building Tujague's occupies is 300 years old and was originally a Spanish arsenal. Tujague's is a formal saloon of the old order, with an exquisite 1856 back bar, tile floors, and a long mahogany front bar which glows with polished attention. The 1856 back bar was special ordered for Tujague's from an English manufacturer, and its slim Corinthian columns add a touch of delicacy that otherwise would be lacking in the old barroom. For Tujague's is still a workingman's saloon, opening and closing early, with an atmosphere of big bellies and wide suspenders—though the clientele at Tujague's today is polite and sportily dressed. It is a quiet spot after hours, with oldtimers in attendance, one or two couples lingering after dinner, and drinks which are reasonably priced. The fear factor is near zero. A friend and I stumbled across Tujague's one evening after a big Chinese dinner at Fun's, and large glasses of icy Michelob at Tujague's mahogany bar were just the thing to erase Fun's Chinese aftertaste. Later, Pepe Citron of the *New Orleans States-Item* provided me with a column he had written on Tujague's, and between my research and Citron's I was able to piece together a bit of Tujague's history.

Otis and Philip Guichet, Jr., run Tujague's today, but their father, Philip Sr., presided grandly over the old establishment for nearly forty-five years, in partnership with the late John Castet. Philip Guichet was born in 1886 in LaFourche Parish, Louisiana, where his father owned a rice mill, general store, and rental houses. The town where Philip grew up is still called Guichetville, and is located on Bayou LaForche near Raceland, Louisiana. Philip came to New Orleans in 1910 to help his brother Philibert run Tujague's, the family's recently acquired saloon. The old saloon has been in the Guichet family for over sixty years now, and if there is a traditional saloon left in New Orleans it is Tujague's. Philip and his partner John Castet made a pact that whosoever died first, the survivor would buy out the dead partner's interest so that Tujague's would remain unchanged. Guichet was obliged to honor that agreement several years back when old John passed away.

The neighborhood around Decatur Street remains seedy, but when Philip Guichet was a young man, it was very much the violent New Orleans waterfront of legend. "Decatur Street was the Old West," Philip Jr. told Pepe Citron. "There were tough places where the seamen went . . . shootings, fights. The streets were mud . . . later they were rock. There were no sewers in the early part of the century. We lived above the saloon and in back, on Madison. We would get up early and empty chamber pots into the gutter. My mother or father would wake me and say, 'Quick while it's still dark, empty the pot,' so I would go out before daylight and the mess would be cleaned up next time it rained. When we were little kids, somebody had to take us to school and bring us home. Dad wouldn't walk out of the place without a gun in his belt. We had iron bars on the second-floor window where we played . . . it was like being in jail."

Philip Guichet kept a good deal of money on hand in those days, as he was unofficial banker for many Decatur Street marketmen who were struggling to recover from a devastating 1915 hurricane which had completely wiped out New Orleans' French Market. The historic bartering place, which had served New Orleans since the eighteenth century, was being rebuilt with WPA labor during the Depression, and Philip Guichet became a backer for many merchants initiating a fresh start. "I kept three stevedores," Philip told Citron, "and doled out their money. Plus meat men, shrimpers, fish men, wholesalers. They'd come to me and say, 'Can you lend me the money to pay for my merchandise until I can sell it?' They were very honest. Very seldom did one beat me out of a nickel. At night they'd give me their money in bags and I'd pile it into my safe. Nobody counted it. They trusted me and I trusted them."

Philip Sr. personally served three presidents in his forty-five years behind Tujague's bar. "I made cocktails for Eisenhower," Philip says. "Sazeracs. They made me drink half of each one first. I thought they were joking but they certainly were not. Truman ate here. Drank bourbon. And I remember young Roosevelt . . . Teddy Roosevelt. He was here in the twenties. I can even show you the table where he was sitting—over there. He was with a party of eight or nine. And entertainers: Martha Raye used to come down from the Roosevelt. Mainly she'd drink the gin fizz. Sometimes the Sazerac or the grasshopper. Sometimes she'd sing. John Carroll too, whenever he was in town, he'd stand up to this bar. Lots of other movie stars. And judges and fighters and practically every mayor we ever had. Governors . . . Huey Long, Davis, McKeithen; the City Council, most every senator we've had; General Ray Hufft was a regular."

Philip Sr. traveled to New York City from 1928 through 1930 to participate in The New York Contest for Cocktail Mixing, and won three years straight. The contest was officiated by Walter Winchell, and Philip's grasshopper mixture of crème de menthe, crème de cacao, cream and brandy was Winchell's favorite. Philip later invented the "dry" grasshopper, employing just a tablespoon of brandy. "But he never registered the name," Otis Guichet told Citron. "Everybody makes it and features it now. Take Sazerac, that name is registered. Only the Fairmont can advertise it. We can serve it, and we do, but we are not allowed to post it or advertise it."

Tujague's serves food from eleven a.m. to three p.m., and five p.m. to nine p.m. and offers a set Creole menu, with no choice. In the old days, a complete meal at Tujague's cost fifty cents—which included a cocktail, all the food you could eat, a bottle of wine, dessert, and coffee with cognac. Today a complete dinner costs four twenty-five and does not include drinks. "We used to make more money in the fifty cent days," Philip says. "We were the first to feature boiled brisket with horseradish sauce . . . now everybody has it. We were the first to serve that crispy 'cap' bread, too."

Today, Philip Guichet's traditional lunchtime convocation is presided over by son Otis, seated at the head of a big barroom table in the chair his father occupied for four and a half decades. The wine still flows, conversation borders upon the outrageous, and food is stacked high along the table. Bemused tourists or sympathetic regulars stand up to the 1856 bar and contemplate what's left: Tujague's beer, the brisket of beef, bourbon, Philip's grasshoppers . . . and an immutable sense of old French Market and her past.

Party Tavern
Route 23, Venice

Party Tavern is a pink frame structure at the end of Route 23 in Venice, Louisiana, the last highway town on the Mississippi. Pilottown is further downriver, but to get there you need a launch. Party Tavern, for all intents and purposes, is the final stop on the Mississippi. It ain't much. But in a town surrounded by swamps, Gulf and Getty Oil camps, and water, it's a damnsight better than nothing.

Party is a Cajun bar, like Duck Blind across the parking lot, and the two are pretty much interchangeable: plain decor, *austere* decor, with formica counter, neon beer signs, country jukebox, cheap beer, wine chasers, and a rowdy assemblage of fishermen, pilots, tugboat captains, and oil roustabouts. Fear factor is very high at both Party and Duck Blind, but on the afternoon I visited there was not much trouble, and I was able to enjoy a leisurely glass of beer without incident. A fisherman across the street by the tugboat docks spat at my companion when he tried to take a picture, but other than that Venice was indifferent to our presence. Party looked like it might get hot on a Saturday night but I was in no shape to stick around. Party is the kind of bar where you expect either to lose a little or win a great deal. Probably shattering something along the way. Louisiana swampland around Party swarms with birds—egrets, coots, herons. To say nothing of aquatic life, the alligators, rattlesnakes, and alligator gar. The patrons of Party and Duck Blind are like hybrids of Venice's wildlife: part bird, part fish, part alligator, with a sprinkling of human someplace. All loud and rusty, clanking like poorly oiled nautical machinery.

Frenchy's
Route 23, Port Sulphur

Frenchy's is a Cajun joint south of New Orleans, with possibly the finest country music jukebox in Louisiana. Name your favorite and he/she appears on the plastic at Frenchy's. Frenchy's is an unassuming white frame house with a big sign, small parking lot, and rectangular bar inside hosting locals, tourists, fishermen, oil workers and trappers. Plus old pal Doc Rock and me. Beer at Frenchy's is cheap, thirty cents for a draft, drinks around sixty cents, and both are politely served. Fear factor at Frenchy's is low to marginal, and the place is clean. A beehived barmaid served us and we chatted for a while about Nashville music and nothing in particular. The mood in Frenchy's is just right. It's a good hangover-afternoon distance from New Orleans and a hot spot to hit any Cajun Saturday night.

TENNESSEE

Downtown Memphis was deserted, its financial district by the old cotton exchange uncrowded, the King Cotton Hotel on Main boarded up and vacant. I ordered a piece of apple pie in a little café off Memphis's high bluffs, and a waitress slapped my pie onto the stove, frying it in butter. "Fried Pies," a Wes Montgomery tune, sprang to mind. I had always worried over that title. What could it mean? Wes Montgomery was dead, sold out to the modern sound, and Memphis didn't appear to be doing much better. Historic Beale Street, where upcountry blues was born and nightspots wailed from 1900 through the 1950s with the music of W. C. Handy, Chuck Berry, Bobby Blue Bland, Johnny Ace, B. B. King, Little Junior Parker, and Furry Lewis—all working their distinctive blues styles and keeping Beale Street hopping with hookers, pimps, hustlers, and speakeasy bosses—was dead now, torn up for urban renewal. A statue of Handy, author of "Memphis Blues," "Beale Street Blues," "St. Louis Blues," and many others, stood in a tiny patch of land surrounded by a traffic island, dubbed W. C. Handy Park. There were no bars of any consequence anywhere. Just black poolrooms and cafés, deserted theaters. I stopped in a liquor store and asked. "We only had liquor two three years in Tennessee," the counterman answered. "I can't rightly recommend nothing." In a black record store, salesgirls knew no bars worth mentioning. I walked and drove the streets of downtown Memphis for an hour before checking my map for Highway 51, Elvis Presley Boulevard and the house I hoped I'd find.

A filling station attendant provided the final clue. "At's it," he said pointing wildly, "at's it down acrost from McDonald's. Stone house. You cain't miss it."

Presley's house was in a miracle mile section of Memphis, and the avenue which bore his name was lined with fast food franchises, gas stations, and Seven-Elevens. A thoroughly unattractive neighborhood, but representative of the New South. A guardhouse stood at the foot of Presley's drive; an iron fence surrounded his property. Graceland, Presley had named the house, in memory of his mother. A figure of a guitar player was wrought into the gate, and I could actually *see* Elvis's house from the road. It was a fieldstone mansion of a suburban "eighteenth century" design—not at all what I had imagined. But what was there left to imagine in the New South? Day before, I had stopped into a no-name bar at Tallulah, Louisiana, and had nearly been killed for disrupting a professional gambling operation toward its rear. I was merely searching for the john. "Is gambling legal in this parish?" I had asked the barmaid. "Well, hadn't ever been no one come around to make it *un*legal," she said. Then, in my frustration, I asked if Tallulah was the hometown of Tallulah Bankhead. "I ain't heard no mention of her," the barmaid said, "but then Conway Twitty is from Talooler, went to high school with me and my brother."

Bars were uniformly bad in most of the New South. The Bible Belt and extensive post-Prohibition legislation was largely to blame. Baton Rouge had yielded nothing; nor Natchez; nor Vicksburg; nor Greenville. And they were not exactly New South towns. At Tootsie's Orchid Lounge, Nashville, a 1966 World Champion bull rider name of Tom Turner had mounted Tootsie's bowling machine, kicked his heels in the air and whooped, "Pull her head up, Tom, I believe she's a goin' to pitch!" Tootsie's—around the corner from the old Opry House, on Broadway, and just a block from George Jones's Possum Holler—was a beer joint worthy of a two-day drunk, which was what Turner'd been pitching. "Worked a rodeo yesterday in Florida, flew my plane to Nashville last evening, been at Tootsie's ever since," Turner said. "I won twenty-seven beers at that bowling machine, and I ain't ate a thing all day. My stomach must think my throat's been cut. I fly to Phoenix tomorrow, but for the rest of tonight . . . let em good times roll."

I knew I would find nothing of substance in Memphis. If Beale Street was dead, there was little hope. Tommy Turner sounded as if he'd charted the proper itinerary. So I slapped a Stanley Turrentine cartridge into my tape deck, and headed west.

WEST

MONTANA

I crossed into Montana at noon, pausing alongside a wheat field to pee and to set back my watch. The sun was hot as a branding iron, the wind dry; when I lifted my hat perspiration coursed freely down my cheeks and I could feel a damp compress working at the base of my spine. US 2 dipped away from North Dakota, its pavement narrowing as it cut through glaciated plains and sloping valleys, etching *into* the land, intaglio—as if descending a ramp. Very much the product of human hands. A man-controlled ethic predominated in this country, and although elements remained fierce, man seemed less at their mercy, less the match stick pawn of entropy.

A butcher in the parking lot of Stateline Club, near Bainville, shouldered half a carcass of beef and bared a rusty Colt at his hip. Fluid trickled from the steer's thoracic cavity, bloodying an already soiled butcher's smock. My VW was the only passenger vehicle in the lot. A sign over Stateline advertised "The Longest Bar in the Northwest." Inside, a white-haired bartender sat alone at the seventy-foot counter, sipping Schweppes and nodding to mournful Western sarabands from a tiny Japanese radio. Stateline was a monster: elongated and narrow-gauge, like a converted bowling alley. I sat midway down the bar and waited to be served. The bartender moved slowly off his stool, drawing a frosty bottle of Bud from the chiller. I'd had my first view of Big Sky this trip; now I was tasting my first cold Montana brew. Everything seemed rare and refined: the air thin as space, mahogany shining like galvanized steel. Butcher came through the back, wiping his hands and cursing. He presented an invoice and relaxed against the bar while Stateline's bartender signed it. The bloody smock hid his Colt. In Montana it was legal to wear a pistol. Stateline looked like a swinger: an evening/afterhours spot, for boogieing and making arrangements to get laid. Very bleak at midday. Dirty beige carpeting led to a dusty ballroom and makeshift bandstand. Someday I'd catch Stateline about midnight, on a weekend. I drained my Bud, ordered another and drained that. Out in the parking lot the sun was broiling, and my locked VW was hotter than the inside of a basketball.

Gray buttes punctuated the stifling plains west of Bainville . . . grim sentinels to Montana's once unfenced, once borderless rangeland. US 2, "High Line" to natives, traversed the northern quarter in nearly a straight line; through towns of two or three houses, one grain elevator and a general store; railroad snaking past, freight cars chugging through an undulation of wheat fields, the north wind— cold, murderous. Here a "breeze that makes a long chain stand out like the tail of a kite isn't so bad," my Federal Writers' Project *Guide* read, "but when end links start snapping off one after another, it is safe to assume that a good stiff blow is about to begin." *

Wolf Point, a nineteenth-century steamboat town on a high bluff overlooking the Missouri, flaunted a couple of crusty saloons—Montana and the Stockman's, both on Main Street. Wretched-looking Indians lounged out front; heavy fear factor. I did not partake. Wolf Point hunkered at the southern tip of Fort Peck Reservation, so many Sioux and Assiniboine frequented its saloons. A bleakness. South of Brockway, Route 253 regressed to gravel, and it was a dune buggy ride the forty-eight miles between Watkins and Terry: rangeland, cowboys, cattle and heavy equipment crowding the coulees, everything recessed; emphasized by its relationship to the stark landscape. Cowpunchers in chaps and red bandannas, whooping and herding stock. You set your watch back one hour at the Montana border, but sixty miles west of North Dakota you were a hundred years into the past.

WOMEN'S LIB
WAS AFTER HIM

MILES CITY, Mont. (AP)—An elderly Miles City man who told law officers he opened fire "because he was being attacked by women's lib," was being held in jail Friday after shooting a man and two police vehicles.

Custer County Sheriff Bill Damm said a sanity hearing in district court for the man was scheduled for Monday.

The sheriff said a resident of this eastern Montana city called police shortly after midnight Friday to say he had been shot in the back.

Police responded to the call and were fired upon as they approached the victim's home. One bullet smashed a headlight while another struck the hood of the police cruiser.

Authorities said additional forces were called. They surrounded

---

* Federal Writers' Project, *Montana: A State Guide Book*, American Guide Series (1939; rep. New York: Somerset Publishers, 1972), p. 224.

the victim's house and got him and his sister out. The wounded man was treated and released at a local hospital.

Damm said officers located the elderly man who allegedly did the shooting after some Billings people visiting in Miles City notified authorities at midmorning Friday that the windows on their car had been shot out during the night.

Damm said officers traced the shots to a trailer house. When he approached the house, Damm said, the suspect greeted him and said he had opened up "because he was being attacked by women's lib."

The officer said the man told him he would not have shot at the police car if he had known its true identity.

An opportunity to ponder this oracle while drinking with salty seniors at Stockman's Bar, Main Street, Miles City. Named for the old Indian butcher, General Nelson A. Miles—Commander of the Fifth Infantry at Fort Keogh during the seventies, and subduer of Chief Joseph, Sitting Bull and the Ghost Dance Sioux at Wounded Knee— Miles City was a northern outpost on the Texas Trail; wild-wooliest of nineteenth-century Montana cowtowns. Nearby Fort Keogh was established as a consequence of George Custer's demise at Little Big Horn in 1876; thus Sioux-baiting in Miles City had long been the order of the day. Several oldtimers at Stockman's looked ready for action—seasoned enough to have served under "Bearcoat" Miles. Stockman's was more ratty and tattered than any saloon I had run across since Iowa: old men lined the bar, their filthy Stetsons cocked back on pink foreheads, antique coveralls and gingham shirts faded but neatly pressed. A battered wooden counter served at Stockman's matched by a once elegant Victorian back bar and long mirror, dingy but respectable. Spittoons overflowed beside a worn brass rail, and dusty trophies grimaced from the walls: elk, antelope, bison. A hand-printed sign over a shoeshine stand read "No Bumming Drinks." The shoeshine boy asleep. Several old men slumped against a rear wall, tipped back in rickety Windsors, communing. They did not require drinks. A grandfather's clock chimed four times, then settled into a constant tick. Beers at Stockman's were a quarter a glass; one had the feeling they'd always been that price, always would be.

The town was filling up. It was Friday afternoon in Miles City and times hadn't changed so much that cowpunchers and ranch hands would not crowd the saloons until closing. Pickups bumper to bumper all up and down Main Street; the hotels crammed. Still, Stockman's remained unruffled. An old man's bar. Remnant of an old man's world. I hurried outside, hoping there was room for me.

The Montana
Main Street, Miles City

An apron of white salutes the patron at Montana. Tile white as alabaster: Ipana white, bleached and scoured white daily. So white you might eat off it, wouldn't mind doing so. Sluiced past that Cerberean stuffed ram guarding the front door, all the way back to Montana's men's room—where marble takes charge as an antique trough urinal—brass tubing on its water jackets buffed to a mirror finish. Tile lies there, white as cocaine; smooth as a saltlick and nearly as tempting. An attendant is at hand, both here and in the barroom. Mopping up. A long mirror slants overhead, flattering, while a patron washes in the antique marble sinks . . . stalls bleached, walls scrubbed, ceiling and floor.

The white runs to brass: cuspidors like golden pumpkins—salubrious as soup tureens, fresh. Brass rail shining like the polished balustrade at Loew's. French ceiling fans with bright blades, revolving slowly . . . revelatory. Brass flanges, knobs, latches, and handles.

The white runs to oak: oak front bar by Brunswick, oak cabinets, oak ice chests, oak back bar, all by that noted Chicago firm. Back booths are oak, as are a majority of Montana's trimmings, except for Honduran mahogany plankwork along the front bar: a deep red, unscarred and richly polished.

A set of six-foot longhorns, cut in 1904, sulks behind the back mirror. Plus assorted animal heads—bison and elk. A pressed tin ceiling overhead. Jukebox, but nothing like a bandstand. Bartenders sweat in starched white aprons and white shirts, open slightly at the collar. Always mopping and polishing; at the ready to serve your next drink. Their beer is glacier cold.

The white is a snowfield punctured by hand-tooled boots, overlong Levis and a jangle of spurs. Stockmen step straight up to the historic bar and are not deterred. There is conversation, hearty laughter, slaps on the back. But most patrons remain . . . subdued. It is the absolute formality of Montana. Its religiosity. The old saloon is Montana's Canterbury, "Our Lady of the Cowtowns." Everything purified. So clean and well ordered. The soul of a puncher is Boraxed white just to stand before the 1904 back bar and take a drink.

Wayne Olson, barkeep at Montana and one of three partners who currently run the saloon, relates a bit of Montana's history: Founded in 1901 by James Kenney, having remained in the Kenney family for three generations. The front-and-back bar set are from Chicago, as are most of the hardwood fixtures. Installed, 1904. Tile laid in 1912. The saloon stayed open during Prohibition as a speakeasy. Miles City had lost little of its rough and readiness by that time: The south side of Main Street was lined with saloons. Respectable folk lived on the north side of Main, toiling as cattle buyers, bankers and pawnbrokers. Life was strained, if uncomplicated; violence was not unknown. "On one occasion," my Federal Writers' *Guide* reported, "a member of Miles City's respectables hit a gambler on the head with a singletree, and killed him. To save the good man embarrassment, his friends hastily hanged the dead man as a dangerous character."

"And that ain't nothing," remarked a cowpoke on my right. "Was gambling dens and whorehouses all up Main Street. You could get what you wanted if you knew what, and if you didn't somebody'd lay it on you anyways. What you drinking?"

Icy draft at thirty cents a glass, with a Jack Daniels bracer at seventy-five. No one seemed to be ordering cocktails at Montana, perhaps in recollection of certain foul concoctions once standard fare in Montana saloons: Tangleleg, Forty-rod, Lightning and Tarantula-juice. Tangleleg, it is written, was a mixture of cheap booze, burnt sugar, flavoring, pure alcohol, rum and plug tobacco. Its name derived from its ability to render an imbiber confused to the point where he could not remember which leg to place in front of the other, and so floundered about tangleleg-fashion before forfeiting consciousness. The Jack Daniels at Montana was undoctored. Smooth and nippy. I tossed it off and ordered another. The old saloon was growing crowded. Cowpoke remained engrossed in conversation with one of the bartenders. I tipped my hat to Montana's exquisite fixtures and headed for Main Street.

Folks kept collaring me out there, grabbing my arm and exclaiming, "Ain't you Chub Fellerman's boy? No? By God you do favor him. Come on then, let's have us a drink. Where you say . . ." Into wee hours, mistaken identity a bane to sobriety, hosts eager to fill me with Tangleleg, gill-high. "Old Chub, I swear we was tight . . ." Through an endless spew of cowpoke repartee, me denying, them insisting, each of us ultimately stumbling to the next bar.

At Golden Spur, Main Street, I discovered an exquisite cherry front-and-back bar set with heavy Empire columns and squat Romanesque arches. Interior design elsewhere in the barroom a tad plush for my taste, but booze underpriced. "Goddam if there ain't a certain *element* on the loose," an elderly rancher remarked. "Not a polite crowd like there was sixty years ago." At Bison, punchers were packed so tight I couldn't get past the front door. A handsome hardwood bar there. Raucous conversation. At Trail's Inn, the boys were dancing with Buck knives on their belts and hadn't even bothered to wash. Rough trade, but with a patter pleasing to the ear . . . Hillbilly roulades from a fadeaway Wurlitzer salvaged from Depression effects. A handsome blond bar at Range Riders, where hundreds of cowboy photos covered the walls, undoubtedly the work of Miles City photographer L. A. Huffman. Tangleleg reasonable, cold draft for a pittance. At none of these Main Street bars was a fear factor noted. Cacophony, chaos, but nothing like panic—for a certain code was adhered to. I saw no fights. No random violence. A puncher invited a lady to dance, and if she accepted they circled the floor granddaddy-style, at arm's length, polite and proper. If a lady refused, she did so with regret, and no one's feelings were hurt. No cutting at these saloons, no shooting. If a man was going to hit you, one supposed he would ask you outside—or slalom genteelly through some accepted form of effrontery. "Let me tell you 'bout the old lady 'an Chub . . ."

New Atlas Saloon
Main Street, Columbus

New Atlas was established in 1906, while Columbus was a stagecoach stop on the Yellowstone Trail; an important trade center and shipping dock for surrounding counties. Travelers required gambling, strong booze and friendly bargirls in those days, and New Atlas was happy to oblige. Not one, but *two* Victorian back bars still preside, and Atlas's antique gaming tables are some of the finest in the state; they crowd in amongst other fixtures like one-armed bandits in a contemporary Nevada lounge. The back bars are nineteenth-century juggernauts which frame a man doubly . . . his backside handsome as his front. There is a well-tended counter at Atlas where a puncher may partake of cold draft beer for thirty-five cents the large glass, twenty cents the short. A shot of bar whisky for sixty-five cents, Jack Daniels for a dollar. Patrons at Atlas are sheep or cattle ranchers, tradesmen, or wheat farmers. An occasional tourist will stop in during summer months, but historic fixtures at Atlas are dusted and polished primarily for the locals.

Stately wooden booths line the rear of the barroom on two levels. A man is comfortable there as a dozing prelate. A mélange of staid artifacts remains from pre-Prohibition days: poker tables, a lovely nineteenth-century piano, gaming chairs, and an old keno table with attached wooden stools—star of the lot. High ceilings at Atlas, of delicately embossed tin, to equal yesteryear's high poker stakes. One feels as if he's drinking in an auctioneer's barn.

The mood at Atlas is quiet, and although no fear factor was noted, dread seeped gradually into the pores of this pilgrim, as if from antique fixtures themselves. Perhaps it was Atlas's menagerie of stuffed heads: ferocious animal faces contorted about a taxidermist's snarl . . . Mortuary of static rage. Including heads and neck of a two-headed calf. "Only lived ten days," Atlas's bartender explained. "Couldn't eat. In one mouth and out the other. Belonged to a farmer south of here. Had to kill him. Cut off his heads and had him mounted 'fore the newspaper'd run a story or the meat got cold."

T. P. Mulvihill owns the old saloon now. His dad before him. The old back bars are from Butte, originally the product of Brunswick-Balke-and-Collender. Somber as mausoleums. A neon sign out front crackled in a nimbus of mosquitoes. Next door at Rec Hall café, cheeseburgers were fresh and the chocolate malts thick. Teenagers advised that if I was heading toward Livingston I would surely want to get my hat blocked.

"Got a whorehouse there which is famous in these parts," a pinball jock proffered. "You might even say it is something of an institution."

The Stockman
Main Street, Livingston

Route 10 between Columbus and Livingston is a calamitous stretch. No daytime speed limit and the curves are tricky. One has the opportunity to observe at close intervals that quaint Montana custom of planting crosses along the highway where citizens have expired ghastfully. Some shoulders with six or eight; the citizenry is reminded but undeterred—Tony Lamas in the gas tank, the length of the Bozeman Trail.

Bartender at Stockman possessed only one ear, the other removed . . . jagged . . . as if by pinking shears. He served me with dispatch. Stockman's bar was long and of some indeterminate hardwood. Cowpokes nursed cold mugs wherever they could escape Livingston's afternoon sun. Stockman was bright at forty-five hundred feet above sea level: two bay windows draped in faded calico. A clean well-lighted saloon. The cowpokes were old; tan as mahogany etched in oxblood. Several sat a stool apart, drinking and shaking sweat from their hats. Stockman was cool. A monster lithograph of three snarling stallions covered a far wall. Animal heads and stuffed fish. Beer was cheap, a standard thirty cents a mug. A hopped-up Indian sashayed in, challenging Bartender to a friendly game of pool.

Ambience at Stockman was fine. A small trail bike parked out front, plus several dust-bathed station wagons minus hub caps. Temperature in the nineties. I strolled back outside. Livingston had been quite a bar town in the old days. The Bucket of Blood at 113 Park Street enjoyed a reputation which stretched across state boundaries. Calamity Jane had been a business partner there before retiring to her log cabin home on Main Street, to shrivel up and mope. Kitty O'Leary, alias "Madame Bulldog," had run Blood's dance hall. Weighing 190 pounds, she served as her own bouncer, working stripped-down most evenings like a proper Olympian. Somebody said the old Bucket of Blood was no longer open.

Longbranch was, however. Also on Main, it featured live country-western music and unrestrained hugdancing. I'd first heard mention of Longbranch in Tom McGuane's *Bushwacked Piano*. McGuane lived in the area, as did Richard Brautigan, William Hjortsberg, and other sensible novelists. It was a sensible place to live. Hemingstein had done his share of barhopping in southern Montana, and Livingston was not without its local writers. The late Patrick T. (Tommy) Tucker, coauthor of *Riding the High Country* and perennial sidekick to painter Charles Russell, was a Livingstonian. Tommy had hustled many an edition while spinning yarns at Livingston saloons. Of course yarns and novel-making were inextricably related. Writers loved bars the way old ladies loved nurseries. The pre-Pro saloon was rest home to the narrative as surely as television was state sanitarium for the stage. People still palavered in Western saloons with a minimum of headline humping—that recap style so prevalent in post-Pro taverns. So grating and lyrically discommoding.

Pioneer ranch and farm artifacts dotted the walls at Longbranch. Some rodeo photos and posters. Beer was cheap and the place looked like it might hoopity-hop. That goddam TV was on this afternoon, though. Bartender and me alone in the Longbranch. But . . . a Merle Haggard special! White line fever, old Merle truckin an cussin his way through the workin man's blues. I ordered another, and Bartender sat down to join me.

The name of Merle's private Greyhound, up there where the Chartered sign should have been, was:

TROLLIN

The Sport, likewise on Main Street, was Livingston's fancy saloon. Specializing in Mexican food, Sport was hardly overpriced but saddled with a slickness which was nearly disheartening. Fixtures were genuine enough—Sport had been founded in 1909—but the ambience was dude ranch. Master Charge and BankAmericard accepted, if you know what I mean. A Montana P. J. Clarke's? Livingston, as a bustling railroad center, was close enough to Yellowstone Park to siphon off a steady flow of Eastern tourists. Still, a cold Bud draft at Sport was thirty cents. Innumerable Wild West/pioneer artifacts decorated Sport's walls; acres of wooden plows, old rifles, and pitchforks. Plus assorted animal heads. A long wooden bar served Sport's patrons, in consort with an ornate Victorian back bar, sort of ice-cream parlorish, with leaded-glass side cabinets and a huge mirror. I drank comfortably, with the mildest sensation of unease due to the filthy condition of my jeans and boots. Was I chic enough for twentieth-century Livingston?

Old Saloon
Route 89 (south of Livingston), Emigrant

A fat man sat sprawled across a wooden bench drinking mint juleps and glassing the Absarokas for bighorn. He did not budge. I walked past him into the coolness of Old Saloon and called for a drink. No one responded; the place was empty. A nautical skreeking from Saloon's front porch, followed by a sigh, and Fat Man was behind the bar. It was Saturday afternoon in Emigrant. "How 'bout one of those juleps?" He served one promptly in a proper glass—mint fresh, just the right touch of sugar. Of course Fats was from Maryland. And he had noticed my plates.

"Near Washington? I see. No, I'm cook actually. Barkeep should be along. I worked in St. Mary's last year. Little joint down there. Sure I know Duffy's. How's that breakwater? Last afternoon I saw Duffy the Chesapeake was ready to wash him out of business. Had fifteen old wrecks piled up around his tavern like sandbags. Claimed the state of Maryland wouldn't help. Had lost a lot of land. Yes, sure. What the hell. But it's important to Duffy . . ."

Barkeep hurried in, a young fellow newly graduated from Princeton. "I know Cabin John," he said, setting up. "Had a girl friend from Bethesda." We drank a julep together and discussed Emigrant. Barkeep was a local. "Hemingway used to drink here," he said. "Combed these mountains thoroughly. Fine hunting around Emigrant. Fishing too. It's a mining community, but you'd never know it now. Lot of dudes summer here. Got a pretty good Saturday night. Hell, we're the only saloon. We are it and we feature live entertainment."

Old Saloon had started to fill up. I ordered a bowl of Fats' homemade pea soup (twenty-five cents) and ate a charcoal-grilled hamburger. Olympia drafts were just thirty cents. I retired to a side table and drank a cup of coffee. The sun was setting over Gallatin Range and a three-piece group called The Discords was tuning up.

Old Saloon had been established in 1902. A variety of mining artifacts hung from the walls—picks, axes, and a beautifully restored miner's pan. An old wooden bar set. Old Saloon was well kept but plain. A high falsefront made it easy to spot from the highway. Drinks were cheap: a shot of Jack Daniels for sixty-five cents. A few newspaper articles were framed and displayed about the barroom. Gold had been discovered at Emigrant Gulch in 1862, and there were hot springs nearby where crusty prospectors had bathed in makeshift vats. During the winter they'd lived in holes dug into the sides of mountains. Inflation ran rampant: a ninety-six-pound sack of flour went for twenty-eight dollars, tea was a dollar a pound and chewing tobacco five. The old boys did a lot of hunting and got used to the taste of game. Today there wasn't much left of Emigrant. Old Saloon being just about it.

The Discords had begun to play, slow and mournful. I sauntered back to the bar. A lovely blonde in stockman's pants and a red checkered shirt came in with two friends. She was very tan. She ordered a julep and asked me where I was from—conspiratorially—as if all this wasn't absolutely the greatest fun. I told her Cabin John and she said is that like Grosse Pointe? I told her not exactly. She was working for the summer on a ranch near Pray. We had a julep together and I invited her to dance. She two-stepped easily, her right arm held straight, deb-style. Her name was Liz and she was from New York. We had another julep, then switched to beer—before long The Discords had quit, and we were out on the front porch singing. A handful of locals sat around the steps, urging us on. Fats and I reconnoitering harmonies on obscure Appalachian ballads. "Sing at George Jones, gawddammit." Old Saloon had relinquished a bit of its cosmopolitan air. We huddled on the front porch in Emigrant's sixty-degree chill, howling at the Absarokas like there was no day after tomorrow.

Chico Hot Springs Ranch
Off Route 89 (near Emigrant), Chico Hot Springs

At Chico Hot Springs Bar the drinks are mixed with mineral water and you can marinate your costive gut in a steaming pool of natural heat—before, after, or during your toot. You simply wander out Chico's saloon door and stumble into those hot springs. The saloon is not swimming-pool oriented, it is a goddam authentic Western hotel bar which happens to be seated next to paradise. You can trap shoot at Chico Ranch, you can ride, hike, fish, and hunt. But who the hell cares when those incredible mineral springs are right past the saloon door. You may also rent a room, which can be accommodating on a sodden Saturday night. Eight bucks in the kitty and you're home free.

There's an antique wooden bar set at Chico, with obligatory spurs and pistols hanging about the walls. Cold drafts; good service. Chico's clientele is far from tourist: they are down-home, health-conscious Montana vacationites. You'll hardly notice an Easterner here. Some students from Montana State; a few kids with their parents. There's a billiard table in the old barroom. Drinks are standard cheap. Chico Ranch is wood and looks to have been around many a year. And you can swab your body in that hot springs pool until ten p.m. Throughout the winter. Floating there in steamy solace as snow flakes drift into your face and a burly cowpoke swims past with a six-pack under his arm.

The Oaks

Main Street, Bozeman

Drinking at Oak's nineteenth-century front bar (modest back bar under a fat mirror, and whisky bottles the breadth of a dusty rear counter) with Ken McCullough: poet and port-taster, with whom I have debauched regularly since 1962, and one Mylo Miles: great-grandnephew to General Nelson A. Miles (of Wounded Knee/Miles City fame), a tall, dendroid young man with shoulder-length blond hair and a Custer goatee which he kept tugging, as if to pull longer. McCullough in regulation Old Ebbitt T-shirt, faded Lees, and Justin rough-outs . . . hirsute from Adam's apple to lacrimal punctum, thick black hair in a ponytail halfway down his back. A dimestore straw cocked over his left eye. Mylo draped in a purple/green sateen Dennis-the-Menace jacket, and wanting a bath. We were crowded up to Oaks's bar amongst whiskered oldtimers and one or two fat women, tossing back Tangleleg at sixty cents a shot and cold draft Olys at thirty cents a stein. Barkeep at Oaks formally attired in white shirt and matching apron. Serving us without expression.

Scarred wooden tables line the back wall at Oaks; rickety stools the front. Bozeman isn't much of a whoop-de-do saloon town. Post-Prohibition ordinances, regrettably, once forbade dancing after midnight; in beer joints, ever. And Oaks's barstools are there for a reason: it had been illegal to drink standing up. Perhaps that accounted for the paucity of mind-boggling bar sets in Bozeman. Who had the nerve to *sit* in the presence of a truly noble back bar?

I was trying to get Mylo Miles to talk about his great-granduncle. The kid seemed reluctant. Too heavy a stigma. Mylo's dad owned a couple of bars in Livingston, was disappointed that his son did not plan to follow suit. Mylo was a poet; folks at The Oaks seemed to recognize him, turning away in despair as if to say, "Lord there's General Miles' kin and wouldn't he shit if ever he set eyes on that." But Mylo was okay. Perhaps a tad "confused" as to his Western role. But commendably chauvinistic. He promised an epic poem for *Saloon:* "The LSD History of the Real Wild West."

I retired early, exhausted from my first week covering Montana saloons. Mylo and McCullough stayed on; later moving to The Hofbrau, also on Main Street, for eight ball and sandwiches.

The Bozeman Hotel waited. My room facing Main Street was spacious and well aired. Fourteen years ago I had slept on the same floor while en route to a summer job outside West Yellowstone. Fourteen years ago Bozeman was the finest hotel in town. Tonight my room cost three fifty, and the old hotel had degenerated into a halfway house for teenage junkies.

Timber Bar
Main Street, Big Timber

A makeshift bandstand had been raised toward the rear of Timber, and a three-piece Western combo was slashing out hits to a rodeo crowd packed tight into the dusty saloon, from men's room to cigarette machine and on out into the parking lot . . . where a herd of brightly colored pickups were paralleled as if at hitching post—cowboys, herders, punchers, shearers, circuit clowns, and dude ranchers all partying in the wake of Big Timber's annual rodeo like there wouldn't be another party any place ever.

It had been a ballbuster of a rodeo, and everyone seemed content—hot dog, barbecue, and beer concessions sold out, hoppers full to the rough pine seats—although no one I had bumped into could recall whether Benny Reynolds had actually won the thing or not; folks weren't worried and neither were we. I was satisfied, except that I had fallen in love with a cowgirl from Cheyenne who'd been "following the circuit" for six weeks, was named Laura, wore a BARREL RIDING CHAMPION 1970 silver buckle and a great big smile. We'd watched Big Timber's last events together on a fat yellow wrecker near the announcer's stand. When I told her of *Saloon*, she'd laughed and said "Want a real book you follow the rodeos. Guarantee you'll write a bestseller. *Behind the Chutes*. Every cowboy west of Sandusky will buy a copy for his mother and you'll be a star." I loved her then and I loved her now, but I had not loved her when she'd disappeared into the camper of a circuit clown named Bunky Boder.

McCullough was having woman problems himself, so I steered clear and took a tour of the barroom . . . noting fixtures, jotting down descriptions, trying to keep my notebook dry from a cyclone of beer and perspiration. Timber had been a cinch to spot from the outside: its tall falsefront sported a hand-painted mural of a lumberjack felling a tree . . . the lumberjack's left hand raised as if taking an oath, saying "How," waving goodbye to the tree or screaming "Timber." Timber's exterior was matched by several murals inside, including a major rendition of the tragedy at Donner Pass and a pastel portrait of Smooky, somebody's favorite dog. A tacky front bar; tacky formica fixtures—but a spirit undeniably Wild West, and the beer cheap. About thirty cents a can.

Regulars lurked about, but it had been hard to pick them out as the town was full today: with rodeo buffs, roustabouts, and no-good hangers-on from every corner of the state. Big Timber was small, consisting of two main business streets and a modest residential section; the most striking footnote I could cull from my Federal Writers' *Guide* was a synopsis of local jurisprudence the likes of which I hoped to avoid: "In early Big Timber, as in other frontier towns, justice was informal but effective. A character remembered only as the Bad Swede, a chronic disturber of the peace, was once sentenced to spend three days in jail. The nearest jail was at Bozeman. As the sheriff had no desire to ride sixty miles with his cantankerous prisoner, he lowered him into a thirty-foot prospect hole. Bad Swede, it is said, emerged from this form of 'solitary' a changed man." *

I eased carefully out Timber's front door and into the Main Street, cowering the half-block to Erv's Bar, fearful, guarded, with an overwhelming sense of the senseless. Crazy Mountains under a haze of purple squatting to the north without enthusiasm, much less comment.

---

* Federal Writers' Project, *Montana*, p. 197.

Erv's Bar
Main Street, Big Timber

Erv's proved reassuring. It was a tiny saloon with a delicate mahogany back bar and sturdy wooden counter, painted red. Erv's bartender was bald except for two curlicue sidescruffs which stood out in the breeze from an overhead fan like a mad rodeo clown's. He was an oldtimer, like the majority of his customers, and was laboring under the stress of Big Timber's celebration. Erv's was nowhere near as crowded as Timber Bar, and there was none of that rowdy element; no dancing, no band, just a sturdy little juke which belched along at an appropriate volume. I bought myself an icy draft for twenty-five cents and settled into a corner. Most of Erv's customers looked as if they'd been soaked in brine beneath a broiling sun for thirty years. There was more crust and by-product on Erv's patrons than in any saloon I had researched for days. Marvelous. I settled onto a squirmy wooden stool between two old goat-ropers who had to have been a hundred the day George Custer died, and sipped my Oly draft like a canty suckling bowser.

Butte

"Montana's largest city," quoth the Federal Writers' *Guide*, "lies against a bare southward-sloping hillside like a vast page of disorderly manuscript, its uneven paragraphs of buildings punctuated with enormous yellow and gray copper ore dumps, and with the gallows frames that mark mine shafts."*

A literary conceit upon which to launch a non-literary pilgrimage. Four grizzled English Majors (McCullough and pals each Iowa City-certified) researching Great Bars in Butte—America's penultimate mining city: gold discovered 1864, silver discovered 1875, copper ignored until 1885, then bulldozed into bonanza by the Marcus Dalys/W. A. Clarks of Butte's early boom days. English Majors

* *Montana*, p. 136.

traipsing the height and breadth of Butte's "Richest Hill on Earth". Ten thousand miles of underground tunnels snaking beneath the decaying city like, yes, Daly's legendary Anaconda. Butte disordered and near death as our Writers' *Guide* suggests. Population shrunk from 90,000 pre-Prohibition to just over 20,000 post-Watergate. A whorehouse district shriveled from 1,500 girls working three shifts, to none noticeable. Gambling until the nineteen-forties, a major Butte industry: today a minor pastime. Chinatown once four blocks deep, boasting tong wars, hatchet murders, *et al:* Deserted. Tonight at the Pekin Noodle Palace, twenty or thirty diners were latched separately in San Francisco cribs with zero commotion. W. A. Clark's palace of red brick, white stone, slender columns and elaborate gingerbread was this evening a rooming house, where elderly miners warmed their suppers over electric plates as a fading light shined multilaterally through stained-glass windows. Evel Knievel: Butte's contemporary prince, residing in split-level grandeur off the sixteenth hole at Butte Country Club . . . Another darling of the media fostered by Daly's copper-wire legacy of interminable electronic overkill.

Stockman Bar

101 South Wyoming Avenue, Butte

Several older saloons reflected the spirit of Butte's gold and silver days, and Stockman was one of the finest. Overjoyed to learn Jack Kerouac had spent time there, had indeed slept in the rooming house upstairs.

Gentle Jack may have loved Stockman: its cool and quiet after a long day trekking across the Hill, its tombish peace after a change in shift, its icy beer. Light filtered amicably through leaded stained-glass windows. An ancient back bar, simple, serviceable, yet with a touch of whimsy its battered filigree could not hide. A front counter oiled dark by the palms of countless miners. Workers lined three deep this afternoon, swilling boilermakers—"Sean O'Farrells" here in Butte, where the drink had been invented: a shot of Tangleleg washed down with a schooner of beer. Speaking of Evel Knievel—"I *saw* Bobby last week. Had him an old junker, was cuttin doughnuts acrost Main Street. Spinnin tires, runnin down lampposts an not givin one shit for nothin." Accompanied by guffaws and loud calls for another round of O'Farrells.

A corny hand-painted mural covered Stockman's rear wall: sentimental rendition of a moose coming out of the mountains to drink from a royal blue stream. Bartenders at Stockman were friendly, as was the clientele. Zero fear factor at five o'clock on a weekday afternoon.

Drinks were cheap. And Stockman remains the only saloon this Pilgrim has researched with a stuffed Gila monster over its back bar.

M & M

9 North Main Street, Butte

A reckless oldtime saloon, near a main street intersection reminiscent of Baltimore's "block." On a minuscule scale. M & M is a sports bar in the classic Butte tradition. That means gambling—light gambling for "fun and chips" supposedly, but heavy sports and poker betting in truth. There is a workaday front and back bar at M & M, matched by a café counter on the opposite side of the barroom. Both areas are crowded to near frenzy: Butteonians of every ilk—eating, drinking, swilling coffee, and communing in a setting unique to the Richest Hill. A cloak room off to one side, filled with serious oldtimers gambling at a half-dozen poker tables and occasionally glancing up at two tall blackboards which chart the progress of various Major League teams. Beer is standard twenty-five cents for a large glass, and shots hover around sixty-five. Food is cheap; bountiful and homemade. English Majors are disregarded at M & M. They blend in with numerous students from Butte's State School of Mines; here one supposes, on a field trip to garner lore from the eldest of Butte's oldtimers. Everyone jammed up to the bar in a crush as sensual —with its odor of sweat, press of damp shirt against bare forearm, jostle of portly miner passing beer to frothy mate—as it is comforting.

Across Main Street, The Sportsmen of Butte, cast from a similar mold, is nowhere near as classy . . . primary difference being an availability of porno magazines and cheap guns. And the fluorescent lights will put out your eyes. Generous fear factor, but . . . intriguing.

Met Tavern, at 1375 Harrison Avenue, is another sports bar, more in the vein of M & M. It was at Met that Bobby Knievel is said to have been christened "Evel." One George McGrath, a county tax assessor, claims responsibility: Bobby had just been released from jail and strolled directly into the Met for a beer. McGrath and cronies were discussing another local hoodlum nicknamed Awful Knofel. When McGrath spotted Bobby, he said "Look at you! You're worse than Awful Knofel! You're Evel Knievel!"

The fabric of history.

Luigi's
1826 Harrison Avenue, Butte

". . . Likewise played spoons with the captain of his spoon band," McCullough was saying, "did some amazing runs making weird sounds playing his cheek. And, like his wife said, the animals love him. He, no bullshit, lifted the lid to the aquarium and put his puckered mouth next to the surface of the water and big goldfish swam up and kissed him. Someone missed so he did it again. Same thing. Then he turned out the lights and had his luminescent spiders dance—in couples yet, in time to the music. Then on with the lights, and he rushes up behind the bar and with drumsticks plays the whisky bottles brilliantly. Later played again with different levels in bottles and one even missing. Just as brilliant. Then he did a rendition of 'Yellow Bird' with hand bells in seeming random fashion, one bell for each note, and always the right bell even though there was no pattern to the way he picked em up and laid em down."

"Luigi?"

"*Loo-ee-gee!*"

Standard fifties tavern exterior; no, a restaurant façade. Blank. Hinting nothing. WORLD'S LARGEST ONE-MAN BAND AND HIS HOUSE OF DANCING DOLLS, THE FUN HOUSE OF ENTERTAINMENT. Luigi's sub-logo. Inside, the barroom dark except for one or two indirects and sunlight from a small window. English majors scooted up to a formica front, comfortable on cushioned stools. Sole patrons.

"No pool table," Bill Bode announced, dropping a quarter into the Wurlitzer (six plays) and punching out three Lee Hazelton tunes. I countered with two Neil Diamonds and a "Jamaican Farewell." It was that kind of sunset. A mummified blonde served us tall Buds at fifty cents a bottle. Eyes gradually accommodating to the gloom. Luigi's was amazing.

Circus artifacts and odd mobiles dangled from the ceiling: plastic cows, wriggling snakes, mechanical spiders, mechanical spider webs, fighter planes, fuzzy insects, lizards, quizzical dolls. At first everything appeared stable; but with the movement of fixtures (doors, cabinets, ice chests) figures were set in motion: a huge plastic hammer dropped toward the bar as if to crown a customer, a spider lowered over the men's room door, fighter planes moved together, then apart, a lizard crawled up a lamp, a hatchet dipped near the bandstand. "This is nothing," our barmaid warned. "Wait for Luigi." A stuffed bird swooped and dived, then swooped again, "like a hanged man getting a hardon," quipped McCullough. Carnival impedimenta crowded the corners . . . posters, puppets, dolls, stuffed monsters. Hard to tell if Luigi's total effect was more nursery than madhouse; although fun house in truth may have been the more acute characterization.

"You wait for Luigi," our barmaid repeated . . . her hair in curlers, scarf about her head, housedress rumpled: The Mummy. "Luigi's don't get busy til after nine o'clock. Then it's the liveliest place in town." I told Mummy of *Saloon*. She feigned interest and introduced me to Pearl, Luigi's pert middle-aged wife. I tried to explain about English Majors and why we were in Butte. She listened patiently, offering stories of Luigi's and famous patrons she had served—one night talking to Georgie Hamilton "and not even knowing who he was." Evel Knievel: "He always behaves himself here. Though when he was younger he'd try to get in underage."

Luigi she characterized as kind of a St. Francis of the Northwest. "Animals *know* Lu," Pearl said. "In the forest they'll eat from his hand. Wild deer, rabbits, squirrels. Birds fly right up to him. Lu speaks to them. He kisses the fish," she said, indicating a back bar aquarium. "They just know it's Lu."

Slovakian by birth, Luigi (Ludvik Jurenic) had ridden into Butte "many years ago on a freight train . . . Butte was wide open then. One hundred-fifty mine shafts working, with over fifteen thousand men actively employed. Butte was Las Vegas of the Mines during the thirties, except there *was* no Las Vegas then. Vegas eliminated the last of Butte's fun. In the forties. All Butte's gamblers, prostitutes and carriers-on migrated to the Sahara Hotel. Minus Luigi, that is. Luigi's the last fun person in Butte. Last of that wild thirties-style character, the sort we grew up with."

Thirties-style indeed. Perched above the Richest Hill, Luigi's seemed an absurd synthesis of Modernism and the pre-Prohibition saloon. All these dangling doo-dads wired together like puppets or booby-traps or silly actors in some Butteonian black comedy.

Luigi came on about nine. He was a tall man, thin, with graying hair and an insidious smile. The barroom had been filling steadily since eight o'clock. Mummy had transmogrified herself with platinum bouffant, satin heels, and electric-green gown into the Last of the Great Butte Hookers. She catered servilely to Luigi's middle-aged patrons—most of whom were trussed up in country club casuals such as pink slacks, seersucker jackets, yellow bow ties and a gaggish array of bright pantsuits. English Majors unharassed because of their appearance. Regulars at Luigi's could have cared less; they were geared up for the show. A fiendish lack of focus apparent. "Looeegee!" Peter Ellis's cry was echoed. But these folks weren't kidding.

Luigi sat on his bandstand warming up. "Warming up" consisted of tinkering with the two dozen percussion instruments and large accordion which comprised his one-man band. Warming up also involved teasing the audience, tantalizing the faithful *Looeegee!* with promises to start "right now," or admonitions like "Go to Helena, I will do it in my own time." Whenever a lady visited the toilet stage-left, a huge hatchet would lower over Luigi's head and he'd whine into the microphone, "Be sure to wash your hands." To hearty laughter. Prompting encores of bathroom humor, personal and direct—Rickles fashion.

"Looeegee please! Begin, Looeegee!"

"You're so dumb," Luigi snarled. And suddenly the barroom came alive. A button had been hit, Luigi had struck a chord, and every mechanical creature in the place began hopping and shuffling to the music. A cry of painful ecstasy rose from the audience. Quickly they were on the dance floor, gyrating and twisting astride the . . . chaos . . . from Luigi's one-man band. Country clubbers bouncing into wire spiders, grandmothers slipping on samba-ing snakes. English majors were struck dumb.

"Whadda tell ya?" McCullough managed. "Whad I say?"

I gripped the bar with both hands and hung on. There was not a fixture in the house that wasn't jerking and twitching uncontrollably. Even the bar shivered with Luigi's infernal beat. All my worst fears had been realized. Unwittingly I had encountered an absolute antithesis to the stability I sought in a Great Saloon: stability as frame to chaos, stability as tradition, stability in capable architecture as bugbear to the demons of an inferior interior. I kept my gaze locked straight ahead. Through peripheral vision I caught lizards snapping, puppets poking, Lord God! a three-foot doll negotiating a tightrope. I had to look. Luigi was sweating fiendishly. He humped and swayed like a mechanical octopus; banging drums, beating cymbals, chording his phantom accordion. It was church music eletronically distorted . . . organisms in the great choir, a witch's sabbath of a satanic Thursday night. Before long it became apparent that Luigi's "little creatures" were up to more than just casual eurythmics. Perusal disclosed countless combats to the death: a crocodile devoured a spider behind the bar, a snake dismembered an alligator, a lizard stalked a spider along a dark shelf. All controlled mechanically, *electronically* from the town which shoveled copper wire to the millions; by shaman Luigi now ecstatic on the bandstand . . . Singing, preaching, salting his repartee with repeated allusions to "victims" and "massacres":

> I was dancing
> with my darling
> to the Mylai Waltz . . .

McCullough held a fifteen-pound ship's bell and was clanging it maniacally. "Yes!" Luigi shrieked. "Yes! Again!" The bell a deafening counterpoint to accordion and cymbals; Luigi's regulars hopping and chirping like crickets at a tea dance. I could bear no more. Luigi's regulars were worse than his puppets. He hurled insult after insult, manipulating them adeptly as he did his dancing dolls. "Go to Helena!" he sputtered over and again. "You're so dumb! Dumb people, dumb dumb dumb!"

Retreating to the toilet, I stumbled against a comatose figure I first took to be a Butte matron, dutifully observing all from the solitude of a dark corner. She fell limply to one side. A mannequin! Cadaverous. Life-size and grotesque as a taxidermist's granny. When I returned from the toilet, Luigi had left and English Majors were whispering among themselves.

We were a long way from Miles City.

Marcus Daly Hotel Bar (Tammany Lounge)
Corner Main Street and Park Avenue, Anaconda

Anaconda is the town Marcus Daly constructed as smelter-center for the copper ore his company mined in Butte, and as monument to himself. Daly's "Big Stack" stands at Anaconda: a chimney 585 feet high and seventy-five feet wide. One million tons of earth may be processed at Anaconda every twenty-four days . . . 965,000 tons of it going to waste, piled high just outside town in a miniature mountain range. Wind blows hellishly along US 10-A to Anaconda, slamming red dirt, mud, and pieces of slag into a pilgrim's paint job. Twenty-five miles of highway from Butte to Anaconda traverses a moonscape discontenting both to substance and spirit. A fact not fully realized until one sits safely ensconced in the coffin-like wainscoting of Daly's 1884 Tammany Lounge.

Tammany, originally the Montana Hotel Bar, is an exact reproduction of New York's defunct Hoffman House Saloon, renamed for Daly's favorite race horse, Tammany, whose head lies immortalized in a mosaic of over 1,000 squares of hardwood at the center of the barroom floor. Remainder of Tammany's flooring consists of alternate strips of redwood and maple. Other woodwork, including Tammany's front bar, is fashioned from Philippine mahogany. There is a massive back bar at Tammany, elegantly carved with megalithic Empire columns and a wide mirror. Fine brass handles on Tammany's drawers and a handsome brass footrail along the front bar. An oversize painting of delicious nudes on a far wall. Thin Greek columns of brass stand as decorative supports at the center of the room. Brass-trimmed moldings square the ceiling. Elegant leaded-glass entranceways, from both street and lobby, lure a hesitant patron toward attractions within. Heavy draperies shield an afternoon drinker from Anaconda's mile-high sun. A diamond-patterned wallpaper of red and gold contributes to the atmosphere of suspended animation. Sturdy oak tables with matching captain's chairs are arranged about the barroom in an uncluttered fashion. A man may stretch his legs and relax.

Daly, a gregarious Irishman, spent many contented hours in this barroom, having personally overseen construction of the hotel in which it rests: a red Gothic horror with Renwickian turrets, once offering "The Most Glamorous Accommodations in the Great Northwest." When his hotel was nearly completed, Daly is said to have stepped across Main Street, studied its two stories and exclaimed: "Doesn't look big enough. Put an extra story on her." Another evening, having arrived late and unrecognized, Daly is said to have complained at the bar that his poor luck might force him to go without a bed. A printer on Daly's paper, departing for night duty, offered the tired stranger his room, "hoping he was a whisky drummer and might leave me a quart." Next morning Daly's hotel manager informed the printer that from then on his rent was to be free.*

Today the old hotel is a period piece visited by fudsy tourists and eager traditionalists—with a gaggle of itinerant businessmen sludged aboard. Daly's barroom retains its air of big business; copper moguls and field representatives standing politely at his polished front counter. Drinks are reasonable: whisky about one dollar, draft beer around forty cents. Outside, Anaconda's "Big Stack" belches out three to four million cubic feet of gas per minute, and the air is rank with chemical waste. But at Tammany one drinks on. Disinterested. The most comfortable trappings of a bellicose Industrialism cancel social regret and insulate the nervous pilgrim from an obnoxious fate.

Adieu to English majors at Bozeman. Zonked; peritonea puzzled; cerebella sagged. McCullough fielding good-byes in Karl Marx Pizza jersey, gesturing with coffee-mug fist and suggesting last minute saloons. "Check Eddy's Club once you get to Missoula," he croaked, "and have a drink with Helen at that little bar in Pony. She is a hardass old girl, but one hell of a rodeo rider." Sure, sure. Possessed of other saloons which John DeHaas, architecture professor at Montana State had provided. Crisscrossing me farther northwest. McCullough waved from his crumbling front stoop. Bozeman. An "experience" fourteen years later I could neither countenance nor contain. Pausing at the Dairy Queen west of town: queued up for a shake and what do you suppose . . . an entire bridal party—groom blushing, bride tearful, ushers rowdy under Big Sky dinner jackets—descended upon the unwary eatspot in a procession of dusty pickups. A Bozoland send-off, double cheeseburgers all around, of dubious pretense.

---

* Federal Writers' Project, *Montana*, p. 370.

Ann's Pony Bar
Off 287, west of Harrison; Pony

Six point five miles of gravel separate Harrison from Pony; Harrison equaling the real world. Six point five miles of shale and debris, alleviated by ice cold Schlitz at Ann's and the aggregation of empathetic company. Pony is a partial ghost and around five p.m. daily every oldtimer in Potosi Canyon stops at Ann's for a drink. They sift out of the hills via pickup or shank's mare, and barkeep Helen serves the crustiest of them. "Old Harold," she says, indicating an overalled gent at the far end of the bar, "has a placer claim he still works. Harold's one of the last gold miners in these parts . . . stops by each evening for his beer. See, our mining companies pulled out in 1943. Was something of a boom during the thirties when gold prices went up. But by the end of World War II our population dropped three quarters. This here's the only bar in town. Gets pretty lively on weekends, or when somebody's celebrating a birthday."

At first I had not recognized Helen; had thought she was a man—her voice so deep, skin so leathery, shoulders broad, hair clipped short. She took a swipe at the bar with a clean white towel and moved to placate another customer. Beer at Ann's was cheap: Bud forty cents a bottle; drinks under a dollar. There were modern fixtures inside Ann's (mostly formica) but that was about the only new gear in Pony. Ann's Pony was a venerable false-front building next to a bankrupt hardware store and Rex Flour distributor. Ruined brick and frame structures posed skeletally around the old mining town. No one walked Pony's dusty streets. The town appeared deserted. But several customers had been seated inside Ann's, nursing beers or playing the jukebox. Now the barroom was filling up.

"There's Bert," Helen said. "Best move your VW. That's her spot and she never parks anywheres else. Bert owns this building." A sharp blast from outside. A seventyish woman behind the wheel of a fifties-ish Dodge waited for me to move my car. I did so graciously, waving. Bert did not respond. She toddled slowly into the barroom and took a seat two stools from Harold. Bert was quite stout. She breathed deeply before ordering.

I told Helen of *Saloon*, and she took an instant liking for the project. I had bought my first two beers, but she bought the next three.

"There's an old bar *here*," she said confidentially. "Next door, locked up exactly like it was. Ann might show it to you." Helen nodded toward a slim, hard-drinking woman seated at the Harold-end of the bar. Extraordinarily well-dressed for Pony. Helen wore Levis, Bert a long ranch skirt, but Ann was chic in a citified shirt-waist and high-heels. As befitted a ghost town businesswoman, I conjectured.

Unlocking the hardware store, Ann exhumed a catacomb of memories from Pony's fancy saloon days. Her old back bar was fashioned of oak. An exquisite 1930s Wurlitzer stood unharmed, as did countless saloon fixtures and rogue antiques. Stray mining artifacts of multi-description lined the walls. What Ann possessed here was a gold mine of a pre-Pro saloon, and I could not understand why she didn't work it. "Bert keeps things this way," Ann explained. "Been cooped up since 1939, like the town and her, and I guess that's how things is going to stay."

Home in the new barroom, I noticed a Victorian upright I had missed; a very nice Victorian piano which, Ann said, "still gets some heavy use on party nights." I shot a game of rotation with two old ranchers who told me they "was going to get drunk proper and sleep up in the Tobacco Roots tonight." Helen bought another beer and I lugged out Vardis Fisher's *Gold Rushes and Mining Camps of the Early American West* so we all could take a look at it. Harold enjoyed the photographs of California forty-niners, whom he resembled. Harold turned the pages slowly, wheezing with satisfaction. Bert spotted the wife of an Ann's Pony regular sulking outside in the front seat of her husband's truck. "Whatsa matter," Bert hollered, having loosened up, "you molting?"

We drank another beer, then another, and before long I was reminiscing with Ann's regulars like I'd been drunk in Pony all my life. An hour later Helen refused my tip, insisting on shaking hands; and I weaved solemnly toward the parking lot.

Bale of Hay
Main Street (Rt. 287), Virginia City

One of Virginia City's twenty restored buildings, Bale of Hay is a turn-of-the-century miner's saloon *cum* museum, purportedly "just the way she was in them good old days." Dustin Hoffman played a scene from *Little Big Man* here, and not an artifact needed to be changed. It's a late Victorian barroom, with comfortable captain's chairs, original card tables and ancient peep shows which still operate. They are hand-cranked devices housing salacious photographs and drawings, operating on the motion picture principle. Nineteenth-century penny-arcade stuff, descendants of which may be patronized today across the Forty-second Streets of our republic. Antique games of every sort are situated around the old barroom and in the children's arcade preceding it. Old posters, including stills of Dustin Hoffman from *Little Big Man* may be ogled. Expensive sandwiches are available; Kristofferson on the stereo, trippy waitresses in tie-dye halters and studded Landlubbers. Folks shaking horses for rusty nails. A negotiable fear factor.

Virginia City is the Williamsburg of the Rockies, a contemporary tourist town gone ape on the restoration dollar. But from 1863 when gold was discovered at Alder Gulch to 1864 when Sheriff Henry Plummer was hanged, nearly 200 men were murdered and Virginia City gained a reputation as the most violent town in the Territory. Plummer's road agents were finally brought to justice by a bloodthirsty vigilante committee which showed no mercy then or later, when "questionable arrests" became the order of the day. Tourists may visit The Site of the Vigilante Hangings, where Plummer's men stretched hemp, or Boothill, where they were planted . . . minus Clubfoot George Lane's star appendage, which may be viewed in fleshy dessication at the Thompson-Hickman Museum. George's clubfoot surviving as Virginia City's most appropriate knickknack from a gruesome past.

The old Territorial capital waned sleepy on a weekday evening. I nursed Pony remorse until midnight at Bale of Hay, then clumped along wooden sidewalks back to my motel. Pausing in various saloons; some intriguing with hand-curved pre-Pro bars—most attractive being Pioneer Bar, likewise on Main Street, which boasted a blind barkeep during the day who "never missed a lick." Blind Bob was off, so I didn't get a chance to monitor his act. Pioneer proved pleasant however; a truly old-fashioned saloon selling sporting goods over the counter, fishing licenses, and light hardware . . . oldtimers sipping quarter drafts. Where authentic Virginia Citizens migrated when Bale of Hay turned tourist.

Stockman Bar
Main Street (Rt. 287), Sheridan

Old miners sitting in the early morning sun, drinking Oly and playing cards. A half cloakroom at Stockman, for card playing and indis-
criminate betting. A handpainted mural of a rocky mining scene.
Sheridan was named for General Philip Henry Sheridan, famed
Union cavalry leader, and has been an important outfitting center for
gold, silver and lead mining in the Tobacco Root Mountains. Most
of the men who frequent Stockman look to be about Civil War age.
There is a handsome back bar of blond hardwood, and comfortable
card tables. A timeless place; static yet ethereal. Old miners like
motes in the sunlight, playing out their hands.

Moose Bar
Montana Street, Dillon

A thirties-style back bar with neon-lit glass columns and scurvy
front counter. Moose was the saloon John DeHaas had warned me
about: shootings, stabbings, wino Indians asleep on the barroom
floor. Just noon and the front counter was already crowded.

"You ain't him!" a drunk blonde screamed at me. "I know you
ain't, you are balder than a duck egg." To snickers from soberer patrons. Then: "It's your round. Goddammit you come in here and
think you can't go a round." I tried to push her away. "Please buy a
drink mister." Followed by intense mumblings.

A gray-haired woman at the far end of the counter made room for
me. I dropped my head, embarrassed. Every eye in the saloon
cocked my way. "Short draft," I managed. A harelip barmaid served
me. Took my quarter and grinned. The gray-haired woman was
laughing.

"You a regular?" I asked.

"Yes," she said. "I am Irish." Then she yawned.

Dillon was a major railroad center and Moose Bar conveyed that
atmosphere . . . a heated Eastern feel, with a hit of Norfolk or Baltimore. Shit City. Moose's block was downtown Norfolk to the core:

a dozen filthy bars, cheap drygoods stores and fleabag hotels. The proprietor of Moose was infamous in these parts. Steve Logan, mayor of Montana Street. Dressed in black—black boots, black shirt, black hat with a silver band. Tended bar that way, with a big .44 on his hip. Had served time for killing a customer in his bar: Steve announced closing time. A drunk ignored him and dumped another quarter in the jukebox. Steve shot him dead. Had spent a couple of years inside for that, but was free now. I had been warned not to patronize Moose after dark. Steve was off duty this afternoon.

"Irish all my life," the gray-haired woman chuckled as an Indian approached me for a handout. I shouldered past and headed for the street. If Moose's fear factor was this heavy at midday, what could it be after midnight? Maybe it was the way I *dressed* or something.

I hurried next door to a drygoods store and bought me a four-dollar cowboy shirt.

Wagon Wheel Saloon
Route 278, Jackson

Paved road ends at Jackson; tumbleweed along the main drag. A post office and several small businesses. A gas station. A frame hotel. To say that Jackson is unobtrusive would be to understate your case. A grizzly oldtimer sat at Wagon Wheel's nondescript bar and tossed his head. He was terribly sunburned.

"Won't go out for twelve dollar," he said, "but I'll go out for fourteen." He was a little tight. "Go all day for fourteen, but they ain't no way I'm goin out for twelve."

An overweight barmaid raised off her stool and drew me a beer. I noted a separate area to Wagon Wheel for dining, as some food was available. Furnishings were formica. What made Wagon Wheel remarkable was its setting. Absolutely bleak. Wind howled through Wagon Wheel's front door and sucked sand, dust, and pieces of tumbleweed out the back.

"Ain't right," my companion muttered, "a man should go for twelve."

The barmaid laughed.

Eddy's Club

428 North Higgins Avenue, Missoula

On the skillet-flat bed of a prehistoric lake at the maw of Hell Gate Canyon, Missoula squatted across Clark Fork–Columbia River like a great Northwestern Detroit. An industrial malaise within this university/railroad town which was doubtless unfounded. But nonetheless mean. I checked into the Palace Hotel (five bucks a night, over the air shaft) and hurried to Eddy's Club.

A somber, sweaty spot. Unconscionably hot. Ancient bohos and sloppy railroad bums mixing quiescently with students. Hangers-on. Kissing the ass of America's collective gerontic. Photos of oldtimers papered the walls. Photos everywhere of grandfatherly hobos. Pool table. Nondescript fixtures, cheap and plain. I ordered a twenty-five cent draw and settled into my notebook. Bugs exploded against Eddy's glaring overheads. A men's room stench mingled with scalp-stink of dirty old winos and putrescence of freak. McCullough's Ginsberg letter:

". . . After Missoula reading we are in Eddy's Club—usual frenzied ecstasies. Old Home Week every time another person stumbles in the door; Jim Welch beams by. Maybe he is the best poet in the country now that he's found his own voice. Finally Allen streams in. . . ."

Circles. I wandered across West Main to Turf Club, testing my luck. I was troubled about Missoula. The town had taken its name from a Salish word, *Im-i-sul-a*, which translated *by the chilling waters.* As Clark Fork–Columbia's waters were no chillier than those of any other mountain stream, interpreters had pondered this translation. Some thought it meant *place of evil omen.* Turf Club was much more of a clean well-lighted place than Eddy's. A handsome back bar of some dark hardwood. Sober bartender. Sturdy fixtures. Less cantankerous clientele. I bought myself an Oly draft and relaxed.

Missoula Club

139 West Main Street, Missoula

Outside the Palace Hotel I asked a group of loiterers where the great saloons were in Missoula.

"Let's go," said a fortyish fellow in flat-top and oversnug Levis.

We hiked around for half an hour before he put his hand on my ass and asked if I didn't think I was cute. He was a lumberjack from Oregon. On vacation. He said I guess you don't like girls and I said afraid so. Ducking into the Missoula.

Photos of MSU greats greeted me at Missoula Club—baseball, football, basketball—all grinning confidently and without spite. I pulled up a stool at the weathered oak bar. A white-haired barkeep with "Tom" stitched across his apron served me a quarter draft with an enormous smile. He looked like an MSU great who'd been warming the bench at Missoula Club for the past thirty years.

"How about a hamburger," I said. No supper for this pilgrim.

"Grill's closed," old Tom said. "But—what the hell."

He fried me a fat burger with onions and pickles, A-1 sauce on the side, and a complimentary sack of chips.

The lumberjack lurched in, swaggering a bit more now, and demanded the same. Offering me a raft of shit in the process. Tom's smile faded.

"Grill's closed," he said with consummate finality. "And so is the bar."

Lumberjack retreated to the street.

I carried a second Missoula letter on my person and reached for it as Tom sidled toward the grill. National Forest Service smoke-jumpers trained at Missoula; I had applied for a Forest Service job earlier in the year, and, combining work with duty, had inquired matter-of-factly if my prospective employer knew any Great Bars near Missoula. A courteous reply from B. R. Van Gieson, Supervisory Forester, had followed:

". . . I am not much of a habitué of the local bars but did chance to know of two that are worthy of mention—both now being nonexistent. The first, named The Dirty Shame, was located in the Yak Valley north of Troy, and catered to a diverse clientele including radar base employees, movie stars (John McIntyre and friends), displaced (by popular hometown request) Virginia hillbillies, loggers, miners and assorted hybrid locals. Outspoken and physical differences of opinion were the customary order of business.

"The other bar, known as Liquid Louis, was located in the Swan Valley about thirty miles north of the small town of Seeley Lake. It was the social center for various backwoods locals who made a 'living' by logging, trapping, poaching, farming, etc. The proprietor (Louie) was, as is often the case, his own best customer and sometimes gave away his stock when in his cups. His death is reported to be alcohol connected. His patrons had a habit of declaring they could 'Lick any man in the house.' Of course, everyone can't lick everyone in the house so it led to some spirited contests. Don't know if these class as Great American Bars but they did have a local notoriety."

Old Tom spotted me reading and asked what it was I had there. I showed him and he laughed. No, he didn't recall those two. But he wasn't surprised. Nothing in this world surprised him anymore, he said, much less Montana saloons.

We drank to that.

Silver Dollar

West Railroad Avenue, Missoula

Into the Silver Dollar next morning by eleven. Old fellows in spotless coveralls were cashing Social Security checks and calling for drafts. A few sat at one side shuffling cards. Everyone clean. Bright sweatshirts, carefully oiled boots. The place was half formica, about like Eddy's, but nine times as orderly. Retired brakemen, engineers. Some still on the payroll. Younger stiffs would be in later. Across West Main you could hear freight cars crashing around the yard. Tonight I'd be in Idaho.

IDAHO

Owl Club
Main Street, Salmon

The boys were stacked up at Owl's front counter like cordwood and I had to wrestle my way forward, under straw brims and denim sleeves, to get an honest shot at a drink. Owl's barkeep loped by four times without serving me; I screamed on the fifth, and he turned to reveal the pink holster of an empty eye socket. "Half blind," he hollered over the din. "Sware t'god I never seen you." He was dirty, unshaven and dark as an Indian, but he sold me my first Coors of the trip and I blessed him for it. Frosty draft at twenty-five cents a glass. Clear as an Idaho trout stream. Somebody jostled my arm and I spilled about half down the front of my shirt. Not caring, bellowing for another carried at a trot by Owl's raggedy snake of a bartender.

A snowy white owl sat stuffed over Owl Club's back bar; its plumage anomalous to the plenary dinge of Owl's barroom. Back bar was well kept and sported four columns that looked to be mahogany. Scarred front bar of identical hardwood, having seen better days. Both were still eminently serviceable. Had the nearby ghost of Leesburg provided this set? Salmon was a subalpine city encircled by waves of the loveliest Rockies in Idaho. Likewise headquarters for Salmon National Forest, and the supply center for an extensive livestock and mining community. Owl Club its preferred oasis.

Antique wooden tables at Owl, small but comfortable. Matching chairs. Some Western murals and paintings about the barroom. An obligatory pool table. A balcony where Owl's band of the moment performed. A tarnished brass rail at the bar where I rested my foot. Owl's Coors was delightful; apoplectically delicious. Folks around the barroom seemed to be enjoying a hellacious good time— cowpokes, miners, wilderness adventurers. What a town to pack out of; what a saloon to pack back into.

Galena Lodge
US 93, Galena

They were pouring concrete for a new fireplace outside Galena Lodge as I drove up and somebody yelled "Grab a rake," so I obliged. A forest ranger, two kids, and the young couple who ran Galena's bar. We worked for half an hour spreading concrete, then trouped inside for a well-deserved round of drinks. Galena Lodge had been built in the late nineteenth century, I was told, as supply post/hostelry for Sawtooth's transient miners and loggers. Eight thousand feet into Galena Pass, it was today a welcome way station before tackling seven miles of narrow summit road. Beer was reasonably priced. Drinks professionally mixed. Galena's ambience was rustic log cabin. Paintings of Western history and native fauna, by William Pratt, hung in the main lodge. The view from Galena was stupendous. A Conoco pump out front had replaced water troughs for mule and man. A pilgrim departed sufficiently primed to carry on.

Ketchum's bars were all ghastly. Joints like Pioneer Saloon and The Grizzly Bear. Overpriced, underquality, trying desperately hard to be chic. Crammed with goatish Sun Valley types and Gucci bozos, loud-mouthing about "the Islands" or "downhill at Kitzbühel." Tan, bejeweled, and unctuous. The old saloons were finished. Hemingway would have hated Ketchum in the seventies. All its mining camp bravado was gone.

O'Leary's Saloon
Main Street, Idaho City

Twenty-nine miles from Boise, Idaho City is a mining town which has survived. Down from a population of 15,000 to 187, Idaho City nevertheless supports a handful of saloons and keeps its rutted streets peopled with a desirable tourist trade. Oldtimers still malinger on benches outside the Idaho *World*, perusing its latest edition and booting whatever stray dog might be nagging for attention underfoot. Eighteen sixty-two saw gold fever strike Idaho City—"the boomer paved with gold"—placer literally having been collected in the streets. Today all that is a memory—pursued commercially at various saloons, or disregarded entirely by sportsmen who speak of nothing but game.

A fat stone fireplace warms the pilgrim at O'Leary's. There are antique guns (muskets, rifles, pistols) to assault his eye and an occasional trophy to whet his appetite for the hunt. Beer is cheap at O'Leary's and so are mixed drinks. Fixtures are standard formica but the mood is Old West. Saturday night a large crowd from Boise may be expected and there is always live music.

Wiegel's Miners Exchange Saloon
Main Street, Idaho City

Miners Exchange is the oldest saloon in Idaho City (1865), having endured numerous Main Street fires for its sturdy brick structure. Interior is slightly seedier than O'Leary's but the fixtures are more authentic. Same cheap beer, same country-western music on Saturday night. Same hunters, fishermen and rogue oldtimers laying back and slurping up the Coors.

Violence is not unheard-of at Miners Exchange; it is traditional: "Several parties were found in the streets on Tuesday morning," an 1863 Idaho *World* reported. "Some with fractured skulls; some with bunged eyes and swollen faces, indicating very clearly that there had been a muss somewhere during the night. Blood was freely sprinkled about the town on woodpiles and sidewalks. As the puddles of blood were distributed over a large district, it was impossible to locate the fight." In 1863, only twenty-eight of the 200 persons buried in Idaho City's cemetery died natural deaths. A large percentage were alcohol-related. Those old miners liked to drink. According to an 1866 *World*, one Pat Mahaffey returned home of an evening "the worse for liquor. Turning sick, he sat by the stove and vomited into a box in which his wife had placed several goslings. After a bit, Pat looked down and saw them and roared: 'God a'mighty wife, when did I swaller them things?' "

Bouquet Eats Drinks and Sportsman's Center
Main Street, Boise

Bouquet possesses the most beautiful back bar I have seen in America; its arches, columns, and cornice more ornately carved than the reredos of many a Renaissance cathedral. The wood is light cherry and it is highly polished. The entire piece stands nearly twenty feet tall, the highest point a magnificent arch capped with a Baroque cupola and supported by two heavy Ionic columns . . . the whole framing big mirrors, diamond-dust bright. I walked into Bouquet at eleven thirty Sunday morning. Not a seat at the bar. The place looked like a casting office for a Sam Peckinpah film. Old men were lined up at the bar drinking double shots of port with short beer chasers, and not one stool was free. Fortunately, Bouquet had an adjoining café counter where I could sip a cup of coffee and dodge cue sticks from the several pool tables behind me. But I felt like a puppy who had been left in the car. Bouquet's old men drank as a single organism, fleshed elbow-to-elbow like scissor dolls. A few would speak, either to neighbors or themselves. But the rule was silence. Not one of these men would have sat at the café counter, that much was obvious. Bouquet's back bar was why they were there. I felt as if I were in church; promising myself I'd come back later.

When finally I did, about six that evening, there was one free stool at the bar dead-center and I grabbed it. The perspective from that angle was like a front pew seat in a Borromini chapel. I felt enveloped by the bar, swept up by its huge wings and coaxed to its center, which contained the big back mirror and a positively holy image of me. I stared until beer was set before me and an oldtimer to my right broke heartily into sermon about the sorrows of drink and how a man never could find the Lord in church anyhow. He spoke as freely as if I'd been a regular at his elbow for the past fifteen years. He introduced me to the night bartender, owner of Bouquet, a dark-haired man of about forty who managed fighters, and . . . I could see as he leaned over to shoot pool . . . favored elevator shoes. Bouquet's owner had been offered fifteen thousand dollars for his back bar alone, and now that this entire block of Main Street was threatened by urban renewal—and Bouquet was the last of the old saloons open for business—he probably would have to sell. A lovely primitive (oil

on wood) of an Indian buffalo hunt hung over Bouquet's cigar case.
A photograph of a boyish fighter named Joe Cortez sat on a glass
shelf behind the bar. I asked if Cortez still fought, and someone
pointed to a tall figure at the other end of the room, a quiet man
about forty-five who stood aside, drinking alone. Talk soon drifted
to famous saloons, to local history, and the wild gold rush days of
Boise Basin when placer was plucked from wagon ruts and Idaho
City was the most successful mining camp in the world—two
hundred and fifty million dollars taken before it was all over, more
than from Klondike of Alaska or the entire forty-niner scramble.
Bouquet's old men remembered into the night. As I departed, an
oldtimer seated next to me was deep in reverie about what he swore
was "*the* most beautiful bar in the Northwest," a carved mahogany
back bar he'd seen as a young man in The Dalles, "with naked
wooden women butted out from every post, like bowsprits in the
wind."

Basque Center
Sixth Street, Boise

Fixtures at Basque may be modern, but they are immaculately clean
. . . as clean or cleaner than The Montana in Miles City. Spanish
posters and artifacts hang about Basque's modest barroom. An L-
shaped counter to the right of Basque's entrance: spotless. A
toothless woman with a wide smile and many shakings of the head
tends bar as you point to the brand of beer you desire. She laughs
and serves it promptly, flashing fingers to indicate the price. Spanish
music clatters from a corner. Several Basques in starched white
shirts and tight trousers joke at the bar. You are the only blond in
the club. Only non-Basque. The Basque men are very physical,
grabbing each other about the neck and wrestling bearfully between
awesome shots of whisky. There is a lot of *machismo* at Basque Center, fast heavy drinking being one attribute. A black-haired woman
with deep brown eyes and oriental skin has sat down and the men
are vying for her attention. Loud jokes. High-pitched singing. Much
masculine banter in Basque, obviously akin to courting. The young
woman smiles, dropping her eyes. Her escort seems annoyed but
takes the kidding good-naturedly.

One feels that if Basques could afford a bar as stately as Bouquet's they would grab it up. For the ambience of Basque Center is quintessential Old West. The second largest colony of Basques in the world is said to live around Boise. Around, because Basques are sheepherders (fellmongers some), mountain men who since the eighteen-seventies in America and pre-Roman times in Spain have lived an isolated existence, speaking a language which is related to no other, wandering the hills and resisting assimilation. They have fought off Romans, Visigoths, Charlemagne, Moors, and Franks to insure their independence. They remain fierce traditionalists who have consistently opposed those who would change their way of life.

Basque Center is intensely formal. Although outside patronage is not encouraged, you attract no more than a curious stare. Fear factor is heavy at first but levels out. Drinks are standard-America, but you notice several old men sipping unfamiliar brands of wine. Beer is forty cents a can. What you get to go with it is well worth the price.

Old Boise Saloon

100 South Sixth Street, Boise

At three o'clock in the afternoon, Old Boise is quiet as a country railroad station. The 1906 opera house fairly dozes. A tinsel static, the texture of cobwebs, jabberwocks about the rafters but Boise's floor level is nearly silent. An elevated stage seems to ponder the entertainment it has hosted; most assuredly that it will endure tonight. A clack of leather heel against stone. A tink of spoon against glass at Old Boise's afternoon ice-cream parlor. A squeak of dry timber as stools are mounted. The sigh of Old Boise's bartender drawing yet another Coors at his exquisite turn-of-the-century front-and-back bar set.

The set is from Silver City, bartender is quick to explain. By way of Pittsburg. "All these old bars were fashioned back East," he says. "Only one or two companies made the dandies. This set doesn't have a tag on it except 'Made in Pittsburg.' Otherwise I could tell you for certain." Four dolmenic columns grace Old Boise's back bar, filigreed with handcut medallions and etchings. The wood is dark veneer, and both front and back bars support marble counters. Back mirrors are "antique original, shipped all the way from Paris." Old

Boise's ice-cream parlor stands off at one side. Assorted sandwiches are available there, as are soft drinks. But Old Boise's pride is her ice-cold Coors on tap at thirty cents a glass.

Once titillated with *Saloon*, bartender soars to attention. "No, there aren't too many old ones left with fancy trimmings. Old Boise's special. Was a church as well as an opera house, you know. Before we got it. Damn place is haunted, but in a friendly way. Late at night if you're real quiet you can hear voices: people singing, people speaking parts from back behind the stage. You got to see Silver City. It's a rough road in and an even rougher road out, but Silver City is unique. Idaho Hotel there has a bar. That's original. Talk to J. J. Spencer, he's a friend of mine. Publishes the Owyhee *Avalanche*. One of the oldest newspapers in the state. He can tell you all about Silver City. Probably knows other bars too. And come on back tonight. Got a band playing I guarantee will pop your shorts for you."

At eleven o'clock in the evening, Old Boise is blasphemous as a lower-Broadway disco. The sepulchral opera house shivers with the sound of Zeppelinesque rock. A Boise band; loud but extraordinarily tight for a hometown group. Old Boise's floor is packed with good-looking kids, bopping and bumping to the electronic grind. Eyes calcified, stomachs lubed. Hips popped asunder, all sweat and honey-sweet. "What I say?" bartender shouts, throwing an arm about my shoulder and buying a Coors. "Are we groovin? Is Boise a bust? Have they fucked us, or maybe is we fuckin them?"

I shake my head. Grinning broadly.

"*Silver City*," bartender shouts, pointing toward his statuesque back bar. "Understand?

"You try it."

Idaho Hotel Bar
Jordan Street, Silver City

The road south of Murphy is little more than a trail: twenty-five miles of rut and ravine, traversing shale, limestone, basalt, and granitic scarps carved eerily across the Owyhee batholith; ultimately climbing 6,000 feet into the Owyhee Mountains to the ghost town of Silver City. A two hour drive at ten miles per. Not to be attempted in bad weather with poor tires and shock absorbers, or minus a full

tank. I passed two Jeeps that had foundered in the switchbacks; I could offer only water and a lift. But don't count on company out there, especially after dark. Or in winter months. You'll stand a better chance on a snowmobile then; Idaho Hotel will be waiting to service you, and garner fifty cents for your upstairs floor privileges.

Idaho Hotel is a ramshackle demirep of weathered clapboard and sagging summer-beam, which throughout the eighteen-sixties maintained suzerainty over Owyhee County and enjoyed repute as the most glamorous hostelry in southwestern Idaho. Today an American flag still flies from her balcony, and the hand-printed sign across her front door reads:

NO ANIMALS

ROWDY KIDS

OR

SELF-PROPELLED

VEHICLES

ALLOWED

IN THIS BUILDING.

If that were insufficient to attract a sensible man, there is the addendum in fire-engine red:

BEER

Idaho's lobby is packed with antique furniture—rough and ready desks, tables, and chairs, all in unfinished wood—as the upstairs quarters are now vacant. A patron may sleep there, as previously noted, in his own bag, on the floor; for fifty cents a night. Idaho's bar is at the rear of the building; it is a simple room, rustic as the lobby but more spacious . . . with similar unfinished card tables, sideboards, dining tables, and chairs. Victorian nudes replete with adoring cupids hang about the walls. A simple front-and-back bar set, in light oak, serves Idaho's clientele. A simple mirror to match.

An antique slot machine with real playing cards instead of fruit, stands next to the bar. You pull the handle and playing cards spin; the correct combination wins. There is also a "Mills Chicago," a musical slot machine popular about 1900—constructed over a music box to circumvent local gambling laws. Other antique music boxes are situated about the barroom.

Beer is sold by the can (fifty cents) at Idaho Hotel, as proper refrigeration for draft is a problem. Only ten people inhabit Silver City year round, so clientele tends to be regular. The Owyhee

County Cattlemen's Association holds its weekend convention at Silver City each summer, and that brings in about a hundred visitors. A dozen or so campers can be counted on any given evening at Idaho. Plus assorted daytrippers. For Silver City is a ghost not to be missed.

The entire town looks like a set for Robert Altman's *McCabe and Mrs. Miller*. Buildings are remarkably well preserved; many gussied up with carpenter-gothic barge boards and Bavarian gables. Hills around Silver City are so steep that most privies are two-storied— perched on stilts and anchored to principal structures by rickety catwalks. Some are roofed over, to protect delicate patrons. Silver City knew its finest hours during the eighteen-sixties, when Owyhee mining fever was at a peak. Gold was discovered in 1863, and a sampling of ruby/silver crystals from Poorman Mine won a gold medal at the 1866 Paris Exposition. Thousands then called Silver City home; as late as 1898 the town boasted six general stores, two hardware stores, a tin shop, two meat markets, two hotels, four restaurants, a photographer's gallery, a brewery and a bottling plant, a jeweler, a newspaper, two lumberyards, a tailor shop and three barber shops, four lawyers, two doctors and eight saloons.* In 1935, Owyhee County's seat was moved to Murphy, rendering the *coup de grâce*. Except for a handful of crusties and one or two summer businessmen, Silver City folded.

The camp seemed void of tourists this weekday afternoon. A party of five o'clock poker players had gathered around Idaho's tables, preparing for the evening grudge match. Somebody said J. J. Spencer's Owyhee *Avalanche* was no longer in business, and its old home was now a beer parlor on weekends. I bought a six-pack for the thirty-eight mile jog to Jordan Valley, hoping I had enough gas and daylight to make it out.

---

* Federal Writers' Project, *Idaho: A Guide in Word and Pictures* (1937; rep. New York: Somerset Publishers, 1972).

OREGON

Scotty's Tavern
Main Street, Baker

A light cherry bar waited at Scotty's, its two nicely balanced columns capped with handcarved cherubs, scowling gargoyle-fashion; its entablature placid overhead. An unmatched front counter with formica top hosted several farmers and an outrageously tiny woman seated next to me—sipping a twelve-ounce Heidelburg and taking time to crack a hard-boiled egg. The eggs were fresh at Scotty's and just ten cents apiece. I ordered one; it was still warm at the yolk. Ordered another and to hell with serum cholesterol. The little old woman had just gotten hers peeled. A bird-sized peck, and then back to her beer. That maneuver wasting the best part of a minute. Guess you learn to take your time.

Baker certainly had. The "Denver of Oregon," a major supply center on the Oregon Trail and wildest stop between Portland and Salt Lake, Baker had atrophied to four or five saloons and a coopful of oldtimers who couldn't recall secondhand stories of the good old days. Mining camps of Rye Valley, Willow Creek, Gem City, Sparta, Eldorado, and the Mormon Basin had once depended on Baker, both for supplies and for R-and-R. Gambling halls, blacksmith shops, livery stables and saloons were Baker's principal industries during the eighteen-eighties. Baker Hotel at ten stories was one of the tallest buildings in Oregon, dwarfing every structure in town and prattling its own grandeur. A General Grant behemoth, it was still lovely inside, but seedy as a bus station. Indeed, its lobby now served Baker as the local Greyhound depot.

Draft beer at Scotty's was Heidelberg at fifteen cents a short glass. Hardware and grooming accessories for sale under the back mirror. Everybody talking slow and moving around on gum shoes. That little woman still hadn't finished her egg. I bought a nail clipper keychain for a quarter and gave myself a manicure. The old woman wrapped the last of her egg in a paper napkin, stuffing it into her purse. Both of us shuffled outside.

167

Stockman's Bar and Café
Main Street, Baker

A scintilla of boomtown fervor lingered at Stockman. The brassy barmaid served ranch hands repartee which would have made Lyndon Johnson blush; punchers kept their quarters lined along the edge of Stockman's pool table waiting for a game, and the jukebox croaked out a Powder River samba. A unique Western-style back bar of white oak or ash stood at the far end of the room, its thin English columns more like those of a pulpit than a saloon piece. A heavy oak front bar, worn and sodden, stood in protective counterpoint. A Scots Guard of a front counter. Several old men dotted its length, but the majority of Stockman's patrons were restlessly young. Beer was cheap at twenty-five cents a stein, bar whisky reasonable at sixty-five a shot. Cowboy paintings hung about the room . . . mostly of Western flora and fauna. Very amateur; very endearing. So long and kiss the kids.

Elephant and Castle
201 S.W. Washington Street, Portland

A pseudo-English pubroom, peopled with lumpenproles pitching darts at three p.m. and nibbling cheesy Reubens. First stop off the freeway, a dart's throw from Willamette River—newly sanitized as the result of Oregon's extraordinary program of reclamation/revitalization. Salmon now frolicked where shit once had befouled the shore. Elephant was perfectly nice, but I wondered if Governor McCall's sympathies had extended to restoration of Portland's saloons. Elephant was in an old building, near the site of Portland's first log house and peripheral to the oldest business district. Like I say, perfectly nice: A big oak bar, clean toilets, and a reading-room ambience which was peaceful. I might as well have been drinking in Philadelphia. No sense of the Pacific Northwest had permeated Elephant's a-regional hide.

"Hoyt Hotel had two old bars," a sixtyish barmaid told me. "Hotel's closed now for renovation, but should reopen. Don't know any others."

We'd just have to see. My Federal Writers' *Guide* proved encouraging: During the last quarter of the last century, Portland had been so saloon-blessed that lumber baron Simon Benson had donated drinking fountains to be placed at many busy corners, hoping that if "good water were available his loggers would not consume so much alcoholic liquor while visiting the metropolis." One Portland saloon, Erickson's, had stretched the full north side of West Burnside Street between N.W. Second and Third Avenues and was once "*the* most widely known saloon in the Pacific Northwest." Erickson's mahogany bar had run to 674 feet. Loggers, seamen, "dirt movers and hobos from everywhere" met at Erickson's. When Portland's 1894 flood had swept into the saloon, proprietor Erickson "quickly chartered a scow, anchored it at Second and Burnside, stocked it, and business continued more or less as usual."

That sort of thing was plain enlightening.

Beer at Elephant was sixty cents a stein; sandwiches about two dollars. An amiable afternoon spot. But dull, my god.

The Bowery

436 N.W. Sixth Avenue, Portland

Hoyt Hotel, not far from Union Station, was indeed closed; boarded up, its windows sheeted with polyethylene. I strolled down Sixth Avenue, through a light rain, admiring Portland's verdure. How green everything was. Desert passed, West won, I had crossed the Cascades and from here on would bask in Oregon's temperate clime . . . compliments of the Japanese current. Pacific Northwest was the East on stilts, minus traffic congestion. Same cosmopolitan air, same sophisticated dress. Business folk hustled along Portland's streets with the determination of Eastern counterparts. Portland was nearly a mini-San Francisco. My first hit of "city life" in so many miles.

Bartender at Bowery said he thought Hoyt would reopen, but not to bet the baby on it. A massive fellow in white T-shirt and apron, with a complexion pinker than salmon. Served me a cracked-porcelain bowl of homemade pinto beans, with a side dish of lumberjack chili, for less than one buck. Cold draft at thirty cents a stein and cook's stews available. Plus pickled pigs' feet, Polish sausages, and ice cold hard-boiled eggs. Bowery was far from sophisticated; it nestled on the fringe of Portland's skid row district without really being skid row itself. Patronage was half black, half white, and the races mixed well. TV was on: *Wide World of Sports*. Heated conversations about the Yankees, or Roger Staubach's shoulder separation. Friendly. A dayglo ceiling over a rectangular formica bar, but . . . ambience at Bowery was standard pre-Prohibition. A comfortably dingy tone to the fixtures, but the floor was swept. And food first rate. Couple of stevedores played shuffleboard on Bowery's old-fashioned set—sawdust over shellacked maple, with those heavy pucks. Three blocks south, Indians and blacks were cutting each other to ribbons in the mission taverns. But here at Bowery all was peace.

Don's Beachcomber Inn
Bay Street, Florence

Heavy fear factor at Don's; one wondered precisely why. Off Siuslaw River, on a little front street two blocks from the coast, Don's appeared affable. Old automobile hoods hung from the walls . . . a species of decor I'd not yet encountered. An exquisite yellow Caddy hood over a far pool table; assorted Fords and Chevvies—vintage stuff. A logger/fisherfolk/freak tavern, but with little of the melting pot tolerance called for in a superior bar recipe. Longhairs drank at one end of the barroom; cueball loggers and teamsters at the other. Territories inviolate.

A cueball collared one of the freaks and squawked: "Buy you a beer, son. I am feeling generous. Little woman done me proud: Baby's eight months old today, and y'oughter see the *balls* on that boy."

Timber Inn
Route 126, Mapleton

A quiet, clean, efficiently run tavern in the heart of Kesey country. Ken Kesey had set his lumberman epic *Sometimes a Great Notion* near Mapleton, and Timber Inn was straight out of the novel. Surrounded by green hills and ever-threatening flood waters from the Siuslaw, Timber nevertheless held an illusion of permanence. Loggers in calk boots and green twill pants—checked Mackinaws draped across their shoulders like flags, sawdust in their whiskers, hair stinking of gas and oil—swilled draft Blitz at thirty cents a stein. Occasionally retiring to shiver a slambam game of pool. Hard-boiled eggs *fresh* at Timber, and gourmet picnic tins available to go. Loggers guffawed scarily as each tourist-stranger entered; huddling together like clumps of stout trees.

Something about logging bars that rendered them less congenial than other watering spots of the American outdoorsman. Oregon had yielded few Great Bars during weeks of research; Pendleton, The Dalles, Eugene, Springfield, and countless smaller towns had offered nothing. Loggers were a breed apart from lesser men. Cruder, more violent, less sympathetic. One recalled Henry Stamper's motto in *Notion:* "Never Give An Inch," and his constant refrain: "We'll whup 'er." Loggers were, by nature, a dull and cloddish lot; lacking the style and exaggerated sense of fashion which even the most rustic cowboy possessed. Service in logging bars was slow, humor abrasive, conversation loud. Perhaps it had to do with loggers' relationship to the land. Something as simple as that. Loggers slaughtered, where farmers cultivated. Loggers raped; farmers inseminated. Fishermen and ranchers? One had long felt that the death of a single tree was worth that of a hundred animals. Instinctive prejudice. But these Oregon lumberjacks bore it out. One had only to drink in their bars for three weeks—or precede them once down a curving highway, truck horn blatting, fifteen tons of freshly murdered sequoias hurtling toward your bumper—to feel such a coolness.

Thank God for Timber, whose fear factor proved minuscule; whose setting was as gorgeous as its draft beer was cold.

Sporthaven Restaurant and Bar
Route 101, Brookings Harbor

A singularly plastic establishment of minor interest except for its situation on Chetco Cove, where salmon run like wildfire in August and big trucks may be viewed from Sporthaven's back window carting away flatbeds-full of sport salmon, freshly caught. You can charter a boat at Sporthaven or sit at the slick formica counter soaking up fishing stories the likes of which you'll hear no place else.

Right *on* the Pacific Ocean, catering to sportsfishermen, charter-boat captains and crusty Pacific Coast mates, perfumed with fish slime and bejeweled of scale. Beer is fifty cents a can and food is serviceable. Get in there about seven thirty a.m. before the boats go out or after four p.m. when they dock. You'll inhale some blarney and the beer won't hurt. Buy fishing gear from Sporthaven or just a wide beach towel. For less than a mile north or south waits Oregon's legendary coastline . . . the most beautiful emerald green, craggy-deserted beachfront in America.

WASHINGTON
Seattle

Sunset

First Avenue (Belltown), Seattle

Two blocks east of Puget Sound and an astronaut's step from Space Needle Lounge, Sunset proved a lazy afternoon saloon frequented by septuagenarian loggers, commercial fishermen, carousing S.I.U., and itinerant bindle stiffs from the four corners. A majority of Sunset's patrons were retired; Belltown existing on land platted in 1852 by three founding families and surviving as the eldest of Seattle's several Skid Road neighborhoods. Sunset possessed a back bar reminiscent of Seattle's boomtown days when lumbering, legerdemain, and the Alaskan gold rush kept slips and saloons filled round the clock. Veneer over Sunset's four graceful columns was dark, and a peaceably worn front bar stood as silent mate. A big Fisher system tooted gently from behind the back bar . . . outside it was extremely hot. My first cold draft at thirty cents a mug quickly assuaged tourist angst acquired at Space Needle Park. An oldster to my right was telling Nick the Bartender about "this elk I saw up-country with antlers wider'n a Volkswagen." Most of Sunset's customers drank wine by the short glass (twenty-five cents). Plain whisky bottles with orange plastic stoppers lined Sunset's back bar, refilled with many different brands of wine.

In an hour or so Sunset would change shifts as patrons wandered down Western Avenue to Millionaire's Club—a Skid Road service center where bunks were cheap and the evening meal free—or strolled purposefully home to more commodious flops such as the Downtown Y, where I had registered. Wine would continue to flow at Sunset, as old men who were skipping supper, or avoiding it, resolutely toasted nightfall. Quietly visiting with friends. Seattle's Skid Road was a vital organ of the city; many of its residents retired widowers living in furnished rooms on small Social Security checks. Few were alcoholics. Saloons such as Sunset and Belltown Bar, further along First, provided special services for these gents. They were cheerful places where a man might sympathize with his peers or razz younger fellows still able to work. Usually these saloons offered the sole opportunity for social contact with women and families. Far from a nursing home, Sunset was a lively saloon with good times to be had, extraordinary tales to be overheard, and cheap booze to be drunk. The name of the game.

Central Tavern
207 First Avenue South (Pioneer Square), Seattle

Pioneer Square was the original skidrow. In 1853 Henry Yesler built a sawmill there, at the foot of present-day Yesler Way; had skidded logs down through the high timber to his doorstep, thus establishing the neighborhood's moniker. Skid Road from the beginning was haven for every sort of tough; Yesler's cookhouse hosting the earliest activity, quintupling as civic hall, jail, church, and saloon. Later Madame Damnable superseded Yesler in popularity, her Conklin House surviving many seasons on a reputation of tasty cooking and hospitable lasses. By 1900 Seattle had become principal supply center for the Alaskan gold rush, and a scuttle of bagnios, gambling dens, and hurdy-gurdies sprang up around Pioneer Square. Fleecing comers-and-goers, the ready and unwilling alike. During World War II a comparable boom occurred. Today about Pioneer Square similar loggers, sailors, Indians, cripples, beggars, trappers, and tramps might be encountered; but most of Skid Road's original saloons were gone.

Central Tavern proved an exception, but even it had suffered restoration in step with a Pioneer Square urban-renewal project, which had brought health food stores, ice-cream parlors and silky boutiques to a neighborhood where previously only mission houses had flourished. Missions were still operating—as were the honkytonk skin joints which had been Skid Road's pleasure from the start—but they coexisted in nebulous harmony with arty newcomers.

Central was very much an artist's saloon, catering to those of the snazzier sensibility who had taken advantage of Skid Road's low rents and large spaces to nuclearize a private community. Which was not to say you might not observe factions of the old neighborhood partaking at Central: "All humanity hep and weird," as Kerouac described them, "amazing me out of my eyeballs—Indian girls in slacks, with Indian boys with Tony Curtis haircuts . . . families of Okie fame . . . drunks—*drinkin*—my God they been drinkin! Everyone is a lush, I can see it—Seattle!" * Drinks hovered about a dollar, beer half that, and palatable sandwiches could be purchased for less than two. A plain oak bar had been refinished and stood before Central's bare brick walls monolithically. Numerous plants added a touch of Pacific Northwest green. Tables were of old wood, as were captain's chairs. Soothing tapes on deck: Gordon Lightfoot, Bob Dylan, Leonard Cohen or some other North Country bard. Pool tables and cold draft. Oly on tap. Well-dressed, peach-complected locals mingled with the Skids. Opportunity for action, unrestricted. Madame Damnable would have been proud.

Place Pigalle

81 Pike Street (Pike Place Market), Seattle

Pike Place Market was the solar plexus of the city, a three-block agglomerate of truck stalls, fish counters, flower marts, second-hand shops, rooming houses, diners, and saloons . . . like Pike Street Tavern with its handsome pre-Pro bar set and collusion of polite Skid Roaders (Pike Place functioning as shopping center/forum for Skid Road's salaried upper-crust), and Athenian Tavern with its sunny drinking rooms, fresh seafood, and quarter drafts. Seattleites from every neighborhood mingled at Pike Place; joining Skid Roaders, farmers, and fishermen in a crush of industrious humanity—intent on the satisfaction of primary goals. (Largely gratified.) If you couldn't find what you wanted along the boardwalks of this 1907 public market, it hadn't been imported yet. The motion, colors, the *smells* . . . I purchased a sack of bright pink kippered salmon chunks, munching them between beers at Athenian; later picked absentmindedly at a head of Kelly green romaine as I strolled from stall to stall. Bartered for an entire sturgeon and nearly acquired it. Finished my last hunk of salmon at Pike Place barber college where I bought a Bubbs Creek haircut for fifty cents, no sidewalls and close-clip the rest.

Place Pigalle was a half-hidden little dive at the southwest end of the market, strung out over the hillside like a clothesline. Stumbled across it inadvertently and don't think I'd have found it if I hadn't been tracking strange bars. Sun was setting over Puget Sound and

---

*Jack Kerouac, *Desolation Angels* (New York: Bantam Books, 1971), pp. 118, 119.

Pigalle's two big windows permitted a flood of red to bathe the barroom. There was an old oak bar at Pigalle; nary a modern fixture in the place. I called for a thirty cent draft and settled astride a sturdy ash stool, head cocked to monitor action in the harbor. Ferries and steamers chugged toward Bremerton; freighters hooted out to open water. As fine a view as I'd enjoyed in a Great Bar to date. A mélange of freaks, merchant seamen, Skid Roaders, hip blacks, and prostitutes comprised Pigalle's clientele. Freaks were well fed and healthy, but typical in a comforting way. Jukebox was a tad spacey. But controlled. One did well to recall that Seattle was Hendrix country: A cliffdweller city milky with contrasts . . . Space Needle to houseboats; stormy hillside solos to gutbucket bass riffs; all waterfront and back bay.

A jimjamming poet slumped next to me nagged for beer, then offered poems from a frayed portfolio at a dollar a sheet. No thanks. Samples were real vague. I drank another draft then switched to bar whisky (sixty cents) to cut the evening chill. Moving toward Pigalle's front window, to watch a tug turn a liner in the Sound, a blonde chatted me up, and suddenly I was engulfed by Seattle freaks fusillading queries about the East Coast ("Yeh I made it there once, far as Detroit."), digging on *Saloon*, and demanding to know what bars I'd researched in the Pacific Northwest. Everyone clustered around a corner table, candle in a bottle neck, 200 feet over the harbor . . . friendly! "Victrola time," somebody hollered, and everyone piled out of Pigalle down through market fish stalls to—

Victrola

91 Pike Street (Pike Place Market), Seattle

A sliver of a saloon, in the bowels of the old market, jammed with what can only be described as . . . hipsters: cats in berets and goatees, lankhaired blondes in black turtlenecks and Levis, spades whoopin and finger-poppin to *jazz* on the juke, like the sixties never happened. A section of Victorian back bar encircling whisky bottles reflected in Victrola's modest back mirror; a serviceable front counter cluttered with glasses. Draft beer was a quarter a stein; naturally the most popular option, but bar whisky was cheap at sixty-five a shot. Pigalle's friendly blonde grabbed me and before I could pay had us out on the dance floor laboring to Fats Domino hucklebucks and Bing Crosby hugabears. Victrola's juke was nothing but oldies, mostly real-oldies. Took a break and immediately got involved in an insane conversation with a shortass Brother in black beret and leathers about whether dogs possessed the gift of reason. "A dog can *decide*," this Brother insisted, "but he cannot *choose*." Me nodding yes, yes, of course you're right—separating best of friends. Bolt to piss and Pigalle's blonde, who, it turned out, was herself waitressing days at Athenian, followed me straight to the men's room, whoops! her mistake, a wink and into the growler next door. Fats Waller on the box as we emerge *"Want some seafood, mama"* and back on the floor; blond ponytail swinging, leather aviator's jacket slapping . . . old bums in the alley snorting rotgut and clapping hands to the lunatic beat.

Waterfront Bar
Bellingham

Hangover afternoon saloon, well-suited to recovery and remorseful self-vendetta. Perched at the lip of Bellingham's industrial waterfront, commanding a sober panorama of harbor and outlying Puget Sound. Beer ridiculously cheap at thirty cents a can—cold and bracing to shaky nerves. A pierside clientele composed of brackish oldtimers, cowlick barkeeps, and burly Skids. Had spent the day sloshing through snow atop Mt. Baker, angling for a view of Desolation Peak: 6,085 feet of penance where Gentle Jack had sobered up one summer as fire lookout, and encountered the void. Picked up a backpacker driving down who'd been out two months. Told him of *Saloon* . . . mildly interested. Asked was I camping. Told him no. Said, "You'll kill yourself in those YMCAs, man." Very Teutonic and ascetic under two months' culture of mountain slime. Prompting comparisons in my mind-box between wilderness backpackers and seekers of the Great American Bar. Each hunting a spot where it all might come together. Each practicing a life of restraint and sacrifice. Each a distance man of sorts: Gaffed on marathon-dementia.

Backpacker had withdrawn at Shuksan. I pushed on to Bellingham: A murky seaport town with spectacular vistas of two mountain clusters and a shrouded bay. A former associate lived nearby. Poet and alcohol-aesthete of the old school. Word had it that he was heavy on the sauce these days. Booze finally getting the best of the old porcupine. So I did not telephone. Sat at Waterfront instead, nursing personal regrets, plumbing gods of the hop, and girding up for San Francisco.

CALIFORNIA
San Francisco

Checked into the Chinese Y as Old St. Mary's tolled seven bells and a florid dawn eclipsed the variegated roof tops of Chinatown. Four bucks a night and I was home free. Half a block from Grant Avenue, five blocks from North Beach and three down from Nob Hill . . . Chinese Y was a bargain of the first order, perhaps the last such in San Francisco. I never stayed any place else. Halls were a trifle dingy, rooms were cramped—but there was no hair in the shower drains (a racial plus) and guests proved friendly to a man. The building's bright pagoda façade overlooked a children's playground, whence trilling Cantonese rose to swab this pilgrim's exhaust-blatted ears. One nurtured few illusions about San Francisco; its alcoholism, narcotics abuse, and suicide stats were common knowledge to the most vacuous Golden Gate tourist. Our Beauty by the Bay, America's axiomatic End of the Road burg. A death temptress since gold rush days. Yet in Chinatown one was permitted to fantasize. Chambers might be too close to bathroom and phone, bedclothes a bit ratty, the sign overhead

WARNING!

LOCK YOUR

DOOR

EVEN WHEN

GOING

TO

THE BATHROOM

sadly prefixed by: "Jerry Tubin of Malaysia/Singapore was here, 16 to 21, August, 1972," hinting loneliness and ego-crush of the bleakest variety. But even a jaded weektripper like me cheered to realize he'd be breakfasting on *deem sum* at Hang Ah Tea Room by three (certainly splurging on ginger ice cream and lotus bean buns at Fong Fong Bakery) before hitting City Lights Bookstore by five, for a ritual browse . . . followed by an evening's carouse of North Beach boho saloons. Over twelve hundred bars were licensed in San Francisco, not counting beer joints. One couldn't hope to research them all. But with six hours sleep and a good Chinese feed underbelt, one could take his best shot.

Vesuvio Café
255 Columbus Avenue (North Beach), San Francisco

Vesuvio is North Beach to the core, from its leotarded blondes in Landlubbers and motocross boots to its full-bearded painters in splattered turtlenecks and heavy cords. The fifties happened at Vesuvio, and then continued to happen. Every legendary beat has imbibed here—Ginsberg, Corso, Ferlinghetti, Kerouac, Cassady—and the feel of the place is that any moment several might tumble in again, crash up to the bar, and order "brews" all around. Vesuvio commands a pleasant view of Columbus Avenue, tit shows, and bisex discos notwithstanding, and comfortable window seats encourage the dalliance of seeing and being-seen. Atmosphere is strikingly like that of the departed Figaro in Greenwich Village; with draft beer at an agreeable fifty cents and bar drinks below a dollar. Vesuvio is a lounging café (one feels he might set up shop in a dim corner, break out notebook or sketchpad, and drink unharassed the livelong day) with lazy table and chair combos; but V's front counter bustles and bar service there is brisk. Homer Ansley's "Double Exposure" hangs behind the back bar . . . a painting reputedly Kodachromed on thousands of postcards home. A curtained booth for "private parties" is available upstairs, dubbed John Wilkes Memorial Booth, and from it the view of proceedings below is indeed theatrical. Best time at Vesuvio is any time, from eleven thirty a.m. when it opens to two a.m. when it closes. Vesuvio is the first bar I hit in North Beach, and usually the last.

Tosca Café
242 Columbus Avenue (North Beach), San Francisco

Tosca has been coddling North Beach Italians (San Francisco's largest ethnic minority) for over fifty years, and its dark mahogany fixtures are matched in richness only by the hue of its coffee drinks. Espresso machines dominate decor at Tosca, and some of the best capuccino in town is fashioned behind the old front counter. Capuccino at Tosca is not your garden variety; its made with chocolate, not coffee—steamed with milk and brandy. The result (at ninety cents) is a potable which will melt your socks. Venetian coffee, the same drink but with *coffee*, likewise goes for ninety cents. A hundred selections of Grand Opera grace the juke at Tosca; clientele is old neighborhood Italian or traditional boho; and if your mission is to cut the chill some dank North Beach evening, Tosca is the spot to accomplish it.

Coffee Gallery
1353 Upper Grant Avenue (North Beach), San Francisco

Born of the San Francisco poetry renaissance and a stubborn Beat invasion, Coffee Gallery preserves the exacerbated optimism of that fifties North Beach era. Front room is a saloon with suitably weathered fixtures and a jostle of paintings/drawings/sculptures, which changes weekly. Beer up front is forty-five cents a glass, and you should have no trouble encountering conversation. "Look like a fucking Nazi," one regular exclaimed, noting my Bubbs Creek haircut and leather aviator's jacket. Then he bought me a drink.

Take your beer and wade back to the Showroom, a betabled and benched auditorium of perhaps thirty feet, with stage forward for whatever harangue a patron might offer. Wednesday is poetry night, highly recommended. Although readings verge on the surreal, many sober poets persist in peddling their wares in the time-tested San Francisco tradition of shouts and supplication. (A sodden black read from a typescript thick as a telephone book before his woman physically dragged him offstage: "You *drunk* Jim, make a fool yo'sef.") Monday, Tuesday, Thursday evenings are reserved for sounds; bring your axe and saunter forward. Weekends, Coffee's management provides pro entertainment, but the aura surrounding these professionals is often shattered by scenes transpiring in the audience. A boho, silver-spectacle crowd, with the occasional Hell's Angel tossed in. Modest fear factor. Superior chaos. No hard booze.

The 1232

1232 Upper Grant Avenue (North Beach), San Francisco

A handsome back bar at 1232, looks like mahogany. Lovely entablature indented by a Rococo shell, hand sculptured below the cornice. Matching front bar. Possibly the liveliest of Upper Grant's saloons, quite boho and loose on the cuff. "Awright, whoever's smokin dope, *cut it out*," shouted 1232's gamy Italian barmaid. Palmed fifty cents for a bottle of Coors and rang it up on the old-fashioned, handcrank cash register.

Buena Vista Café

2765 Hyde Street (The Cannery), San Francisco

Dodder on down Hyde Street some hangover Sunday and set up your shakes to a glass of Buena Vista's world-renowned Irish coffee. Ninety cents across the bar and you'll own a blend of the freshest Colombian, finest confection, tangiest Tullamore Dew, and heaviest hand-whipped cream this side of Dublin. Buena introduced Irish coffee to American palates in October of 1952 and today sells over 2,000 glasses of the stuff per weekend. To sit at Buena's weathered front counter and observe Jim Stafford mix twenty Irishes at a time, each one a masterpiece, is to share a trice of bartending majesty (Jim's no slouch with tequila sangrita or the Ramos fizz, either). Buena exhausts one hundred cases of Irish a month, one eighth of all Irish whisky imported to America. Buena tends to be crowded, but not impossibly so. The crush is reassuringly chaotic and one usually can wrestle up to the bar. Buena's expansive windows overlook San Francisco Bay, providing a sober view of Alcatraz Island. Buena has held this location since 1903, having moved across the street from original 1880 digs, known as Billy Nieman's Saloon. Today Buena is touted as San Francisco's most famous and largest grossing saloon.

A generous selection of imported beers is available at Buena, and Aquavit (served properly, frozen in ice) is a favorite of owner George Freeberg. Sunday brunch is traditional; dishes such as Coney Island clam chowder, prawns with sauce, crab or shrimp rémoulade, veal cutlet with tagliarini, and Bavarian cheesecake are typical fare.

Lunch or dinner is reasonably priced. Although tourists are noticeable, San Franciscans predominate. San Franciscans treat Buena
as a metropolitan asset to be patronized frequently. One *knows* one is
in San Francisco at Buena Vista; fact that the old saloon's popular
just goes to show.

San Francisco's best-known lounge is undoubtedly Top of The
Mark, in the Mark Hopkins Hotel (California at Mason), a short hike
up Nob Hill from the Chinese Y. Certainly Top is the most famous
skyroom in town, if not the world. Its view, upon opening in 1939,
was unsurpassed. Today, Fairmont Crown Room, in the Fairmont
Hotel (Mason at California), offers a comparable view—if you can
stand the approach by outside elevator—and boasts a platform which
rotates, providing a 360-degree panorama. But Top is still king, a
tourist must since the nineteen forties when *de rigueur* for partying
military off to the Pacific theater. Design-wise Top's not much, too
slick and forties-deco to qualify as a great saloon, and too removed
from business of the city—greatness of bars partially contingent
upon proximity to land and the American road. But Top *is* earth-
bound in that, originally, it served as private quarters for copper
baron Daniel C. Jackling, a hardrock miner from Cripple Creek who
struck it double rich with his patented process for milling low-grade
copper ore. Mark Hopkins Hotel opened in 1926, and until 1937
Top of the Mark was parcel of Jackling's rooftop estate. Twenty-foot
ceilings remain, but Jackling's heavy Victorian decorations, his rare
tapestries, and huge oil paintings are gone.

Mark Hopkins still accommodates guests with trappings after the
nabob manner (thirty-four suites feature grand pianos), but Top of
the Mark is awash in tourist gush, a-clatter to the strains of a weak
cocktail orchestra, and fudsy with its drinks. Top's bar, as Lucius
Beebe remarked, before his death, is simply "not noted for the liber-
ality of its martinis." *

Pied Piper, however, in the Sheraton-Palace (Market at New
Montgomery), most assuredly is—their martinis a full three ounces,
their bar whisky a generous two. Palace Hotel's place in the history
of San Francisco is another book. Beebe redux: "The hotel was conceived . . . at a time when California was riding the very crest and

---

* *Gourmet*, March 1965.

apex of the Comstock bonanzas in Nevada. From its very inception, the Palace was the paramount showplace of what was easily the most ostentatious city in the world." Post-1906 earthquake, Palace was rebuilt "on the same princely scale as had guided its architects in the seventies." To the tune of twelve million bucks. A Maxfield Parrish painting was commissioned for Pied Piper (of the minstrel himself), and craftsmen were engaged to swath the new barroom in mahogany. From 1909 to present day, Pied Piper has remained San Francisco's preeminent hotel bar. Today, sadly, you're more likely to encounter traveling salesmen than nabobs, but drinks are reasonably priced and caricatures of celebrities (by Tony Sotomayer) diverting. Pied Piper is traditionally a men's bar—legend having it that the only woman to darken its portals, before sex restrictions were dropped during World War II, was Lillian Russell.

Pied Piper's open for lunch, between eleven and two.

Hoffman Café and Grill
619 Market Street, San Francisco

Hoffman claims the honor of being San Francisco's "oldest continuously operating bar in the same location," having conducted business *during* the 1906 earthquake, in a privy-sized shed before the wreckage of their still-smoldering saloon. Menu of Hoffman's makeshift canteen read:

CHEER UP

HAVE ONE

ON ME:

WIELAND'S LAGER,

WILSON'S HIGH BALL.

ALL THERE IS

AFTER ALL.

COME IN AND

SPEND A

QUIET EVENING.

Once rebuilt, Hoffman carried on after the fashion of legendary San Francisco saloons such as Duncan Nicol's Bank Exchange (world-famous for its Pisco Punch), or Barry and Patten's, San Francisco's first gentleman's saloon, combining the sanctity of a library (three-month-old newspapers from Boston and New York hung about the room on racks) with the amenities of a well-stocked bar. That tradition prevails today at Hoffman as it did seventy years ago, and mood is that of genteel, Before-the-Fire saloon—orderly, restrained, in sober defiance of all Barbary Coast barbarities.

A forty-five-foot oak counter, with matching back bar, is situated saloon-right as the patron enters. Draft beer there is fifty cents a glass, and one would do well to stand a minute at the hundred-year-old counter (shipped round the horn) and partake of Hoffman's special ambience: A recollection of bonanza kings, of bullish trading, and gargantuan investments. Hoffman remains a banker's saloon, keeping banker's hours of eleven to eight weekdays, closed Saturday and Sunday. Best time at Hoffman is either lunch or after five, when what's left of San Francisco's financial aristocracy gathers before polished oak to hoist the first of the day. All fixtures are authentic old-saloon, from period tables and chairs to sentimental Victorian oils which grace the paneling. Hoffman's most famous painting is probably Domenic Tojetti's "Lily Maid of Astrolat," a reclining figure on a floating bier, poled before a turreted castle as knights weep along the shore.

A menu of hearty American food is served: clam chowder, steamed Alaskan cod and braised shortribs, to blue cheese or Leiderkrantz with apple pie. Reasonably priced at under three dollars per entree. Occasionally, owner Joe Betz will serve up "some gourmet hors d'oeuvres," most popular of which are oysters on the half shell. Bar drinks run an ounce and a half, and martinis are generous. A favorite house drink is the rum Manhattan, a standard Manhattan cocktail embellished with a dash of rum. Betz brags to have "the heaviest hands in town" when it comes to mixing drinks. Another San Francisco tradition faithfully observed at the timeless Hoffman.

Hink's

29 Second Street (Market Street), San Francisco

Likewise a Before-the-Fire saloon, Hink's during the eighteen-nineties served Market Street clientele at Montgomery and Sutter, before succumbing to earthquake shakes in 1906. Hink's reopened at its new location in 1908. Photographs of the old shop, hung conveniently around the barroom, show wreckage incurred post-quake and a general confusion of the neighborhood. Hink's hasn't changed much in its present incarnation. Ceilings are incredibly high, nearly two stories, and walls are paneled in oak, with matching oak booths and bar. It's dark in Hink's, but comfortably so. (Three outside tables are available "for sunbathers.") There's a small back room affording a modicum of privacy. Fixtures are ubiquitously brown, but a warm brown. Hink's back bar sports plain columns in well-cared-for hardwood, and a complementary front counter.

Draft beer at Hink's fills a fifteen-ounce glass, your choice of Miller's or Pabst for just fifty cents. Bar specialties include martinis and Manhattans. Owner Bernie Hink (who changed his name from Pollack, "to keep the bar passing from generation to generation") says he serves the biggest martini in town—a noble three and one-half ounces, for only seventy-five cents. Liveliest time at Hink's, as with most Market Street saloons, is noon or after five. Other hours the old saloon rests, like a matron napping out her dotage. That's a good time at Hink's too. Then you'll really get the feel.

House of Shields

39 New Montgomery Street (Market Street), San Francisco

Eddie Shields opened his saloon in 1936, across the street from the incomparable Palace Hotel. Eddie had his bar set fashioned in exact replication of the mahogany front and back bar in Palace's fabled Comstock Room, long gone. Shields' old barroom is paneled in musty hardwood, with fluted pilasters and a gilded Baroque ceiling. A saloon has occupied this location since 1908, and several period photos still hanging date from the era. There are no stools at Shields' bar, no jukebox, no television, and no clock. What a string of blessings! Until just a few years ago, there were no women. A dining room on the balcony has long welcomed ladies, but policy toward women at the bar is stern. Eddie Shields, now deceased, is remembered to have led something of a crusade against patrons' pleas to install a television set. "I run a saloon, not a theater," he insisted. Barkeep Pete Ragan has been on duty since 1936, and serves a mean whisky on the rocks for about eighty-five cents. He is averse to mixing cocktails. Atmosphere at Shields is that of an oldtime urban saloon, with no fuss, no frills. Except for the extraordinary hard-wood which everywhere buoys a patron's spirits and reminds him where he is.

Breen's

71 Third Street (Market Street), San Francisco

Breen's owns the longest uncurved front-and-back bar set in San Francisco—absolutely the longest I have encountered in America. Breen's set was shipped round the Horn from Brussels to Virginia City, Nevada, nearly a hundred years ago. It is indeed a sight: hand-carved mahogany, seventy-two feet of it, with four nude caryatids adorning the back bar, chandeliers, and bright, wide mirrors. The bar is so long one feels as if he's drinking in a railroad car. Breen's opened for business in 1919, engaging Brunswick-Balke to reinstall the Virginia City bar. A bierstube had stood at this location since 1880, and Breen's continued the Hofbrau with a leaden selection of bratwurst and sauerbraten.

A twelve-ounce stein of Lucky Lager sells for thirty-five cents, and San Francisco's traditional Anchor Steam Beer is on tap for forty. Löwenbräu, Guinness, and half-and-half go for fifty. There's a diversity of clientele at Breen's, unlike other Market Street bars, due to Breen's history as a newspaperman's saloon. Four metropolitan dailies once crowded the neighborhood, and Breen's served shift after shift. Breen's employed twelve bartenders to staff the seventy-two-foot bar, and kept them busy. Breen's stayed open during Prohibition, much to the chagrin of San Francisco's Dashaways, a blue ribbon temperance group known to "dash the proffered cup" from a tippler's lips. Atmosphere in the old saloon remains surprisingly Wild West, thanks to the joyous bar set with its attendant memories of Virginia City; this mixes oddly with Breen's tone, but not adversely. Breen's is possibly the most comfortable Market Street saloon—one feels he would not be disturbed at a corner table if he relaxed with a newspaper or perused a book. Bartenders are gray and white-aproned. Food is tasty and filling. A commendable spot.

It's worth a pilgrim's while to ferry across Golden Gate some evening to *Sausalito*, if only for drinks and dinner at Trident, 558

Bridgeway. Sausalito is as close as you'll come to the cramped elegance of St. Tropez in these United States—residents as well turned out and . . . beautiful as any you'll knock elbows with. Trident is the acme of Sausalito's hip cafés; a pleasure to both eye and palate. John Grissim, C & W aficionado and *Rolling Stone* roustabout, informed me that Trident was the spot to observe off-duty Mill Valley rock stars, Mick Jagger having thrown at least one celebrated birthday party there. View from Trident's terrace is spectacular. Best view of San Francisco from across the bay. Get to Trident early enough so that you can dig the view before dark while colors still explode; and after when lights start blinking, a full chandelier's worth, like Cannes from down the coast.

There's a small bar at Trident where one may sip draft beer at seventy-five cents a glass, ululate to a vituperative sound system and ogle. You'll catch every sort of costume at Trident, Hi-Backed Paydays to Givenchy gowns. Everybody looks as if he's been cultivating his tan an entire fiscal year. There are more hand-tooled leather boots per foot at Trident than at any other American café.

Potted ferns engulf Trident's interior; Lord! it's like drinking in a silk arboretum. Trees, plants, odd grassy things dangle from the ceiling. Rough wood is a design staple here. There is an outside bar on the rear deck, patterned in mixed hardwood, Aztec-style. Wood mosaics predominate inside, where barrel arches provide shape, and tables, close but uncrowded, vie with loud music for most effective space control.

Meal options at Trident accentuate the positive, offering an extensive menu of fresh, natural foods. Sashimi is reportedly excellent, as are steak tartare, "Sunshine" gardens salads, yogurt dishes, fruit and fruit juices, stone ground whole-wheat waffles with nuts and raisins, sandwiches with thick whole-grain bread, something called "Magic Spyder" loaf, brown rice pilaf, and carob for dessert. Wines are California's finest, with the usual foreign brands available.

Trident is a seventies spot if ever there was one—as representative of its time and place as was Chicago's Pump Room during the thirties, and nearly as chic.

And of course there's First and Last Chance Saloon, 50 Webster Street, Jack London Square, *Oakland*. London is said to have imbibed here, and management has seen fit to retain Jack's favorite table (where he supposedly did some writing), just as it was sixty-five years ago. Photos of Jack around the barroom; even a beer glass enshrined in his memory.

If you crave a more comprehensive listing of every sort of Bay Area bar, scrounge a copy of Green, Everett, and Gong's *Fun and Serious Drinking in San Francisco* (VCIM/SF Guide Publications, 1971) to which I am indebted for many facts and figures quoted herein.

Trader Vic's, 20 Cosmos Place, calls San Francisco home, and founder Victor Bergeron still presides over the preparation of his legendary cocktails and often first-rate cuisine. Vic's rum drinks are familiar enough to American's so that a catalogue is uncalled for here. Suffice it to say, they are as potent and well mixed as any you'll run across in San Francisco. And reasonable, at two to three dollars per large glass. Design-wise, Trader Vic's is far from what we have come to expect in a Great American Bar, and traditionally his clientele is a trifle Anaheim for our tastes. But no one can argue with Vic's drinks . . . and memories they conjure of Constantine, at the old Florida in Havana, to whom Vic tips his mixologist's cap.

One pre-Fire bar, which as Lucius Beebe noted in *The American West*, "antedated Trader Vic's by nearly a century as a San Francisco landmark," was Abe Warner's Cobweb Palace, at Meigg's Wharf, in an alley off Francisco Street—"a combination saloon and museum, its name derived from Abe's belief that it was bad luck to discommode the spiders." In the half century or so of its existence, Abe never wiped away a spider's web . . . the result, as photographs show, was a clutter of noble proportion. Atop spider's webs, Abe collected tusks, beaks, heads, and swordfish snouts of every ilk, lending his place the South Sea air for which it became famous. Abe also kept "parrots of legendary profanity and monkeys who had the run of the shop," Beebe reported. Abe always posed for photographs in silk top hat and morning coat; prints that remain show a wizened little man with slits for eyes, who seems to be enjoying a perpetual last laugh.

San Francisco in the nineteen-seventies, for its wealth of pre-Pro saloons, could have salvaged a bit of Abe Warner's spirit: fewer tourists, fewer drugheads, fewer End of the Road alcoholics bellied up to the bar; more profane parrots, masturbating monkeys, and barkeeps like Abe.

NEVADA

Delta Saloon
C Street, Virginia City

Of the dozen or so saloons left in downtown Virginia City, Delta is probably the most famous. Cited frequently in low-life chronicles of the eighteen-seventies, Delta has served more riffraff at the same address than any other C Street saloon. Lucius Beebe was a regular during his tenure in Virginia City, from 1950 to 1966, as tippling recluse and outspoken publisher of *The Territorial Enterprise* . . . as were Mark Twain, Bret Harte, and other luminaries of the journalistic trade. Over one hundred saloons operated in Virginia City during the eighteen-seventies; for Comstock Lode was the most successful silver-mining venture in the world. San Francisco, "over the hill," owed the development of its nabob architecture to Comstock cash. Virginia City was the epitome of an eye-popping boomtown. Today, as Beebe noted before his death, tourism had transformed Virginia City's "once raffish and seedy grandeurs into an outpost of Disneyland."

At Delta, where Bonanza kings once "bucked the faro," dropping a casual $38,000 on the turn of a card, a row of slot machines was pumped mechanically by preening tourists. Where dandified gamblers once stood sizing up their next mark, short-sleeved moms and pops hunched over chromium stools, before Delta's polished front counter. A gift shop had been tacked on where a casino once sufficed. Few antique fixtures remained: Tiffany lamps, dog-eared photos, steer horns. Back bar was modest, as was an unmatched front. "Solid Comstock Cedar," fashioned by McIntosh, architect of the long departed International Hotel, was Delta's principal decorative note. Wide mirrors, reflecting tourist hijinks in the gift shop behind. History gone to seed.

A trip to Delta early some morning encourages one to pretend, though. Or in dead of winter when mountain roads are slick. Virginians are still mad as hatters—fine company, despite survival tactics they've employed to keep the ghost town running. More Williamsburg than Disneyland. Nevertheless: Cash had been the motivation for Virginia City's existence in 1870, and is a prime moving force today.

Crystal Bar
C Street, Virginia City

During Virginia City's infant years, *The Territorial Enterprise* ran a daily column: "Last Night's Violence." On one occasion, according to Beebe, "The victim of a stabbing in a C Street saloon lay for two days under a billiard table before the coroner bothered to sign a certificate permitting its removal." * Such litter would never have been allowed at Crystal, from its opening night in 1867, "Most Elegant Bar on the Comstock."

Today, Crystal maintains that elegance only in its surviving fixtures—moved from their original location years ago. For like Delta, Crystal suffers from an influx of tourism and artifacts of a successful come-on. Not so disreputable as Bucket of Blood down C Street, but crammed to the lintels with tourist souvenirs, post cards, booklets, etc. Crystal's Eastlake bar set remains a pleasure to behold, despite the addition of stools before its carved front counter (brass hand and foot rails polished, mahogany aglow), and tacky drink ads pasted to the back mirror. Crystal's bar set is elegant and high style; not to be missed. The old saloon entertained its share of chawbacons during the Rush, but a tone of high style persisted. Crystal's chandeliers, its most famous item, are indeed crystal: blue and pink gas lamps on a gold plated base, pride of the Comstock. Antique clocks, an original orchestrion, weathered photographs, such as that of U. S. Grant inspecting Sutro Tunnel, make Crystal a rubbernecker's delight. Ledger of the International Hotel is on display, boasting autographs of every famous personage of the period. Crystal is noted for its mixed drinks—concoctions such as Comstock Lode and the Bonanza fizz. Drinks are reasonable for a tourist saloon, and beer is cheap. Once again, get to Crystal some time when tourism is at a low ebb and you will enjoy one of the West's loveliest and most famous barrooms. William H. Marks is owner/manager, associated with Crystal since 1901.

Other Virginia City saloons, many of which date from boom days, are Brass Rail, Bonanza, Bucket of Blood, Cabin in the Sky, Iron Door, Kitty's Longbranch, Michele's Silver Stope, Old Comstock,

---

* *The Lucius Beebe Reader* (New York: Doubleday, 1967).

Red Garter, Silver Queen, Sundance, and Virginia City Vintners. All are located on C Street, the main drag.

Cal's Saloon
Route 50, east of Carson City

Cal's translates nineteenth-century Comstock bawdiness into a contemporary cement-block makeshift, reminiscent of the mud huts and hide tents of Nevada's earliest grogshops. In other words: "Done thrown up this temporary structure, gawdied her some with neon and fancy formica, best we got, and yes we are out to make a buck—" but not at the customer's expense, so to speak. Cal serves a hearty free dinner several nights a week; that's right, *free dinner;* tonight you'll get Italian spaghetti, French bread, and all the salad you can eat. Go on back for seconds, boss don't mind. Draft beer at Cal's is twenty-five cents and it is cold. Bar drinks go for seventy-five. Just a few steps to the rear is Kit Kat Ranch, one of Storey County's "legal" whorehouses. A trailer camp in truth, painted pink, and I say "legal" cause there's not exactly a law *for* em, but there ain't no law *agin* em. So there they sit. And you'll see a few in here from time to time. About ten bucks a throw. One there, shootin eightball with that trucker. Will disappear directly. Another by the bar, cashing in on Cal's free supper.

"Girls work out of here, you might say; case of one hand washin the other. Cops never bother us, just inspect Kit Kat every so often, see the girls're clean. And performin up to snuff. There's other love stores in this area—Moonlight Ranch, the Mustang. Mustang has its own saloon, Mustang Bar, off Interstate 80, east of Reno. Same sort of prices, same freewheelin folks. Yes, girls work out of Mustang too. Very relaxed. You best try it."

UTAH

"We *had* an old saloon in Salt Lake City—" clerk at the Newhouse Hotel said, between shouts from a Dare to Be Great convocation under way in an adjacent conference room.

"—but goddam if the sumbitch didn't burn down last week."

Poplar Place Saloon
Main Street, Moab

Utah was 3.2 beer country, no liquor, no wine sold publicly from behind the bar, which was okay by me. My system needed a break; I was flabby, ill-tempered, and puffed up like a toad from too much drink. A little disco called Crow's Nest, State Street, Salt Lake City, had provided necessary chaos for a time, but as the night clerk at Newhouse indicated, there were no Great Bars in Salt Lake. Park City, a nineteenth-century mining town turned ski resort, boasted one or two oldtimers, but nothing worth cataloguing. Over hard-boiled eggs and beer at one such disreputable, I plotted my next move. Colorado was an obvious must, but no need to rush it. What was left in Utah? Map indicated the little town of Moab, less than two hundred miles southeast. Something clicked. Was it recollection of Butch Cassidy, who had commandeered this Mormon outpost as headquarters, or was it Zane Grey, who had set many of his novels there? No. It was Arches National Park, where Edward Abbey had spent several lonely seasons as Park ranger; a vigil which had resulted in *Desert Solitaire*, one of the Southwest's noblest polemics.

Poplar Place proved conspicuous as I circled Moab for a preliminary look; I had spotted it immediately. Would come back later. Must get some exercise. Jog, do a few pushups, trip out to Arches before reconnoitering supper. Would return in time . . . but, alas, Poplar had closed by ten of this Sunday evening—suck a rock, I should have known. Arches had been worth it, though: Had hiked a half-mile into the desert by moonlight . . . sculpted arches distinct, stars bright, sand rippled and untrampled by human feet. Had collected a small vial of fine red sand from Abbey's campsite. But had meditated too long for Poplar. Information would have to be gleaned from exterior notes and a telephone interview.

Poplar was a handsome structure of adobe hand-pressed brick, oldest commercial building in Moab, a saloon once again after several incarnations as ice house, post office, lumber yard, and general store. Decorated outside with globe lanterns and a stark wooden door, it appeared a winner. Peeking in, I spotted a twenty-five-foot back bar with two large mirrors, plus a heavy wooden counter. Odd fixtures were all oak, owner Joe May later told me, handmade by his staff. Poplar's back bar was from Helper, Utah, where it had been fashioned by local craftsmen near the turn of the century. Wood was mahogany. May had found it necessary to cover his old front counter with oak, as it had suffered irreparable harm during Poplar's previous stints as Frank's Tavern and the Frontier Bar, popular beer joints of Moab's nineteen-fifties uranium boom. An occasional prospector still wandered in, May said, a few jack Mormons and miners—but the majority of Poplar's clientele was younger folks from Moab and tourists on weekends. May had kept the design of Poplar as close to Moab-natural as possible, earning a pat on the back from *Preservation News*, journal of the National Trust for Historic Preservation. He'd removed six layers of exterior decoration, *Preservation News* reported, the end result so remarkable that other Main Street businesses had been prompted to shed "their mid-fifties plastic and aluminum façades to expose the original designs."

"We fixed up the original floors and ceilings," May said, "adding a stairway to the second floor, and a skylight. Installed a wood-burning stove downstairs, which is very comfortable in winter. It's a rustic look. Our prices are reasonable: Thirty-five cents for Bud or Coors draft, the ten-ounce glass. No booze or wine sold in Utah bars, I guess you know, but Coors claims there's not really much difference between 3.2 and standard. Less than you'd think. We sell pizza; certain nights we show films; we have a ladies' night and Sundays we serve Mexican food. Feature bluegrass or blues bands periodically. Try to keep it mellow, though."

May and I spoke for some time. His was a pleasant voice; sounded young. Pleasant music wafted over the wire. He inquired pleasantly about *Saloon* and when a copy might be available:

"See, I do a lot of traveling," May said, "and your book sounds like just the ticket."

COLORADO

Winchester Hotel Bar
204 Railroad Avenue, Rifle

Horses stood hitched before Winchester, next to Harley Davidsons and the ubiquitous pickup. Rifle's streets were empty of pedestrians; her outskirts void of motels. One or two antique hostelries operated downtown, as did several general merchandise outlets. Horseshit bemired Railroad Avenue. Although one had overheard troopers brag of speeders busted, in a diner ten miles west, the twentieth century seemed quite distant. Rifle remained an Old West cattle town, largely unchanged since the advent of the railroad.

Winchester Hotel was a rambling, two-story, pink stucco/adobe structure, veteran of numerous Colorado winters. Inside, a dimly lit barroom. The usual leathery oldtimers huddled around, drinking alone or in company of cross-country motorcyclists. Sad Western music floated from the jukebox. Preposterously. To a lightly carved, English back bar, of cherry wood, "Cut in 1890," barkeep informed me. "We got her cheap. From the old Albany Hotel in Denver." A huge mural of the Colorado had been slathered across Winchester's back wall, a river which paralleled Highway Six hereabouts. Beer was standard cheap: Coors, my first in Colorado. I indulged in several. No one affected Eastern clothes at Winchester, unless you counted leathers; the entire town felt like Big Timber, or maybe Wolf Point, Montana. A Southwestern tone, however. Most definitely Southwest. Enough to make a man thirsty.

Doc John Holiday Tavern
724 Grand Avenue, Glenwood Springs

Passed up Glenwood's 450-foot, spring-heated swimming pool, at eighty degrees, for the hundred-foot outdoor "therapy tank," at one hundred and five degrees, plus a shot at the Vapor Caves. Floated nonchalantly amongst palsy and brawn (Glenwood serving as both health spa and heavy-duty outfitting center), bumping intermittently against paralytic and mountain man while I inhaled a surreptitious six of Coors, and studied Dad's memo:

"The place I want to talk about in relation to my son is the Doc Holiday Tavern in Glenwood Springs, Colorado. They have a back bar there that is 120 years old. It came from Cheyenne to the Tabor building in Leadville, Colorado, and was brought to Glenwood Springs in 1934. There I met the owner, whose name is Greg Klassoff, and during the course of the evening I ran into a guy named Vic who was in the Navy during the battle of the Coral Sea, and he got shot up on the fantail of the *U.S.S. Turner*, which was a destroyer, equipped to hit the beaches and back off and supply gunfire for Marines landing; also the islands from Guadalcanal on up.

"This fellow is a boomer, who runs heavy cranes and heavy equipment.

"In 1954, his wife and three children were killed as they turned onto a highway and were hit by a truck. Since then he's been moving around, running these heavy cranes. The way he got wounded on the fantail of the *Turner* was, as enlisted-man officer of the day, he went in with three Jap prisoners and one of them grabbed a gun and shot him in the belly twice, but Vic, with his .45, was able to kill the Japanese that got him.

"Greg is a nice guy, very fond of this old bar, and I want to make a record of this for my son who is writing a book about old-fashioned bars."

Dad had spent some days at Glenwood Springs, awaiting a bungled pack trip, and had seen fit to help out with research. Which I appreciated, though I had spotted Doc Holiday's two years earlier, en route to some other adventure. A different point of view never hurt, and Lord knows my father had hit enough saloons in his time to qualify as a connoisseur.

The ancient back bar was still in place at Doc's, as was its matching front counter. There existed a seediness to the set which underwrote the miracle of its age. Deteriorated some since my last visit, but then what hadn't. Its cherry wood glowed solemnly in the dimness of Doc's, its four Doric columns, heavy, with minuscule embossing overhead, carried the same weight stoically. Outdoorsmen—the work force of Glenwood—stood drinking and gossiping about the barroom. Although Glenwood on occasion looked oddly like a Catskill resort, nought but tough Western manners prevailed at Doc's. Coors sold for forty-five cents a bottle, and I strapped a couple on. Overheard a drover standing next to me say, of an arthritic: "You oughter seen him, warn't no bigger'n your fist."

A trucker to my left, castigating marriage vows, snickered: "One mouthful of cum is worth a thousand I do's." Doc's big stone fireplace smoked dully. Couple of fellows to the rear shot an able stick of pool. Song was proper on the juke, and my brand new Wigwams were soft as raccoon fur inside my boots.

Hotel Jerome Bar
330 East Main Street, Aspen

Jerome, founded in 1889 by entrepreneur J. V. Wheeler at the height of Aspen's silver boom, was not bad: its barroom compact and intimate, its prices less haughty than downtown's gamier saloons, its fixtures a Victorianophile's delight. Back bar was modestly cut, a light English-style module, probably mahogany, with matching front counter. "Jerome used to be Hunter's favorite bar," Sandy Thompson told me, and one could see why the sentimental Gonzologist might prefer it. Mentioned frequently in Thompson's writings, the room gave off an ethereally masculine feel, as if the ghosts of silver barons prated elbow-to-elbow along the bar. Quiet during most of the day, Jerome sprang to life around five, and again after supper. Best bet for Jerome was to rent one of her rich old rooms, small but elegantly appointed, and dip into the bar all afternoon.

Silver Dollar Bar
Harrison Avenue, Leadville

Leadville, once the second largest city in Colorado and a magnificent boom camp, was now little more than a skidish ghost with none of Aspen/Vail's chic, but with plenty of class. Over two miles high in the Rockies, enjoying a climate adumbrated by my Writers' *Guide* as, "ten months winter and two months mighty late in the fall," snow had been known to accumulate on July 4, grave diggers to employ dynamite in December. Once a metropolis of champagne brothels, nickle-beer saloons, eighteen-eighties mansions, and gilded opera houses, Leadville today was a cold row of faceless houses—those which had not been chopped down for kindling.

Silver Dollar remained a great saloon, however. Host to Oscar

Wilde . . . who'd drunk with miners while dressed in black velvet knee-breeches, black stockings, a Byron collar, and white handkerchief, proclaiming them "not at all rough." Dollar sported a majestic back bar (1879), with two tall Corinthian columns shouldering a carved entablature of some indefinite hardwood. Possibly walnut, for the grain was remarkable; it fluctuated from light to dark in a chiaroscuro so entrancing that the effect was . . . psychedelic. If Dollar's bar had not possessed a plaque testifying that the whole had been manufactured and designed by Brunswick of Chicago, one might have suspected a contemporary craftsman.

Brunswick had been a most influential bar fixture house of its day, and before shifting interest to bowling balls and pool tables, had been responsible for some of the loveliest front and back bar sets of the nineteenth century—indeed of the twentieth, having stayed in the bar business until several years after Repeal. A footnote to the company's eccentricity and wonderful dedication to craft appeared in a 1934 edition of *The Outfitter*, a trade magazine for bar furniture and fixtures:

> An interesting sidelight on the lumbering of the famous Circassian walnut used in the manufacture of Brunswick bars came to the notice of a Brunswick official on receipt of two unusual photographs from the Caucasus Mountains.
>
> These snapshots show two incidents in the lumbering of the Circassian walnut log in its native territory. The first shows the log as it was felled by native workmen and loaded onto a primitive two-wheeled cart to be dragged to the nearest port. The second shows the log at one of the many halts on the way down the mountain being blessed by a local priest.
>
> One reason for the unusual ceremonies surrounding the lumbering of the Circassian walnut may be found in the reverence which the natives have for the Circassian walnut tree. The tree anually produces a crop of nuts which can be sold for enough to support an entire family for months. Because of its great age, the tree has a definite historic value in the eyes of the natives, many of whom live a life as wild as that of the American Indian.
>
> Circassian walnut is most prized when it is found in sterile, rocky regions where the wind and the forces of nature have formed it into a knotty, irregular and gnarled tree. Then its rich beauty is most pronounced in the sworls and finely grained surface of the finished wood. Today this wood, expensive and difficult to obtain, is still used when especially specified in the manufacture of Brunswick bars.

The log shown in the pictures evidently had been located on the site of an ancient battlefield, for there were numerous scars on the surface and spear and arrowheads were buried in the wood.

The Caucasus Mountains! Where Prometheus lay chained and Jason sought the Golden Fleece—you were in trusted hands with Brunswick. Circassia to Leadville with only a brief stop in Chicago, to iron out the rough spots and add little touches like: Silver Dollar's exquisite diamond dust mirror, one of the finest in the West. It was perfectly clear. You could count the buttons on your sleeve in its reflection from forty feet. Only brighter one I had seen hung in Louis Dupuy's Hotel de Paris in Georgetown, Colorado. But that mirror was small and behind a museum mantelpiece, not a working bar.

The floors of Silver Dollar were old tile; they were kept clean. A fancy flocked wallpaper in gold and green *fleur de lis* set off other hardwood which framed the room. Comfortable booths. A large glass-enclosed side cabinet sat off to one side of the bar. There were the customary buffalo heads. Heavy wooden mining beams held up the ceiling. Indian artifacts were everywhere, but well-blended to the whole; there was nothing touristy about the room. Drinks were cheap. Coors beer on tap. Working men of all ages drank at Silver Dollar, content with quiet conversation. Everyone was respectful. There was order and pride.

Buffalo Bar
Miner Street, Idaho Springs

A carpenter Gothic back bar, with matching side cabinets and ice boxes of mahogany awaited the pilgrim at Buffalo. And goddam if there weren't two marlin hanging on a back wall, dogged if anyone would say why. Buffalo was a country-class, downhome Colorado saloon, jammed with real cowboys, uranium prospectors, tungsten miners, and tourists, all getting by famously on Buffalo's thirty-cent Coors. Colorado's first major gold strike happened just a few miles down the road, and folks were still tearing up the earth thereabouts, digging for gold, silver, lead, zinc, copper, iron, bismuth, manganese, molybdenum, you name it. Still a boomtown feel to Buffalo; fine country music cutting through cigar smoke, caterwaulers whining. Stuffed heads hung all around me: buffalo, elk, deer. Men in hard hats, but *clean*, jostled cowpokes good-naturedly. Brunswick was responsible for at least some of Buffalo's beautiful fixtures, nameless craftsmen in blighted industrial cities for others. At 7,556 feet, a man'd better watch what he drank. I ordered another Coors draft and studied my reflection in Buffalo's clear back mirror, humming contentedly to "There's Something in a Spray of Roses." Front and back bar were oak, barmaid told me, made in 1892 and installed at Buffalo in 1906 . . . In stark contrast to City Dump's dayglo accouterments next door, an apt name for Idaho Springs' freak dive, its pine paneling, pseudo-back bar and corny posters atrocious compared with Buffalo.

Crook's Palace
Central City

A handsome brick structure, Crook's Palace was the oldest saloon in Colorado (1859, year of the great strike), boasting a classic 1852 back bar, shipped overland from Boston and fashioned from the most temperate cherry—graced by two Corinthian columns under an embossed entablature. A mahogany front bar (from Denver), with polished brass rail, completed the set, as glorious a pair as could be found in a town that once had paved its sidewalks with silver for a presidential visit. Nothing upper crust about Crook's Palace, however, except her fixtures. Cowboys stood quietly before the statuesque set, sipping Coors at thirty-five cents a glass and ogling her big back mirror. Bartender negotiated with two cowpokes, in rumpled Stetsons and work boots, over the sale of an antique stove: potbelly, excellent condition. One hundred bucks was the figure settled on I believe, and the two cowpokes lugged it from their pickup into Crook's barroom. I watched bemusedly as money changed hands. A tippage of hats, both parties supremely satisfied. Cowpokes counted their cash and split, whisky grins galooted across their faces. I retired to Crook's homey restaurant at the rear of her barroom; see how these Central Cityans liked to eat.

Beaucoup Denver big-bucks summered in Central City, her billygoat streets reflecting tasteful tourism and the understated tonkism of inherited wealth at home in vacation land. Whole town was like a rich child's sandbox: tiny shops, businesses, restaurants, and saloons to be played with, all sanctioned by time and the odd attractive tourist. Even a freak saloon prevailed: Red Bandanna, midtown, not too heavy, just the proper level of mellow freak, nothing outrageous. Two older bars, Gold Coin and the Glory Hole, were worlds more touristy than Crook's Palace, but interesting enough to warrant attention—their antique bar sets solid and well cared for.

World famous Teller House Bar (1872) was today a tourist adjunct to Teller House museum, opening late and closing early, but still resplendent with lovely murals, "The Face on the Barroom Floor," and a modest front-and-back bar set. It was before Teller House that Ulysses S. Grant had alighted from his stagecoach onto a path of silver bricks, straight to the hotel door.

It was midnight by the time I reached Coors Brewery in Golden. Moon full. Sky clear. The road outside was not blocked. I drove straight to the walls of a squat megalithic structure which, for all wonders within, oddly resembled the Pentagon. Discomfitting tales of Joe Coors' John-Birchism had reached me, even in these hinterlands. His nomination to the board of Corporation for Public Broadcasting was in danger of a Senate override. Adolph Coors Company, founded in 1873 by an immigrant German who had fled Europe in 1867 to avoid conscription and seek his fortune in the American West, today was "as self-contained as it is possible to be," a Tax Court judge had ruled: "The company attempts to be vertically integrated throughout its manufacturing process. It obtains Rocky Mountain spring water from wells drilled by it. It purchases hops from Bavaria, rice from California, and barley from Colorado. The seed to grow the barley, a most important ingredient to its product, is supplied to certain farmers by the company." Coors manufactured its own cans, ran its own trucking firm, its own construction company, its own coal mine, its own staff of engineers and agronomists. Owned almost entirely by William and Joseph Coors, a capital loan had never been taken. The company sold no public stock, therefore it filed no report with SEC. A tycoon's individualism, in the grand style of gold-rush Colorado, had produced a beer as emblematic of the Wild West as the Rocky Mountains themselves.

Coors had refused to compromise quality of their brew with preservatives or pasteurization. Thus limited distribution, due to the cost of refrigeration. Coors beer was "brewed cold, aged cold, shipped cold, and sold cold," at considerable expense and vexation; "merely" to preserve flavor. Just eleven Western states sold the elixir, a purist's stance which had earned Coors a suit from FTC, charging "restraint of trade, price fixing, refusing to permit sales to retail chains, coercion, exclusive dealing, intimidation and apportionment of territory."

What a lot of bother. I cracked the tab on a sixteen-ouncer and toasted Coors' megalith, to accompaniment of industrial squirts and gurgles. I toasted the memory of Adolph Coors, who had coddled his talents in this barbaric territory and nurtured his vision until an entire republic was grateful. I toasted Joseph and William Coors for having held this sacred ground. I toasted myself for having reached it. Then I about-faced and toasted the grave of Buffalo Bill Cody, cemented to Lookout Mountain some four miles away. Buffalo Bill, that cataclysmic showman and dime-novel cowboy whose very essence had seeped, via sluices and slurbles of Rocky Mountain spring water, into the Coors I now pressed to my lips.

"—Larimer Street down, green lights glimmering, Denver surrounded by Honeywell warplants, IBM war calculators, selfish Air Bases, Botanical Mortal Brain Factories—"

observed Allen Ginsberg, in his 1972 introduction to Kerouac's *Visions of Cody.** Larimer Street proved more than down, she was submerged; her pool halls and cathouse saloons, her Windsor Hotel and Delmonico's but a memory beneath the collective incompetence of Skyline Urban Renewal Project. The ghost of Neal Cassady's father haunted swishy boutiques and "period" nightspots, such as Bratskellar, My Father's Mustache, Prairie Schooner and Chicago Speakeasy. Ice-cream shoppes like Sobriety Sarsaparilla cooled tongues of matronly browsers who traipsed aimlessly through red brick and tinted glass of yet another restoration boondoggle. Fine old bar sets had been bought up by boutiques and tea shoppes as "display" items. Romanesque back bars which had hosted the likes of Jelly Roll Morton and Babe Ruth—to say nothing of Ginsberg's crowd, who'd lived intermittently in Denver during the late forties/early fifties—today framed reflections of doughy debutantes modeling the latest fashion kick.

---

* (New York: McGraw-Hill), p. vii.

"A successful marriage of East and West . . . a cultural oasis," my *Trans World Getaway Guide* proclaimed, but Denver to me appeared more buffed-at-the-heels Northeast, obsessed with polish and snap, fighting desperately to outlive her raucous past. Downtown Denver was like Berlin after the armistice. Block after block of historic districts leveled, with nothing but vacant lots to show. Larimer Street held one block of Skyline Renewal—the rest was rubble.

Rio Grande Saloon
Corner of Third and Kalamath, Denver

Rio Grande was situated in a forbidding across-the-tracks neighborhood which emitted an odd amalgam of truck drivers, brakemen, construction workers and freaks at lunch hour, all jammed together before a long mahogany bar and lunch counter. Beer was thirty-five cents a glass and Rio Grande's luncheon menu was modest—workingman's fare. A cheerful waitress served me at the counter, and we got talking about Denver.

"This is it," she said, gesturing toward the barroom. "What's left of Denver's hip crowd hangs out here. Come back this evening, you'll see what I mean."

Back I came, and the worrisome drive, via railroad track and underpass, paid off. For Rio Grande housed the heartiest collection of goodtime folks I had run across since Seattle, all dancing madly to a tight rock band and downing every sort of cocktail from the mixologist's bag of one Johnny Guitar—Hawaiian sportshirted owner and Denver bon vivant. Johnny Guitar's drinks sold for less than a dollar and he charged no cover for his band. Husky roustabouts hunkered with bright-eyed gypsy girls in silk bandannas, shouting "Say, we got to talk!" Motorcyclists in oily leathers guffawed amongst lanky cowpokes in handblocked Stetsons and scimitar-heeled boots. Vibrations were contemptuous of stability, coaxing the most reticent patron to the dance floor. It was Denver in the fifties, it was gold-rush Rocky Mountain fever time, without rhyme or season. That sort of joyous insanity, in a comfortable old bar, warehouse district, where the price was right.

Ollie's Roundup
Corner of Morrison and Sheridan Streets, Denver

Ollie's was a fine Country & Western bar in the hurdy-gurdy tradition, where everyone comported with cotillionlike formality, no one feared for impropriety, and the pretty girls would dance with anyone "so long as he asked polite." A dance did not mean a drink, a drink did not mean a fuck—these were separate things which had little to do with fun at Ollie's. Immaculate cowboys—long symbolic, under stylized dress and outmoded manners, of a vanishing West— danced enthusiastically with preferred partners, then escorted them chivalrously to their seats. Insanity vacillated from polka to hug-dance, both equally passionate, but always culminating in a reserved good-bye.

Fear factor was nonexistent at Ollie's, so long as you played by the rules. People could still have fun at such emporiums because there were rules of conduct: not laws, but conventions which were respected. People knew how to behave. It was no disgrace to leave a girl at her table; she was available to dance with as many different partners as possible. There was room for magic though, within these restrictions. Magic via the code.

A rockabilly band catapulted hits toward Ollie's revelers, filling the large ballroom with an earcuffing sound. A fat girl in knee-high white boots thumped a pink Fender bass and skworled "*Hey-ay good lookin, whartcha got cookin . . .*" until the whole establishment was on the floor, your correspondent included, hucklebucking with an industrial blonde whose two-foot wig kept cocking over both eyes. Beer was seventy-five cents a bottle, drinks about a dollar. Same crowd of folks had danced in Market Street bagnios a hundred years earlier, with precisely the same quota of glee.

NEW MEXICO

El Patio Bar
Bank Alley (the Plaza), Taos

Labor Day in Taos Plaza. An Anglo couple sat drinking margaritas, quite intoxicated. Having driven from Denver, same treacherous stretch as I, they were headed farther south. Bartender at El Patio was concerned. A middle-aged Spanish with thick black hair and expensive sports clothes, he felt an obligation.

I was drinking Coors at fifty cents a bottle, my first and only of the afternoon; bartender's margaritas looked awfully good. He mixed a fresh batch and set them before the couple. At one dollar and a quarter his margaritas were a bargain.

A large green parrot behind the bar croaked something in Spanish, scratching at his cage. Hand-fashioned of tin, it hung from rough vigas under an adobe roof. El Patio was some other world. The bar, toward the rear of the restaurant, was comfortably secluded. Entire building was adobe, probably centuries old. Taos was a seventeenth-century town, situated between the Sangre de Cristo Mountains and the Rio Grande. Indians dressed in blankets stood about the plaza. Rednecks in pickups splattered hapless poets from the Wurlitzer Foundation. Chicanos hunted Spanish with high-powered deer rifles, Indians stalked hippies, and the Spanish hated everyone. An Anglo took his life in his hands every time he ventured outdoors. So I'd heard. None of this mattered much at El Patio.

Hand-painted figures decorated the walls, as did impressive photos of mournful Indians. Furniture was Southwest colonial, fashioned from wood. I drank another Coors and settled back on my stool. Bartender was still talking. There was a distance to El Patio which proved hypnotic. The drunken couple got up to settle and the woman slipped on El Patio's tile, falling flat on her ass. "You ought to take it easy!" bartender said, hurrying around the bar. "You got to slow down!" Green parrot spat out a sunflower seed and cursed again in Spanish.

Los Compadres
Route 3 (West), Taos

Reputedly a heavy fear-factor spot. I minded my manners and drank unscathed. Only Anglo in the place, but that's okay, the Chicanos were friendly, band was Chicano/Western and lively, and everybody enjoyed himself tremendously. Beer sold for seventy-five cents, no cover charge for the hurdy-gurdy, and the dance floor was jammed. Talked to another farmer, this fellow Mexican. He complained of the weather, but said he could harvest enough to make it through the winter. We drank together for an hour, watching senoritas twirl and caballeros clomp. Heard no English spoken at Los Compadres, excepting that between my friend and me. Fixtures were Western plastic, à la Ollie's in Denver, but not unattractive. A hot band played each night to a full house, I was told. Number one spot recreation-wise in Taos, but watch yourself.

TEXAS

Menger Hotel Bar
Alamo Plaza, San Antonio

Directly across Crockett Street from the Alamo, Menger Bar was itself a fortress against the night. Teddy Roosevelt had recruited his Rough Riders there. O. Henry was said to have imagined many of his stories before its staid mahogany bar, and to have penned a number at its tables. Founded in 1859, Menger Hotel had been the first large hostelry south or west of the Colorado River. Many legendary figures had cooled their throats at Menger Bar: including the unlikely mélange of Robert E. Lee, Ulysses S. Grant, Oscar Wilde, Benjamin Harrison, Sarah Bernhardt, Sidney Lanier, William Howard Taft, William Jennings Bryan, and "Bet A Million" Gates, the barbed wire baron. Atmosphere of the bar was again religious. The room itself was so perfectly laid out that the whole could have been wrenched from its moorings and deposited without apology as a period piece in Winterthur Museum. It was probably the most perfect barroom in the United States. Everything matched, was original and had been designed to match. Mahogany tables, mahogany front and back bar set, mahogany cabinets, parquet ceiling, balcony, mahogany wainscoting and filigree, all executed in an 1850's Southwestern style which held the feel of a captain's quarters in some sturdy galleon.

Beer was cheap, about sixty cents a bottle. Bar remained open until ten, a fine time to enjoy the Alamo, an historic site of deep natural beauty, unmarred by peccadilloes of after hours tourism. Menger Bar was quiet, reserved. I stood amid the ghosts of Jim Bowie, Davy Crockett, and Bill Travis, contemplating the old Republic of Texas and humming Bob Wills's "San Antonio Rose." Outside, the hot breath of Santa Anna rustled through the palm fronds. Alamo Mission rested her battered haunches in pools of adoring artificial light.

At Barrel House, Eleventh Street, *Brownsville*, I dried my shirt beneath a fifty-degree Airtemp and inhaled icy draft alongside shrimpers, grapefruit pickers and oily derrick workers—as Houston's Astros got the piss stomped out of them on an overhead Zenith.

Brownsville's liveliest bars stood along Eleventh Street, a grab bag of Tex Mex cantinas, most of which served food. Good fat cheeseburgers at Barrel House, a dish I selected in deference to diarrhea I'd contracted in Laredo, a dose of sphincter-dilating bubbleshits which had me jambraking beside every thistle bush between Zapata and Sullivan City. At five p.m. it was still one hundred plus outside; the drive down Highway 281 south of San Antonio had been truly preposterous. Hundred percent humidity, well over one hundred degrees, and nary a breeze stirring. The "watertight" interior of my Volks had parboiled my lower torso, a Brooks County sun had fried my face and left arm like sausage on the griddle.

Brownsville was absolutely the last stop. Stuck to the southernmost tip of Texas's panhandle (an end of the road territory graced with nineteenth-century Spanish houses and verdant streets, oddly reminiscent of Key West), Brownsville, as gold rush stopover and Confederate outpost, was the culmination of an idea. Last gasp for Texas, a region more "Midwestern" than the Midwest, less frontier than Iowa, and megatons more technocursed. Tendrils of Houston Space Center streamed across the entire state, obfuscating tradition and cannonading old bars. If there were five original saloons left in all of Texas, I'd not been able to locate them. Even Texas's alcoholic beverage laws were perverse. In many counties you couldn't buy a drink. Private clubs were the exception. Well, fuck that. Barrel House's Bud was the coldest I'd had, her beer mugs crystalline with a quarter inch of ice around the rim, and sensibly priced. Thirty-five cents a glass. Barrel House was far from an old saloon, but suggested one: long bar, comfortable stools, tables to the rear, patrons jostled together in a preferred crush.

My cheeseburger arrived, a full half-pound of fresh Texas beef piled high with onions and pickle. I doused the bugger down with hot sauce and doubled up on salt. Three twelve-ounce mugs in fifteen minutes and I hadn't touched bottom. Would take me all evening to pay back squandered fluids, a debt I intended to honor. Followed by ten hours death-sleep across some Padre Island sand dune, hopefully light on mosquitoes.

Texas had been some disappointment. Memories I garnered were less of Texas saloon life than of its juxtaposition to technology land. . . . Like Sam and Pete's Saloon, Main Street, Dallas, and its situation two blocks from Assassination Alley's "JFK Plaza," an obscene tourist shill disguised as memorial—Sam and Pete's dissolute winos and what-the-fuck beerheads drinking alongside occasional *turista*, poleaxed with Dallas dyspepsia . . . That two-hundred-pound soda waitress at a Dairy Queen in Abilene who'd laughed: "Saloons? Like cowboys and Injuns? Wild West? *Hawr, hawr, hawr,* you shittin me, *hawr,* come tell" . . . A stubble-chinned puncher (blind, crippled with drink) begging outside a Fort Worth department store—brain so fogged and ear so deaf he could no longer tune his guitar, and one harmonica sufficed for each key . . . That ninety-year-old Mexican hunkered before a clapboard saloon above the Rio Grande, so motionless, awake yet so still that flies crawled over his eyes and the click of my camera was but a minor annoyance. . . .

I paid my tab at Barrel House and cha-cha-ed into the gloaming. Thank God I was a fan of Larry McMurtry's; had seen *The Last Picture Show,* so that expectations were tempered, sensitivities honed. The tiny crossroads of Archer City, McMurtry's hometown and location for *Last Picture,* sat in a dry county—but held sufficient interest for me to have undertaken a side trip.

This is it, folks

crayonned graffiti had read, before Archer City's boarded-up Royal Theater:

The Last Picture Show.

Beautiful Cybill
was here.

Sam's Poolhall was in truth "Anarene Club," a domino parlor for old men and loafers, crowded the afternoon of my visit with gents "who a'tually been in the show." Oldtimer in charge at Anarene, a Sam the Lion with pared claws, had raised himself arthritically from his ratty sofa to retrieve Cokes from an antique cooler. Clippings about *Last Picture* hung on a far wall. "Come to see Billy's broom?" oldtimer had said, "one he swept with in the show? Here it is. Wore her right down. We keep it t'amuse folks. Be surprised how many's comin through now. Wantin to see the town. Theater's shut, guess you saw. So's Spur Hotel. Drug Store up Main is doin fine, sold five hundred of Larry's book, one they took the show from. Town's picked up some. See where he throwed that cue ball, spot right here agin the plaster . . ."

We'd sipped another soda, moving onto Anarene's front stoop to leave the domino players in peace. An odd pickup or two cruised wide macadam streets, a milk truck, a stray semi; other than that Archer City appeared deserted. I'd not have been surprised to see a tumbleweed scurry down the center line. Oldtimer spoke quietly, of local politics, football, LBJ ("Ain't Lyndon a pisser—you seen that mane of silver hair?"), about crops and what a man used to find in Matamoros. Conversation turned repeatedly to "the show." Oldtimer couldn't get it out of his head. Finally I confessed about *Saloon*.

"You a writer!" oldtimer'd wheezed, slapping my knee. "I be damn! Maybe they make a hit show outa your'n!"

Then his face grew dark.

"Hell though," he'd said. "Archer City ain't even got a beer joint . . ." The old man looked puzzled.

"Where is we to fit?"

EAST

MASSACHUSETTS
Boston

Greater Boston YMCA is America's oldest, a Brahmin of a health mission ten minutes out Huntington Avenue from Copley Square, its colonnaded lobby and generous space testament to an era when "Youth Movement" in America bespoke more than just tennis shoes and damp jocks. No one seems to know Greater Y's precise age, but its senescence is commented upon regularly . . . by bladder-nosed busboys clearing your table at supper, by night watchmen and students from Northeastern University, by squash buffs elevating to Executive Health Club, by invalids wheeling to the infra-red bake, by clerks and steam bath pursers . . . even by that yellowed news clipping on Greater's bulletin board, praising the selfless attendant who had plucked a terminal inmate from a fire escape dive which would have insured him eternal fricassee, plus the sizable contempt of Greater's prideful clean-up squad.

Exhausted from my Western hegira, I splurged on a cubicle with private bath, air conditioning and nineteen-inch TV. Twelve-fifty the night. At a liquor store opposite America's oldest Y, a black gentleman pawed a gallon of domestic burgundy, asked its price from the clerk ensconced in a steel cage, balked and let his selection crash to the floor. "Three dollar too much," he said by way of apology, and vacated the premises. I purchased a tallboy of Foster's, plus 600 micrograms of methaqualone from a sidewalk vendor, and retired to my room. In plenty of time for Tom Snyder. Not only did my television fail to work, but none of the room's electrical appliances pulled juice. Twelve-fifty down the hopper. Took my medicine, grabbed a flashlight and reclined with two pounds of Foster's and Lucius Beebe's *Boston and the Boston Legend*. Once again, we'd just have to see.

Locke-Ober Café

3-4 Winter Place, Boston

A most antiquated hangover from Boston's Puritan heritage was that licensing resolve which required the whole interior of a saloon to be visible from the sidewalk. This ordinance was devised to discourage citizens from rallying about standup bars, assuming their embarrassment at consorting shamelessly in public view. Happily this is not now, nor has ever been the case, and the shoddy, wimpsnickle edict resulted in wide expanses of plate glass which advertised particulars of a saloon's interior more effectively than a thousand pasteboard circulars.

Locke-Ober's (founded 1875) dates from this period, as her plate glass attests; and any anxious pedestrian hurrying through Winter Place Mews is certain to be tempted by a full panorama of delights within. Locke-Ober's L-shaped bar runs length and breadth of the barroom, with eight silver free-lunch dishes, suspended from the ceiling by counterweights, gracing it dead center. Locke-Ober's mahogany is manned by white-coated barkeeps, held *in extremis* by a cadre of tosspots crowded to its front. Tables are covered with white damask and overseen by waiters in black jackets, white tie, and floor-length white aprons. The barroom, framed from outside, is a masterpiece of Victorian panache. To delineate its fixtures is to recite a Boston litany, relating a skeletal history of the celebrated café en route.

Locke-Ober's men's bar today exists largely unchanged from Louis Ober's redecorating of 1886. Ober's "Restaurant Parisien," as the establishment was known, had done extraordinarily well in its first ten years; King's *Dictionary of Boston*, published 1883, listed it as "the leading French restaurant of the city," and Ober counted among his patrons many prominent citizens, including Eben Jordan, cofounder of Jordan Marsh Company. Reportedly Jordan lent Ober the funds to get started; though Ober soon repaid his debt, a table was reserved in perpetuity for executives of Jordan Marsh, a custom still honored today.

Ober commandeered his mahogany from Santo Domingo, his mirrors, statuary, and wood carvers from France. His silver steam dishes, spoons, and pulleys were designed in Germany and fashioned by Reed and Barton, silversmiths. His ornate cash register

Ober acquired from Kruse Check and Adding Machine Company of New York. His ceiling was frescoed by some forgotten craftsman. His bronze statue, "Gloria Victis," which had been ordered from France, was placed near the center of the barroom. For his north wall, Ober commissioned an obligatory nude from Tommaso Juglaris, painter; born in Turin but late of Boston. Ober paid eighty dollars for the work, a steal, generations of admirers would agree. "Mademoiselle Yvonne," as the damsel is known, stands undraped in a lush arbor, one elbow resting upon a pedestal, the other raised in benediction, her fingers wrapped about a crystal goblet. Lawrence Dame, art critic for the *Boston Herald*, was moved to compose an ode to Mademoiselle Yvonne—reprinted on postcards currently available from the management. An open dumbwaiter, carrying drinks to upstairs dining rooms, ascended on polished brass poles; a gleaming Tom and Jerry machine was installed. Art nouveau electroliers of exposed bulbs were hung from the ceiling, and Ober's French cabinet makers were loosed upon a forest of Santo Domingan mahogany to carve their way into history.

Fixtures were kept light for the time, with an eye to continental styling. Back bars were set with Ober's mammoth French mirrors and framed discreetly with spiral gadrooning. A Renaissance decor prevailed in the men's bar, with turns of Jacobean filigree. To the left of Ober's free-lunch dishes stood his oyster bar, fronted by wrought-iron stools bolted to the mahogany. These curlicued perches still serve the luncheon crowd, single gentlemen in particular, and extend the length of the long bar.

Not until 1891 did Louis Ober attract real competetion to Winter Place, his fixtures and artifacts king-of-the-row prior to Frank Locke's appearance. Locke's Wine Rooms, adjacent at 1 and 2 Winter Place, outshone Ober's quarters with a display of Gay Nineties frippery which bordered upon the ridiculous. A description of Locke's rooms may be found in that small printed history attainable on request from any Locke-Ober's waiter. Locke's "general appearance," it quotes, was "of an enchanting picture, a fairy grotto, a sumptuous apartment in some palatial edifice." Frank Locke was a retired sea captain who came to this magnificence late: "Hangings of costly plush . . . arched ceilings covered with embossed and quilted satins . . . a broad waterfall upon one side . . . the bar rail a heavy tube of cut and embossed glass clear as crystal, the hollow of which from end to end is filled with artificial roses . . ." were but a few of his contributions. Despite Wine Rooms's decor, Locke offered plain

Maine cooking in contrast to Ober's Parisian fare, washed down by
stern liquors. His Wine Rooms survived until Prohibition, and
thereafter were abandoned. His challenge to Louis Ober endured a
scant three years. During that stint, patrons discovered that although
Ober's food was admittedly superior, Locke's whisky slings packed
the desired punch; thus a constant flow of traffic was maintained between the two establishments. In May of 1894, wholesalers Wood
and Pollard purchased both businesses, finishing the competition.
On the thirty-first of that month, a ceremony was held to collapse
partitions separating the two cafés. Key to the front door was tossed
into Boston Harbor, and the new venture was christened Winter
Place Tavern. Emil Camus became manager and remained so for two
years. In 1898, John Merrow, of Revere House in Bowdoin Square,
purchased the concern, running it to bankruptcy by 1901. Emil
Camus, representing Locke-Ober Company, subsequently acquired
the café, auspicating a reign which lasted thirty-eight years and fixed
the present day character of Locke-Ober's.

"It was his object," Sherman Whipple has written, "to create in
Winter Place, not as Louis Ober proposed, a typical French Restaurant in old Boston, but rather an American restaurant in which
might be found choice dishes from the culinary tradition of all those
civilizations." Camus composed a menu which rallied staples of
Frank Locke's New England cooking against the bedrock of Louis
Ober's Gallic recipes, upon which the latter's reputation had been
founded. Ober's rare wines were offered in conjunction with Locke's
fine whiskys, and a beachhead thereby was established.

Today, Locke-Ober's wine list variegates from ninety-dollar bottles of Châteaux Margaux to seventy-five-cent steins of Old Milwaukee. Her menu lists filet mignon Mirabeau, wiener schnitzel à la
Holstein, and sweetbreads Eugènie, in conjunction with New England boiled dinner, oysters Rockefeller, and lobster Savannah. A
patron may pay as little as two-ninety-five per entree at lunch, as
much as twenty dollars per entree at dinner. Service is polite and in
the grand manner no matter what one orders. Two upstairs floors
are reserved for dining: Ladies' and Gentlemen's Café, one flight up;
smaller rooms on the third flight, available for private parties. But
Locke-Ober's men's bar, no longer restricted to gentlemen, is Boston's loveliest brasserie. A sanctum sanctorum where the pilgrim
may meditate amongst trappings which have enthralled Theodore
Roosevelt, Enrico Caruso, Henry Cabot Lodge . . . indeed, every
notable to have passed by the river Charles since 1875.

Locke-Ober's men's bar still functions as a saloon, patrons lining the 1886 bar any evening of the week. It was here that mixology's Ward Eight was invented—a whisky sour with grenadine—of which Lucius Beebe wrote: "Compared with it, a bolt of lightning is a very mild form of stimulant." First poured in 1898, during John Merrow's occupancy, the Ward Eight was dedicated to Representative Martin Lomasney (a strict Prohibitionist) by several of his cronies, the eve before his election. Bartender Tom Hussion claimed responsibility for the concoction, offered as a toast to Lomasney's home ward and imminent success at the polls. Though Locke-Ober's exists in a rival ward, Ward Eight's name stuck, becoming a staple in barrooms around the world.

Locke-Ober's bar is as well stocked and efficiently run as any in America. Bartenders, though formal of mien, are friendly. Their bar may be crowded with regulars but they will take time to welcome a stranger, patiently pointing out original fixtures with a pride that is authentic. Locke-Ober's cocktail list is long and varied. Ingredients are fresh mixed with Locke-Ober's house whiskys or the brand of one's choice. Rarities such as Martell Cordon Bleu or Gaston Briand Grande Fine, at four twenty-five a glass, are available; as are the likes of Laird's Apple Jack or John Jameson Irish. On tap are Würzburger dark or light, Michelob, Bass, Heineken, or Old Milwaukee—ranging from twelve to six bits a stein. Bottle brew runs the same price gamut, from Ballantine Ale to St. Pauli Girl (German), with seven brands in between. An ancient scrivener, perched on a high stool next to the bar, mans Locke-Ober's cash register. He is a sleepy counterpoint to the frenzied bustle around him.

Gentlemen without jackets are not welcome at Locke-Ober's, but a selection of handsomely tailored sportcoats, hanging about the old barroom on Victorian coatracks, is maintained for the underdressed. A glass and mahogany door marked toilet, at the north wall, leads not to the ladies' lavabo but to a gentlemen's convenience of the last century. Rumor has it that certain of Locke-Ober's upstairs rooms served as *salles d'amour* during Prohibition, as their wallpaper suggests the boudoir. But this indiscretion seems unlikely, as Emil Camus obeyed the law so devoutly during our Great Incapacity (refusing to compromise his wine list with alcoholic beverages of the quality available during those years), that Locke-Ober's nearly folded. The café survived however; as did its men's bar, which remains a monument to those who founded her, a catacomb of reverential tolerance in a season of drink-up and shove.

Union Oyster House Bar

41 Union Street, Boston

Oldest saloon in Boston, and reputedly oldest oyster bar in America, Union has been fueling cradle of liberty topers since 1826, when founders Atwood and Bacon installed their semicircular mahogany bar, narrow private booths and open coal range. At age 150, Union's bar is predated only by one known to me, Old Absinthe of New Orleans, Louisiana. Union's mahogany has held up under generations of salt water and brine, its finish having been restored many times. Yet it wears the patina of age gracefully, as if flaunting its days in service to such luminaries as Daniel Webster, "a constant customer who drank a tall tumbler of brandy and water with each half-dozen oysters and seldom had less than six plates." Today, despite tourist shenanigans underfoot in every corner, Union's oyster bar preserves the ambience of a more merciful era. Boston bankers and merchants of the quarter still partake in company of working-men and sailors, each working his quahaugs or littlenecks with unrestrained glee. Draft beer flows *ad libitum*, and Tommy, chief oyster shucker and barman, with fifty-three years service underbelt, is kept hopping until nine every evening. But that's what he's used to, and from all outward appearances, that's what he likes.

The building in which Union finds itself is so intertwined with Boston's early history that no authenticated date for its construction has been found (Union Street was laid out in 1636). Management does know that previous to 1826 it housed one Thomas Capen, importer of silks and fancy dress goods, who christened his business At the Sign of the Cornfields. In 1742, Thomas Stoddard acquired the property, subsequently passed back to Hopestill Capen (who had married Stoddard's daughter), thence to a younger Thomas Capen, Cornfields' draper. Followed by Benjamin Thompson in 1769, afterward Count Rumford, apprentice to the elder Capen. From this time, and until the hostilities of 1776, Isaiah Thomas published *The Massachusetts Spy* upstairs, with its incendiary motto: "Open to All Parties but Influenced by None." Ebenezer Hancock, paymaster of the Continental Army, used Capen House as headquarters during the Revolution, and Union's management sees no cause to discount the probability that George Washington was a frequent visitor. Louis Philippe, afterward King of France, lived in exile upstairs at Capen, where he taught French to fashionable ladies, and turned a creditable *pas de deux*.

In more recent years, the Kennedy clan has patronized Union regularly, John Fitzgerald Kennedy in particular, who loved to feast in privacy at a rear booth upstairs—still held in reserve for Senator Edward Kennedy and his family. Honey Fitz, it is said, was a loyal patron at the downstairs oyster bar, as were his progeny pre-Camelot. Not that any regular could care today, for Kennedys are absorbed into Union's past as readily as lesser folk. One is content to watch Tommy shuck oyster after oyster at the old bar; ecstatic to keep him shoving half-dozens across the weeping mahogany.

Beer on tap at Union's oyster bar sells: one dollar for imported, ninety cents for Michelob, seventy cents for Falstaff, Rheingold or Bass. Cherrystone clams sell: one dollar eighty-five the half dozen; littlenecks: one eighty; cotuits and quahaugs: approximately the same. Every sort of seafood is available at Union (insist on dining in original booths to the rear of the bar), including Boston scrod, Massachusetts lobster, steamed Ipswich clams, and the legendary oyster stews. Lobsters are kept alive in an open tank to the right of Union's's mahogany, and a common occurrence is the sight of venerable Tommy fishing for a fresh one, then zinging him onto a dumbwaiter for the clackety ride upstairs. Lobsters occasionally scramble from their elevated perch, startling patrons at the bar with an abrupt descent.

Framed clippings hang at the foot of Union's stairs, clippings which detail Union's history in photograph and vignette. One such tells of a Mr. Foster, who in 1887 is said to have premiered his invention of the toothpick at Union, having hired several groups of natty Harvard students to feast well, then produced the tacky picks from vest pocket or wraprascal with great to-do. The subsequent display of bad manners is said to have rocked proper Boston to its molars, but not without the desired result: Mr. Foster's toothpicks became all the rage.

Joseph Milano and family acquired Union some five years ago, much to upstairs' tourist success, but sadly, to the oyster bar's detriment. The bar itself, with rickety stools and ancient fixtures, rests unchanged; but four feet to the rear is a tasteless exhibit of souvenir curios worthy of a carnival midway—inluding Bicentennial T-shirts, fake pewter, patriotic prints, statuettes, and salt water taffy. Lucius Beebe, whose history of the renowned ordinary is quoted herein (and on Union's menu), would have soiled his underlinen at the sight of it. At least one other branch of Union has been opened in Boston, plasticized and grim as a Howard Johnson's, but serving the same hearty food. Although Union's prices are high in comparison to her New Orleans counterparts, she remains a must on any Freedom Trail tour, and through her 1826 oyster bar, a firm step into Boston's post-Revolutionary past.

Pete's

82 Broad Street, Boston

You'll find neither Chateaux Margaux nor sweetbreads Eugénie at Pete's old saloon; if you find the place at all you'll accept frosty Black Label at thirty-five cents a stein, reinforced by agreeable cocktails at under one dollar, plus a panoply of Italian American dishes as heavy on the gut as they are light on the wallet. Pete's is situated in a featureless building with no name out front, no identifying number; the only way you'll locate it is to count from either corner or follow the stream of quickstepping businessmen en route after the five o'clock whistle. Pete's interior is as unpretentious as its exterior, a case of comfort-is-as-comfort-does shorn up by workaday fixtures and the colorless languor of a superior bar. Front counter is mahogany with a worn brass rail, stools are wooden and fixed, back bar is post-Pro fake, and the booths are scarred. Pete's bartender is professionally courteous, serving a jostle of randy executives crowded up to his bar, laughing and hooting their way into third martinis. Pete's martinis are famous around Boston and are said to be the most generous in New England. They are not advertised, however. Nor are any other drinks at the old saloon. Only lettering that strikes the eye is a handwritten legend across Pete's back wall:

CUSTOMER IS ALWAYS WRONG

Pius Sabia, or "Brandy Pete" as he was known to minions, authored that sentiment, one worthy of his attitude toward patrons the extent of this thirty-year reign. Pete's operated as a poolhall during the Depression, serving booze under-table until Repeal, when it officially opened as a saloon. Brandy Pete initiated a detente with his clientele at that time which remained until his death. Pete bridged no infraction of his code of manners, and won his nickname from a penalty often levied, "buying the boss a brandy." Severest of Pete's rules were:

1) Any customer who brings in a new patron *buys the boss a brandy*.

2) Any customer who complains about the food *buys the boss a brandy*.

3) Any customer who strays behind the bar *buys the boss, plus the entire house, a brandy*.

Pete collected many a brandy in his day, and his authority was seldom questioned. So infamous did his moniker become that postcards bearing just the sketch of a brandy glass were known to have reached his address.

Today, Pete's old saloon remains a spot where goodtime folks are likely to congregate (Pete's sons have inherited the business). Though Esh, Pete's regular barkeep, admits that a lot of the old fun has died down. Broad Street is in a wharfish neighborhood, dreary during daylight hours, deserted after dark. In the old days, Pete's roared until morning; now the bar closes at ten. Best time currently is lunch, when a crush of downtowners converges for Pete's hearty meals and niggardly prices. Plus the old Boston feel to Pete's, an odeur of departed draymen and polluted sailors, who were making Pete's a regular stop long before most of us had been born.

Jacob Wirth Company
33–37 Stuart Street, Boston

Stuart Street is the tail end of a transient neighborhood, pockmarked by bus stations, hillbilly bars, Union Oyster House's plasticized branch, and hookers on the make. Stuart Street is most often the first glimpse of Boston a poorer pilgrim may get, comparable in tone to Washington's New York Avenue or Manhattan's Port Authority district. Winding his way eastward, away from hustlers and honky-tonks, a pilgrim may be surprised to find himself before the grandiose clock and wide plate glass of Jacob Wirth Company. Jake Wirth's, as the old saloon is known, has not changed remarkably since it opened for business in 1868. Our pilgrim, upon braving Wirth's threshold, is resolutely catapulted back to the nineteenth century. If well traveled, he may be reminded of Chicago's Berghoff or Milwaukee's Terzan saloons. If uninitiated, he will certainly marvel at Wirth's museum piece fixtures, well worn and gratifying as any in America.

Wirth's mahogany bar set, imported from Germany, stands to the left as one enters. A row of mahogany tables, with matching hairpin chairs, faces it aisle-right. Wirth's back bar is fashioned after a sort of Bavarian Romanesque, with portrait medallion of founder Jacob Wirth gracing its entablature, an ornate clock below that, supported by the architraved legend:

SUUM CUIQUE

Latin for "To Each His Own." Wirth's back bar is appended with old-fashioned electric lamps and eight separate beer pumps. Front bar is unadorned; sandwiches are available there, as are twelve-ounce mugs of Jake Wirth's Special Dark which sell for forty-five cents apiece, and are referred to as "seidels." To the left of Wirth's Suum Cuique motto is the legend:

> He who drinks with grace
> Is ever welcome in this place.
> But he who drinks more than his share
> Is never welcome anywhere.
> —Lord Calvert

Septuagenarian bartenders and black-coated, white-aproned waiters scurry about the barroom, shouting orders. Our pilgrim, if he is smart, will collapse with baggage at a table not far from the bar, command a seidel plus a plate of wurst if he is hungry, and collect his bearings.

Jake's dark is brewed in 300-barrel lots by Dawson's Brewers, specially for the old saloon. Those who know compare it favorably to Bavaria's Münchner Hofbräu. Dawson's began brewing Wirth's Special Dark after Prohibition, when Jake's near beer, supplied by Haffenreffer in Jamaica Plain, was no longer called for. Prior to 1914, Jake Wirth's was sole Boston agent for Anheuser-Busch lagers, New York Hell Gate Lager, India Pale Ale, and products of the Narragansett Brewing Company. Today, only Wirth's Special Dark and Dawson's light survive on tap, reinforced by a sizable selection of cocktails and mixed drinks. The old saloon's wurst, braunschweiger, thüringer, salami, tongue, frankfurts, pig's knuckles, and Westphalian ham are supplied by Carl Weitz Butchers, a firm which has grubstaked Wirth's menu for many years. Sauerkraut is made on the premises every three weeks, in huge hogsheads numbered one to ten, and emptied consecutively. More than twenty tons of sauerkraut are prepared each year, all ladled down the throats of happy patrons. Wirth's cheese cakes, raisin cakes, shortcakes, and apple strudel are made by a small bakery in Jamaica Plain, and bread is specially baked for the saloon by Green and Freedman. Liederkranz, Camembert, Limburger, and Muenster cheeses are imported. A most satisfactory menu, formulated to accompany the potation of fine beers.

Jacob Wirth was born of wine growers, owning vineyards in Rhenish Prussia, from which he imported Rhine wine for wholesale and retail distribution, as well as for use in his saloon. Wirth operated across the street at Number 60 from 1868 until 1878, when he moved to the present location. A plate glass façade was added, fixtures were installed, and sawdust strewn about the floor. Wirth's remained unchanged until 1890, when the ground level of an adjoining house was annexed, doubling available space. Sportsmen such as John L. Sullivan were regulars at this time; ladies were allowed in the restaurant proper, but were not permitted to smoke. Jacob Wirth died in 1892, leaving the saloon in charge of his widow who ran it until her death in 1899. Jacob Wirth, junior, then a freshman at Harvard, took over the business in 1902. Jacob junior initiated the sale of spirits at Wirth's, hitherto *verboten*. With the exception of Prohibition—when Jake's old saloon prospered on the sale of an extraordinary near beer and traditional fare—nothing much has changed.

Waiters still pay checks at the brass cashier's cage and cigar counter, before hurrying to deliver a customer's order. Steam tables remain out in the open where waiters may collect orders, and where many dishes are prepared. Wirth's legendary staffers, Fritz Früh and Fritz Heuser, with 122 years service between them, are sadly gone; but others of comparable dignity are present to assist. Although Wirth's is a far cry from fancy, service is after the grand manner. Single patrons are not rushed if inclined to dally over an extra seidel. A pilgrim feels sufficiently comfortable to spread out maps and reconnoiter. Or, if he is leaving town, glut with Special Dark before toddling down to Trailways. A handsomely printed booklet of reminiscences, published in 1964 to commemorate Wirth's ninety-fifth anniversary, is available from the cashier. Sufficient history and remembrance to ameliorate a worrisome trip south. Brace of bratwurst to go, one last sip off the seidel, and Boston *auf Wiedersehen*.

NEW YORK
New York City

I premiered at King Cole Bar of the St. Regis Hotel in December 1943, as a zygote. It was the first bar my parents took me to. We sat in a leather booth before the Maxfield Parrish mural of Old King Cole and nursed morning-after cocktails. Eighteen hours earlier my father had stepped off an airplane at LaGuardia, where a Red Cross nurse had handed him a glass of milk. That was the first cold milk he'd drunk in over a year and it nearly took the top of his head off. He and several other officers shared a cab down Fifth Avenue, overwhelmed by the Christmas decorations, crowds of elegant civilians, bright lights, traffic, and buildings which were not bombed-out ghosts of themselves. My father stopped at St. Regis but his officer pals said wait a minute Doc and began fishing Berettas and service-issue .45s out of his duffel. There stood my father on Fifth Avenue before the St. Regis Hotel passing pistols into the back seat of a taxi cab. St. Regis's lobby was jammed. A desk clerk spotted my father's white cover, rumpled blues and deep tan, and said "Lieutenant, you looking for a room?" An elderly bellhop showed my father upstairs and sat on the can talking to him while he soaked in a hot bath. The old bellhop spoke jerkily in that special New York cadence, with the special accent, and that eased my father's nerves. Then he pressed my father's blues, which had been wadded at the foot of a duffel for thirteen months, and helped him find a white shirt and black tie. Downstairs, King Cole Bar was crowded with the best dressed people in New York. My father ordered a Scotch and water. Then another. He had not telephoned my mother. Bartender asked what's the trouble, Lieutenant, and my father confessed his predicament. He couldn't decide whether to call or show up or what. "How long you known you was comin back?" King Cole's bartender inquired. Three days, my father said. "You had three days," bartender said. "Don't you think she's entitled to thirty minutes?" My father headed for the phone.

That evening my parents ate Italian food at Grand Ticino, with my grandmother and grandfather, and had their picture taken at Ernie's. The picture shows my father in his freshly pressed blues, toasting the photographer. My mother, wearing an oversized fur with a camellia pinned to her lapel, clutches his arm. Later they went back to the St. Regis Hotel and said hello to me.

The St. Regis, then and now, was one of New York's special hotels. Completed in 1904, it was for its time the highest hotel in New York. Designed by Trowbridge and Livingston after the Beaux Arts style, it had been financed by Colonel John Jacob Astor, whose son Vincent enlarged it in 1928. King Cole Bar opened after Repeal and has remained New York's epitome of a post-Prohibition lounge. The room is dominated by Maxfield Parrish's portrait of Old King Cole and his Court, a mural commissioned for the Knickerbocker Hotel in 1906 and subsequently rescued by St. Regis upon Knickerbocker's demise. An expansive semicircular bar, suggesting King Cole's crown, is situated before the Parrish mural and fronts the barroom at its far wall. The bar is mahogany with a polished brass rail, but quite nineteen-thirties in style. It is standup and flanked by a row of leather banquettes. Heavy iron chandeliers, forged medievally, hang overhead. I have often wondered, in my peregrinations through America's gothic saloons, if prenatal exposure to the medievalisms of King Cole had not fixed my taste. Certainly such exposure must have influenced it. King Cole wields too heavy a scepter not to have infected my mother's womb with a whit of regal reserve.

"Hey Jack," a conventioneer spat at King Cole's bartender—wondrous specimen of pink skin and powdered hair—"bring Luther'n me two more them stingers and les see some *fruit* on top this time." The prospect of default had whisked much of the glitter from New York's mantle; King Cole, with other hotel bars, had suffered. During the day King Cole retained most of its pomp, but after seven when New York professionals had fled, the bar was relinquished to a handful of name-tagged double-knitters and the odd dowager supping with grandchildren. Shriners logged Oak Bar at the Plaza, a Latin band beat congas for tips before Hotel Pierre, and bums swan-dived into Pulitzer Fountain, wine jugs held aloft, in mock celebration of Scott and Zelda. Fifty-second Street was finished; Harlem desperate, the Village dead; midtown remained sordid, the upper East Side an abomination. In waterfront leather bars, pop-sadomasochists continued to rehearse unspeakable acts. Scattered throughout Manhattan existed a handful of respectable saloons. I tossed off my Hennessy and laid three dollars on the bar . . . two-eighty for a thimblesize shot of fourth-rate cognac. My conventioneer peers called for another round. I stared deep into Maxfield

Parrish's mural, aching to lose myself in its storybook tints and hues.
I noticed something—that mournful attendant at King Cole's left.
He appeared the image of me! of what I'd come to resemble in
these last frantic months. His expression was precise: moody, aloof,
desensitized. I'd faced him in a thousand back-bar mirrors in a thousand backwater saloons. He was me alright, anxious and morose
before a nursery rhyme king, paying the tab, then shuffling quietly
along.

Artists and Writers Restaurant
213 West 40th Street (Midtown), New York City

Fortified with a vintage copy of Lucius Beebe's *Snoot If You Must,* our
pilgrim proceeds east from Port Authority bus terminal to the
weathered sanctuary of Bleeck's, formally christened Artists and
Writers Restaurant, but affectionately known to generations by the
surname of its founder, Jack Bleeck. Light inside is dim, but our
pilgrim descries a safe spot to stow his gear and steps boldly forward
to Bleeck's scarred mahogany. What'll it be, a dignified barkeep
queries. Draft beer . . . seventy cents across the counter and the potion is his. Quickly quaffed; another. Our pilgrim's eyes accommodate to the gloom: Bleeck's bar is long, perhaps forty feet, and extends the length of a front barroom. Tables line Bleeck's rear wall,
numerous prints and photographs overhead. A second room is visible toward Bleeck's rear, a third beyond that. Bleeck's barroom is
empty but for two couples seated at side tables, plus an expensively
attired garment executive standing at the near corner of the bar.
"You don't know how it is to be stuck with ninety percenters," he
complains. "You don't know how they can hurt you come tax time."
   Lapping the littoral of New York's garment district, several blocks
from Macy's, Gimbels, Times Square, the theater district, Madison
Square Garden, Pennsylvania Station, and Port Authority, Bleeck's
has long attracted outspoken clientele. Before *Herald Tribune*'s demise, Bleeck's functioned as the official saloon of that newspaper,
counting among its patrons *Trib*'s publisher, editor, columnists and
copyboys, and including in its fixtures a hot line extension to the
city-desk telephone. Lucius Beebe has suggested that, excepting
composition and printing, business of the *Herald Tribune* was con-

ducted *in toto* before Bleeck's mahogany. Other New York journals sought representation over the years—in the persons of *Times*'s Skipper Williams, *World*'s George Buchanan Fife, *New Yorker*'s Joseph Mitchell, Harold Ross, and Wolcott Gibbs, *Daily News*' Red Dolan, and an army of lesser functionaries. Each was heartily embraced. Thurber's cartoons festoon the wainscoting at Bleeck's, as does a moth-eaten tarpon caught and donated by J. Pierpont Morgan. A cement-filled suit of armor guards Bleeck's middle room, before a huge fireplace and life-size portrait of Babe Ruth—another loyal customer. Broadway notables such as Noel Coward, Tallulah Bankhead, Mayor Jimmy Walker, Helen Hayes, Charlie MacArthur, Jimmy Cagney, Frank Sullivan, John Garland, and Owen Davis, Jr., made Bleeck's their regular after-theater stop. All these luminaries in company of standard Bleeck's loonies such as Crazy Bob Clifford, a Newport undertaker known to regulars as "the Merry Mortician," who always carried a pocket rule and whose custom it was to surreptitiously measure patrons at Bleeck's bar, then suggest a proper casket . . . shouting "Death, it's hilarious!" before weaving away. And Harry McCormack, barkeep at Bleeck's for many years, who imagined a complete poultry farm and apiary to exist behind his bar, and, in Beebe's recollection, "was forever scattering cracked corn to his flock among the duck boards back of the ice bins."

All of which seems decidedly archaic today. Newsfolk still hold Bleeck's in special esteem, but light years have passed since Stanley Walker moaned: "Cirrhosis of the liver, the occupational disease of the reporter!" When Bleeck's opened its doors in 1925, as one of 32,000 speakeasies in the city of New York, newsfolk and everyone else were drinking with an abandon before which our drug-addled seventies pale by comparison. Frontage of Bleeck's was camouflaged as a fruit stand during the twenties, but everybody knew a speakeasy was hard by. Bleeck's bar was hidden in the back room but any gentleman with entrée and a reasonable sense of hearing could find his way.

Our pilgrim carries his drink rearward, perusing memorabilia . . . and stumbles upon two members of Bleeck's staff napping in the far dining alcove. Stretched full length along the back pews, aproned, soup spackled, with arms crossed like a pair of Crazy Bob's stiffs. Our pilgrim starts, afraid he may incite some terrible fit of busman's wrath. He pauses. The pair rest like mummies entombed in Bleeck's back dining room, surrounded by artifacts of the great saloon's past, coddled by spirits, perhaps even snuggled up to by a literary ghost or so—deflated by spent exuberance and the perfidy of some long forgotten toot.

Billy's

948 First Avenue (near 52nd Street), New York City

What strikes one first about Billy's is its tidiness. Like a little old man with his boots polished. Billy's mahogany front and back bar set is buffed to a glow, as are his eighteen-eighties side cabinets and ice chests. Back bar mirror is bright, tile floor is scrubbed, and Billy's wide front window provides a spectacularly fresh view of First Avenue and the florist next door at Fifty-second. Billy's brass, copper, and bone-handled ale pumps shimmer like an old gent's cuff links. As do his copper pails and pitchers. Billy's red-checked tablecloths, which dot the tiny barroom at irregular intervals, are splotches of color in an old man's cravat. Billy's is where you go when what you're after is the very best—Manhattan's parry to Miles City's Montana Club, or Anaconda's Tammany Lounge: the classiest gerontic in town.

Billy Condron, Jr., an irascible Irish gentleman in his sixties, still owns the old saloon and oversees its operation in much the same fashion as his father and grandfather before him. Billy's did not become "Billy's" until after Prohibition, when every New York drinking establishment was required by law to assume some appellation which might be registered on the books. Previous to 1933 Billy's possessed no legal name, the case with most corner saloons, but was known informally as "Mickey's Place" after the moniker of its founder, Michael Condron. Since Billy Condron, Sr. had inherited the old saloon from his father in 1922, and had been its proprietor for nearly twelve years, the signboard eventually stuck out front read BILLY'S.

This was Billy's second location, the great one, which saw three generations of Condrons come into the business, and which survived from 1880 until 1966 when it was demolished and Billy Jr. moved down First Avenue to the present address. Michael and Bridget Condron had opened their first saloon in 1870, between 55th and 56th Streets on First Avenue; the original saloon was near the middle of the block, and catered to Irish and German workingmen. "Was nothing but breweries and Burns Brothers Coal Yard then," Billy Jr.

recalls. "No fancy apartment buildings in the neighborhood, no fancy Sutton Place. My grandfather opened up early for the breakfast trade, worked all day until two or three, closed, took a nap, opened up again until ten p.m. My grandmother prepared the free lunch and laid it out about noontime. Was strictly working class in those days. My grandparents, they wanted a corner slot—that's where saloons did best—but one man, a brewer named Peter Dolger, owned the entire block. You couldn't sell your place, you couldn't buy somebody else's. You had to wait for someone to die or make a trade. In 1880, they got a trade; took the southeast corner of 56th Street and First. Breweries set you up in business and you paid them back out of profits. That's where the original fixtures come from. I'm pretty sure Peter Dolger set the place up. Fancy ale pumps, I know, were made by a man named John Burns, at 125 Grand Street. Copper, brass, and bone-handled spigots—they pumped beer with a bellows. John Burns made McSorley's pumps, too. A real craftsman."

Other fixtures, which Dolger appears to have installed, were mahogany wainscoting, mahogany front and back bars (back bar a delicate English-stick style), bentwood chairs, heavy tables, and the exquisite cabinet work, including ice chests and side cases. "My grandfather was something of a politician, Democratic Club, that sort of activity, and he needed a handsome place. He helped a lot of people out. He always ran a clean joint, no bums, no hookers, Bridget saw to that. My mother, too. Hookers used to say, 'Don't go near there, Mrs. Billy'll chase you down the block.' We stayed open during Prohibition legally, selling near beer. You were a regular you could buy a drink: whisky, gin, whatever. Under the counter. Come thirty-three we had some trouble. Liquor board said we was too much like an old saloon, didn't want to give us a license. Said our fixtures were too saloonish, our way of running things and our clientele too rough. Well, there was ways to get a license. A Mrs. Shepherd helped us out, she had pull with the board; but that's when we had to fix a name and that's when we started serving food—one of the conditions. Later, when we moved again, they tried to pull another on us, saying we were within a certain-number feet of a church, and no saloon could open that close. We got around that one by proving we'd been in operation years before the church. There's always somebody ready to take a bribe, and I ain't saying we ever resorted to that, we never had to—my grandfather Michael had his connections.

"His place was an institution until we was forced to move. We had WPA artists painting the joint; there's a painting down there now in the Natural History Museum or some place. Smithsonian has been up here asking questions. What happened with the second move was somebody finally sold the whole block. We had a shot at this present location four blocks south, so we took it. We shut the old joint October 22, 1966, and reopened March 13, 1967. Only time we ever been closed. Some people say we're the oldest family-run saloon in New York. I mean continuous, from father to son. My daughter Joan is taking a big interest in the place now—she greets people, acts as sort of a hostess during dinner, helps with the business end—that makes four generations. We moved most of our old stuff down here in '67. Important fixtures, like the bar and cabinets. We lost a few old customers who couldn't make the hill. We pull a different clientele now. Very famous people. We serve some of the most famous people in New York. I don't name any names. Used to be, back in the old place—which I took over in '44 when Billy Sr. died—we catered to elevator operators and truck drivers. Plus the neighborhood crowd. Today it's classier and our food is first rate. Steaks, chops, you can look at my invoices, we buy the best. Prime meat. We don't turn nobody away though. We never been that kind of joint. Long as I'm alive we won't be."

By three thirty of a midweek afternoon the luncheon rush is finished and a few oldtime regulars start shuffling in, to line Mickey Condron's eighteen-eighties front counter and gaze absent-mindedly out the window at the bustle along First Avenue. Billy's day barkeep is mixing a first batch of martinis for these regulars, mostly older folks living in the neighborhood who get lonesome about midafternoon and congregate in twos and threes before Billy's mahogany. Barkeep serves them respectfully, greeting each by name, Mr. this, Mrs. that, in most cases not bothering to inquire what they'll have to drink. Prime spot at the bar is street-side next to Billy's front window, behind the front door. A protected alcove exists there, where a patron feels most comfortable and least vulnerable. Heineken's and Schaefer beers are on tap—a dollar twenty-five and seventy-five cents respectively. An ice-cold Coke may be purchased for fifty cents; Billy's is an excellent spot to repair a hangover. Coke comes in the six and one-half ounce bottle, no cheap tap-Coke, and is served with a full glass of ice. Billy's barkeep is working steadily now, restocking his bar, getting ready for the cocktail rush. Old regulars sip their martinis. Billy's barkeep whips fresh cream daily for the famous Irish coffee (two dollars), and proceeds to do so between answering the phone and pulling an occasional draft. Drinks are not cheap at Billy's, but for New York, reasonable: a dollar seventy-five for Jack Daniels on the rocks, bar whisky less, most fancy cocktails under two dollars. Food is simple: steaks, chicken, and Billy's lamb-chops which are the finest in town. Standard to moderate prices on the dinner menu: entrées five to eight dollars, sandwiches during lunch considerably less. And what you get is excellent.

Later, after the dinner rush, regulars will drift in again, lingering until one or two a.m. During the forties and fifties, my Grandfather Nichols was one of those regulars, stopping either at Billy's or the Mayfair on his eleven p.m. jaunt. He'd walk Lady, my grand-mother's Bedlington terrier, and pick up the early *News*. Plus knock back a couple, all in the same trip. I have a vision of my mother on a raw winter night in 1935 thawing her frozen hair before Billy's pot-belly stove. She'd attended an indoor swimming party, left with her long hair wet, and it had frozen. She stopped into Billy's with friends and stood there laughing as it thawed out. She was modeling then, my uncle was acting in Group Theatre productions, and Billy's was a popular rendezvous. Katharine Cornell, Billy Rose, Nancy Walker, Dane Clark, and other show business types lived in the neighborhood. My grandparents resided at 425 East 51st, as did my mother and uncle, and Billy's just always seemed the logical spot. In the fifties, when my uncle was writing for television and practically running *Your Hit Parade*, I recall evenings at Billy's with stars of that show—plus all-weather New York eccentrics like Xenia Cage, the painter, musician, and pop artist before her time, who had been married to John Cage. Grandfather Nichols was head of the New York Convention and Visitor's Bureau, my uncle an ac-tor/writer . . . and my mother had been a beautiful young woman during Manhattan's most glamorous era, the nineteen-thirties. Cer-tainly there must have existed scores of similar families. All of it centers in my mind around Billy's.

"Remember those antique gas fixtures we had at the old joint?" Billy Jr. says. "We still got em but they're not hooked up. In the old joint they worked, and you know, night of November 9, 1965, the Great Blackout, we stayed open for business and never missed a lick. Bet we was the only gaslit saloon in Manhattan. That a hell of a thing? For a while there, till they cut the goddam juice back on, felt like old times."

White Horse Tavern
Hudson at 11th Street (Greenwich Village), New York City

The white horse has forever been an arresting symbol: It is said to represent swiftness of life to Britishers—implying, when encountered upon a tavern sign, that one had best pause and embrace life before it gallops him by. Sacred horses of Greek, Roman, Celtic and Germanic cultures were traditionally white. In Jutland, a knight astride a white horse is said to appear whenever sea dykes burst and catastrophe threatens. In Germany and England, to dream of a white horse is thought to be an omen of death. "I want to go to the Garden of Eden," Dylan Thomas whined on the eve of his final binge, "to die . . . to be forever unconscious. . . ." Then he toddled down to White Horse Tavern and knocked back eighteen straight whiskies in ninety minutes. A feat from which he never recovered.

That morning of November 4, 1953, is the keystone to White Horse's reputation as a writer's bar, but in truth the old saloon had been hosting Village scribblers since the days of Piet Vlag, Upton Sinclair, the Liberal Club, Mabel Dodge, Edna St. Vincent Millay, Eugene O'Neill, and the redoubtable Joe Gould. It is a safe bet that any twentieth-century American artist with the least *éclat* has at some time or another visited White Horse; it is that much of an institution. Founded in 1880 as the archetypal corner saloon, it has always counted along the backbone of its constituency a clatter of truck-drivers, warehousemen, cabdrivers and workers-in-general who have crowded Village streets for over a century. During afternoon and late morning hours at White Horse, they still predominate. But not in such numbers. White Horse is a West Village saloon now, typical of a certain stratum of West Village's population: the boho painter, ratty writer, and the incurable romantic.

Dylan Thomas spent many a happy hour at White Horse; it was one of his favorite New York saloons. The Beats all loved White Horse (Kerouac, Corso, Ginsberg, Cassady) and patronized it faithfully. Norman Mailer chaired innumerable round-table discussions in White Horse's back room during the fifties, as did Bob Dylan a decade later. The folkies descended upon White Horse as had the Beats and various Village movements before them. The place has an irresistible draw . . . it is seedy, smelly, brazenly run, and occasionally hostile . . . but it's awfully tough not to stop in for at least one beer. There is a fantastic jukebox and between twelve and four a.m. on a good night you can count on a raucous crowd. After midnight the old saloon seems nearly afloat, isolated truly, like a bar from some other country where everything's green outside and in a couple of hours you'll be out there milking the goats.

Cheeseburgers are delectable at White Horse, broiled over an open hearth, to order, and with a tall draft on a bitter fall morning, the ideal breakfast. I have never had less than a perfect cheeseburger at White Horse; nothing fancy, mind you, a quarter pound of good beef with a slice of melted cheese, Bermuda onion, dollop of Heinz, all for a dollar-five. Sit at the bar and watch Horse's counterman fix it. Light floods the old saloon like last night never happened, young writers with open notebooks are already gathered at tables by the big front window, and a bum or two is commiserating with White Horse's manager who nips steadily from a bottle stashed beneath the bar. Cheeseburger comes, and it is so fresh, so clean and shaped on its white china plate, so tight on its bun against the filth of White Horse's front bar . . . the unswept floor, the begrimed fixtures . . . that it's like your first homecooked meal in prison. White Horse's draft is reasonable—sixty cents a glass—and that's another reason you'll encounter simpaticos at this hour. White Horse is a dreadful place, a way station on the turnpike to Hell. But somebody's punched up an old Bobby Dylan tune, there's everyone you'd ever want to hear on that juke, most of whom have sat where you're hunched over now. "Don't ask me no questions about *Dylan Thomas*," Manager groans, sneaking another short one. "We got articles on the back walls; you can read that shit, *I don't care*." A reporter for a high school newspaper in Jersey takes this scolding shakily, but heads for White Horse's back room, notebook in hand.

The stench of piss is overwhelming. I have wiped my plate clean and call quickly for a second draft. A feeling of absolute contentment washes over me—why? This saloon is a mess, a fucking insult to proper bartending. "Let's keep those cheeseburgers coming," I hear myself yell. "Maybe a shot of something on the side." My reflection in White Horse's wide back mirror is one of demented satisfaction. . . . Eighteen straight whiskies in ninety minutes. . . .

Four or five had undoubtedly been more like it, as Thomas was so far gone (on drugs, bleeding internally) the number hardly mattered. He made it through that last night and was strong enough to return next morning for a couple of White Horse drafts. That evening he was hospitalized at St. Vincent's, where he died five days later.

Cause of death, according to St. Vincent's autopsy report, was "Insult to the brain."

There are bars in Greenwich Village, such as Anvil, on 14th near the waterfront, where "you can watch a man grease his arm with Crisco and shove it up the rectum of another man, who is wearing a motorcycle cap and chewing gum," Richard Goldstein has written.* "This is called fist-fucking and it is the apocryphal gesture of pop-SM. . . . There is nothing like standing in the Anvil . . . and watching a man insert three feet of chain into his rectum, to convince you that you are living in a Visconti film." Homosexuals have overwhelmed café society in lower Manhattan to such a degree that it is difficult to locate a "straight" bar in which to pretend the world has not changed. Other SM bars, such as Eagle's Nest, on the north waterfront, and Keller's, on Christopher Street, are crowded with celebrants of this dark art. Also a goodly number of tourists and hangers-on.

San Remo, the old Cedar, old Louie's, and coffee house Figaro are long gone. Lion's Head, in Sheridan Square, persists and it is something of an old-fashioned Village writer's bar. Pete Hamill called Lion's Head home, before he went on the wagon, as do numerous other newspaper writers. I have always found Lion's Head to be coldly exclusive. A dingy basement dive with terrible fixtures and a high hauteur factor; acceptance based upon whether you're a regular or not. Max's Kansas City, 213 Park Avenue South, endures like some brontosaurus from the Jurassic sixties—jammed with androgynous Warholites (mostly from the suburbs these days) and crowded as Maxwell's Plum. Pete's Tavern, 18th Street at Irving, claims to be one hundred-seven years old and a past hangout of O'Henry's; it remains popular with writers and longtime residents of the neighborhood. Chelsea Hotel Bar, 222 West 23rd Street, has always been an amiable spot. There's a long bar, drinks are reasonable and food at the adjacent restaurant tasty. Spanish, if memory serves. You may drink in the company of any number of famous New Yorkers. Dylan Thomas, Brendan Behan, Thomas Wolfe, John Sloan, Diego Rivera, Bob Dylan, Jimi Hendrix, Janis Joplin, Viva, and a slew of others have lived at Chelsea. Permanently, or in dilatory domicile. Bar at Chelsea is comfortable and you never can tell whom you might run into.

---

* *The Village Voice*, July 7, 1975.

Village Vanguard, 178 Seventh Avenue, where Jack Kerouac read his poetry and jazz greats have been performing for decades, is still going strong. It's a cover-charge spot, a jazz club like Village Gate, Bleecker at Thompson, another timeless Village standby for first-class music. A folk-club renaissance of sorts has erupted over the past year, with oldtimers like Bob Dylan and Joan Baez dropping in for unannounced sets at Folk City, 130 West 3rd Street, and The Other End, 149 Bleecker Street. These are likewise cover-charge clubs, but with something of an old Village atmosphere. The Bottom Line, 15 West 4th Street, is another of the genre. Best bet for latest music info is an up-to-date copy of the *Village Voice, New York* magazine, or *The New Yorker*.

Country music has taken Manhattan by storm, and two clubs I know of, O'Lunney's, 915 Second Avenue (Midtown), and The Cow Palace, 19 St. Marks Place (East Village), offer both bluegrass and Nashville-style entertainment.

McSorley's Old Ale House

15 East 7th Street (East Village), New York City

*"You young people don't realize how sweet—sweet and sad—New York was before Prohibition. But now, who'd want to paint a street strewn with automobiles? The skyline? It's like a comb in the restroom of a filling station. A tooth here and there missing, and all filled with dirt. . . ." ***

McSorley's is Manhattan's oldest saloon and doubtlessly its most famous, if not from the paintings of John Sloan then from a single essay published by Joseph Mitchell in *The New Yorker*, April 13, 1940. Mitchell's profile, "The Old House at Home," is probably the finest piece of writing ever done on an American saloon; if you care about American bars and American bar literature, get yourself to a competent library. The essay is contained in a 1943 collection of Mitchell's work, titled *McSorley's Wonderul Saloon*. My personal copy is a claret-hued War Edition, sparsely bound and bearing the incription: "Lt. Charles W. Thompson U.S.N.R. Arzew, Algeria 1943." My father's signature. I had stumbled across the volume in a stack of

---

* John Sloan, quoted in *Three Hundred Years of American Painting* by Alexander Eliot and Editors of *Time* (New York: Random House, 1957), p. 164.

old books, and had carried it in my pack the full sixty thousand miles of my journey. It had comforted me in more tanktown hotels and fleabag YMCAs than I cared to recall. Its Ash Can sentiment on many an evening the only soporific which could lull me to sleep . . . facing the agitation, hysteria, and brake-start flagellation of another day's research.

Mitchell's volume had accompanied me on my first visit to McSorley's in 1973, and was tucked securely in the folds of my leather aviator's jacket today. McSorley's appeared much the same—same sawdust on the floor, same mugbeaten, wood front counter and somber back bar, same memorabilia dangling from every millimeter of wall space, same potbelly stove, same ale or porter for forty cents a mug, two mugs for seventy—but the place was busier, seedier, boasting more college kids, more articles concerning itself, more self-conscious junk. McSorley's "has taken on a busy patina of little doodads," Eugene McGarr had quipped in a telephone interview, "buttons that say Class of '69, that sort of thing." McGarr, a painter/film maker who'd lived two doors from McSorley's between 1958 and 1961, remembered old Ukranians huddled next to the potbelly stove, men who spoke together in Ukranian and whose patois was interspersed by the brogues of Irish bartenders, "twenty-two-, twenty-three-year-old kids, straight off the boat." McSorley's had always seemed more an Irish pub than an American saloon, though its credentials were impeccable. Carrying my brace of ales rearward, I eased a spindle-shanked Windsor chair closer to the potbelly and sat down to mull over Mitchell's essay.

McSorley's had been founded in 1854 by Old John McSorley, an Irish immigrant who fashioned his saloon after a pub he had frequented in Ireland. McSorley's was originally called the Old House at Home, but, according to Mitchell, about 1908 the sign blew down and Old John replaced it with one which read "McSorley's Old Ale House." Old John instigated the policy against women (one which survived until 1970) and bragged that McSorley's motto was "Good ale, raw onions and no ladies." There has always been a back room at McSorley's, but Old John nailed a sign outside reading "Notice. No Back Room in Here for Ladies." According to Mitchell, the only woman ever willingly served in those early years was a vendor named Mother Fresh-Roasted, "who claimed her husband died from the bite of a lizard in Cuba during the Spanish-American War and who went from saloon to saloon on the lower East Side for a couple of generations hawking peanuts, which she carried in her apron." Old John would sell her an ale.

Old John likewise initiated McSorley's tradition of displaying memorabilia—blanketing walls and wainscoting with photographs, engravings, lithographs, legends, and admonitions. Over the entrance to his back room he hung the sign BE GOOD OR BEGONE. On a side wall he placed portraits of Lincoln, Garfield, and McKinley, brass-tagged with the caption "They Assassinated These Good Men The Skulking Dogs." Old John served as president of an organization called the Honorable John McSorley Pickle, Beefsteak, Baseball Nine, and Chowder Club, and tacked numerous photographs of this group about his barroom. A few remain. Old John drank unremittedly until he was fifty-five, then quit, saying "I've had my share." He possessed a bull-frog bass and "enjoyed harmonizing with a choir of drunks." His favorite songs were "Muldoon, the Solid Man," "Swim Out, You're Over Your Head," "Maggie Murphy's Home," and "Since the Soup House Moved Away." All composed by Harrigan and Hart, who then were known as "the Gilbert and Sullivan of the U.S.A." In 1882 they made McSorley's the scene of one of their slum comedies, *McSorley's Inflation*. Old John was "pleased exceedingly."

Though Old John did not die until 1910, he turned head-bartending duties over to his son, William, around 1890. Mitchell noted that Bill McSorley "inherited every bit of his father's surliness and not much of his affability. . . . He was so solemn that before he was thirty several customers had settled into the habit of calling him Old Bill." After Old John died, Bill secured each of his father's photos and souvenirs to McSorley's walls with hammer and screwdriver. His principal concern thereafter was to keep McSorley's exactly as it had been during his father's reign. "When anything had to be changed or repaired, it appeared to pain him physically," Mitchell wrote. He had the bar shored up in 1933, the ceiling painted, and in 1925 retired his father's pewter mugs for earthenware. He installed a pay telephone, which he refused to answer. His contributions to McSorley's memorabilia were minimal, but included a portrait of Old John, a poster of Barney Oldfield in a red racing car, and a poem titled "The Man Behind the Bar." Bill knew this poem by heart, and would recite it, emphasizing the last verse:

> When St. Peter sees him coming he will
> Leave the gates ajar,
> For he knows he's had his hell on earth,
> Has the man behind the bar.

McSorley's stayed open during Prohibition, serving near beer and strong ale, which was washtub-brewed in McSorley's cellar and which was anything but weak. McSorley's never suffered a raid. Doubtless because it was the haunt of Tammany politicians and minor police officials. Bill swore allegiance to peace and quiet, but it was he who installed the fire-alarm gong still secured to the seven-foot-tall icebox behind the bar. "If someone started a song, or if the old men sitting around the stove started to yell at each other, he would shuffle over to the gong and give the rope a series of savage jerks," Mitchell reported. Bill reserved his affection for cats, owning eighteen at a clip. They had the run of the saloon and would amble about, nuzzling patrons' pantlegs. Around 1911, John Sloan, George Luks, Glenn O. Coleman, Stuart Davis, and other painters began frequenting McSorley's. Sloan produced five paintings of the old saloon, including one titled *McSorley's Cats*, which shows Bill about to feed his brood. "He fed them on bull livers put through a sausage grinder," Mitchell wrote, "and they became enormous. When it came time to feed them, he would leave the bar, no matter how brisk business was, and bang on the bottom of a tin pan; the fat cats would come loping up, like leopards, from all corners of the saloon."

In March of 1936, Bill sold McSorley's to Daniel O'Connel, a retired policeman who had been a steady customer since 1900. One of Bill's conditions was that no changes should be effected. O'Connel respected the agreement, harboring nearly as much pride in McSorley's as Bill. Bill McSorley died September 21, 1938. Daniel O'Connel was proprietor less than four years. He died in December 1939, leaving the saloon to his daughter, Dorothy O'Connel Kirwan, the present owner. She has honored McSorley's traditions and changed virtually nothing. She had not even lifted the ban on women customers—visiting the saloon herself only on Sundays after hours—until a Federal edict forced her to. On August 11, 1970, McSorley's opened its doors to women, after one hundred-sixteen years' sanctity. There still is only one toilet, and gentlemen relaxing before McSorley's cathedral-like urinals are sometimes startled to see a pig-tailed distaffer stroll past, heading for the enclosed stall.

An acceptance of women has been the major alteration in McSorley's mood and appearance, no oldtime regular could deny. "The *tone* of a place with women in it is different, and has a different quality to it, than the tone of a place with just men," Eugene McGarr had observed. "In the old days they'd ring that bell at anyone who tried to hustle a lady in, usually some stranger who had heard about the old bar but hadn't heard of the restriction. The tone of a place with nothing but men, is that of men who want to be by themselves and drink . . . with all the pejoratives you can put to that, drinking is an activity that men do together. The same place with women attracts men who are chasing women. In 1955 when you walked into McSorley's, you didn't expect to pick up a girl. You went there to have a beer, and lean against the bar, or sit at a table— and talk. That's what you *did* there. Now, you can walk into McSorley's with the possibility of picking up a girl. To that extent, it's become a different kind of bar.

"In the fifties there were old Ukranians, people from the neighborhood, me, Hunter Thompson, John Clancy, and friends. Friday and Saturday nights were bad, uptownish, but on Tuesday afternoon around three o'clock . . . McSorley's was the greatest place in the world to have a drink."

At three thirty of a Wednesday afternoon, I laid aside *McSorley's Wonderful Saloon*, plus the notes of my conversation with Eugene McGarr, and looked about. A plethora of college-age kids crowded the bar, but the same old men both Mitchell and McGarr had described sat slumped in rickety captain's chairs nursing warm mugs of ale. Here and there they'd been joined by jocular coeds, a conflagration the old men did not seem to mind. Several smiled agitatedly at young girls sharing their tables, gesturing with canes. One or two initiated conversations. The same odor prevailed, one which Mitchell had painted as "a rich compound of pine sawdust, tap drippings, pipe tobacco, coal smoke, and onions," adding that ". . . for many mental disturbances the smell in McSorley's is more beneficial than psychoanalysis." I tapped Mitchell's volume gingerly with the tips of my fingers and reclined against the slats of my chair; absorbing whatever it was that remained.

Fannelli's

Prince Street at Mercer (Lower East Side), New York City

An 1877–78 license hangs behind Fannelli's black-with-age, Renaissance-style back bar, lending credence to tales of the saloon's antiquity. Old man Fannelli claims his establishment to be one hundred and twenty-six years young, which would give it primogeniture over McSorley's—an unlikely probability. In any case, Fannelli's survives as a relic of Lower East Side's mid-nineteenth-century boom as a commercial and entertainment nexus. Beerhalls jammed the Bowery early in the 1800s, and theaters began springing up about 1826. The advent of grand opera in Astor Place touched off a veritable explosion of Bowery theaters, dancehalls and cellar dives. Numerous fancy saloons attracted a booming business; Fannelli's remains, the lone heir.

With the emergence of SoHo as an artists' quarter, the old saloon has taken on new life. But nothing much seems to have changed. A venerable mahogany counter fronts Fannelli's statuesque back bar; two or three tables crowd the rear wall, where a hodgepodge of painters, sculptors, and neighborhood working types are served by a crew of elderly waiters: deaf, doddering, but inordinately courteous. A "Ladies and Gents Sitting Room" is maintained toward the rear of Fannelli's barroom, where remarkably inexpensive meals are likewise available. Cuisine is largely Italian, featuring hearty workingman's portions of stuffed chicken breasts, spaghetti, or braised lamb, each for under three dollars. A large draft sells for sixty cents; bar whisky for about a dollar. A fat orange cat naps fitfully at the far end of the bar, periodically roused by bustling waiters. Fannelli's kitchen is situated directly in the barroom, and waiters vie for chefs' attention while tripping over supine customers. Nobody seems to mind.

The tile floor at Fannelli's is scrubbed absolutely white. Oversize photographs of prize fighters adorn the walls. The bar is close: there, exists a nineteenth-century comraderie and zero fear factor . . . in a neighborhood often as cold as its cast-iron façade.

Paris Bar and Restaurant
South Street at Peck Slip (Fulton Market), New York City

Fulton Fish Market has been slated to be torn down by 1977, so get to Paris before the final carnage. Paris is not physically part of the old market, but spiritually is so close as to garner small chance of survival. Truckers, fishermen, fish mongers, longshoremen, and every other figure of Fulton's long night's journey into day patronize Paris, as they have for over a hundred years. Paris is situated on the ground floor of Meyer's Hotel, an old steamship hostelry, constructed 1873. Today it houses pensioners and officers of the Fishery Council and Board of Trade Association. I did not know about Paris before I interviewed Joseph Mitchell, and was not reminded of it until I encountered William Warner's article, "At the Fulton Market," in *Atlantic Monthly*.

There is a neon café-counter at Paris, where breakfast is served all night to ravenous marketers. Business of Fulton commences about two a.m. and slacks off before noon, so if you want to see Paris in prime time, heed those hours. There is a big front and back bar set, matched, of oak, thirty feet long with a turn-of-the-century back bar framing three tall mirrors. Café royal is drink of the morning, a plain cup of Paris coffee laced with anisette. Oldtimers and tattooed journeymen sit around Paris's side tables shooting craps or playing cards. Some of them carry bailing hooks over their shoulders and affect wool skull caps. They all wear some sort of rubber footgear. You will blend or you will not. In either case, they'll pay you little mind. Paris represents the end of a certain way of life; it is soon to be demolished, and urban renewal is the bugaboo which haunts them, would cause them to lurch out of chairs ready for a fight.

Other saloons well worth a nip on any Manhattan tour are—
  The Gold Rail 2850 Broadway
  The West End, 2911 Broadway
  Oyster Bar, Grand Central Station (42nd Street)
  Old Town, 45 East 18th Street
  Luchow's, 110 East 14th Street
  Pedro's, 251 East 81st Street
  Kettle of Fish, MacDougal, near Bleecker
—further particulars of which may be found in David Yeadon and Roz Lewis's comprehensive *The New York Book of Bars, Pubs & Taverns*.

NEW JERSEY
Hoboken

Duck down into the Hudson Tubes at 33rd, 14th, 9th, or Christopher streets, pick up a PATH train, and take a trip on a time machine—emerging in Hoboken at the 1907 Erie Lackawanna terminal, two blocks from Washington Street and a nineteenth-centuryman's El Dorado of pre-Prohibition saloons.

First Stop: *Hotel Victor*, corner of Hudson and Hudson, an old steamship hotel with a proper bar where you can purchase a short draft for twenty cents and a nourishing lunch for less than a dollar. Across from Deutsche Seaman's Union, Victor once was prosperous, but has fallen on hard times. There still exists a lovely mural of the Manhattan skyline behind Victor's back bar however, and company is pleasant if a trifle bestubbled.

Clam Broth House, 30–38 Newark Street, although founded 1899, is a disappointment. Possessed of a busy men's bar, its mahogany is antique but vulgarly shellacked. Oysters are unfresh, horseradish too mild; but Clam Broth does serve a cheap, cold, sizable draft.

Court Grill and *Brass Rail* saloons, both on Washington Street not far from the terminal, serve excellent drinks and are reputable Hoboken saloons. Helmer's, corner of Eleventh and Washington, across from Maxwell House coffee, runs an exceptional bar: fancy for a Hoboken establishment and famous for its German cuisine. Interior is wood-paneled with high-backed booths, suffering much buff and polish. More a restaurant than a saloon, but worthy of a stein on any Hoboken tour. Maxwell Tavern, also on Washington Street, is just a step across from Helmer's on Eleventh, and . . . need one note . . . good to the last drop.

Café Elysian, corner of Tenth and Washington, is Hoboken's *pièce de résistance*, serving short drafts for twenty cents beneath a Baroque pieplate ceiling with soaring cherubim, encircled by hand-painted murals of the Hudson and ancient steamships which float above the wainscoting. Floor is white tile and scrubbed; service is by a pink-faced barkeep of Repeal vintage who will offer tales of Hoboken during the Great War, when she was a major port of embarkation and under strict military law. Café Elysian is a sleepy place, doubtless named for nearby Elysian Park, where the first organized baseball game was played in 1846, between Hoboken's Knickerbocker Giants and New York. Oldtimers sip beers before a period front and back bar set, and are not averse to conversation. Elbow on through Elysian's extraordinary cut glass doors—partake of the timeless Victorian sensibility.

Hoboken, like most decent American towns, is suffering from the cancer of urban renewal. Its entire riverfront (where *On the Waterfront* was filmed) has been demolished to make space for highrise apartment buildings, intended to house an influx of workers at the new World Trade Center. River Street, famous for half a century in ports round the world, was leveled in 1969. With it went such classic saloons as Nelson's Marine Bar, "founded" 1933, but with precursors dating through Prohibition. Nelson's had been a favorite of the polite Manhattan set, as well as seamen, ex-pugs, and stevedores. Mayor Jimmy Walker made it a Hoboken stop, always pausing to praise Frankie Nelson, a champion middleweight boxer, on the propriety of his establishment. Martin and Dolly Sinatra were regulars. Jim Hans had reminisced about Nelson's, in the September 8, 1971, *Hoboken Herald:* "Frankie was a fighter, but he was also a kind, sincere person, and very much an entertainer. My wife and I enjoyed many a night at Frankie's . . . It was interesting to hear him tell stories about his past. Sometimes while talking about his boxing days, he would suddenly reach down under the counter and ring the old official fight bell he'd installed there. One could spend hours in the place, and we did. It was like a museum with the walls covered with rare old fight pictures and posters. The collection is now in the Hall of Fame, Long Branch, New Jersey." Frankie's saloon was a favorite of literary folk as well as seamen. Edward Abbey had tagged his introduction to *Desert Solitaire:* "E.A./April 1967/Nelson's Marine Bar/Hoboken," having composed it there. Tonight at the corner of Third and River, Frankie's corner, I spoke with two old German Americans—one a night watchman guarding a highrise apartment building hunkered over the rubble which had been Nelson's.

"We remember," they said, responding emotionally. "Such a place."

"Such a *street*," the night watchman muttered. "For blocks we had saloons. You could not stroll five feet without banging against a swinging door. Look—" he said, gesturing along River Street. "Emptiness. One apartment building, others maybe never, and for what? That we should lose a saloon like Nelson's?"

PENNSYLVANIA

Chadds Ford Inn

Route 1 at Route 100, Chadds Ford

Though Chadds Ford Inn is very much an eighteenth-century tavern (founded 1736 in a house built about 1707) its barroom is nineteenth century to the quick. Paddle fans hang above a twenty-foot expanse of oak bar, a large mirror is framed by a mahogany back bar with four Ionic columns, a brass rail extends along the foot of the front bar over a white tile trough. Tables line a rear wall in the nineteenth-century manner, and a magnificent narwhal tusk hangs above the back bar's mirror. A collection of unusual Toby mugs is displayed atop the back bar's entablature. Bartenders are formally gruff and one is as likely to encounter Main Line Pennsylvanians, upper crust Wilmingtonians, or well-heeled tourists from Brandywine River Museum, as musicians in T-shirts, or painters in splattered tweeds.

Chadds Ford has hosted an artists' colony since 1898 when Howard Pyle opened his academy there. N.C. was the first Wyeth of Chadds Ford, and his progeny, including Andrew and James, grew up within walking distance of the Inn. In fact, Andrew Wyeth sketched the cover for Chadds Ford's menu and Betsy Wyeth authored the brief history printed on its back. Jamey Wyeth's Cobra was for many seasons stabled in Chadds Ford's parking lot, or so it seemed. Wyeth's painting *Draft Age* was a gift to innkeeper Dorothy Theodore and hangs today in the Inn's vestibule. Jimmy Lynch, model for *Draft Age*, has been a regular at Chadds Ford since the early sixties. During those years he often could be seen lounging about the Inn's front porch, trying to look as hard as his portrait. Chadds Ford artists consider the Inn their corner saloon; no one makes a fuss when they are noticed.

John Chads founded his inn as a way station for travelers crossing the Brandywine at Chadds Ford, and for anyone who wished to dally beside Kings Highway. John Chads died in 1760, leaving his inn to a nephew, Joseph Davis, who remained proprietor until Battle of the Brandywine—September 11, 1777. George Washington and his staff are said to have honed their battle plan at Davis's tavern. American officers were quartered at the Inn prior to their retreat,

244

and British officers certainly must have superseded them. Chadds Ford was so mercilessly plundered in those days of British occupation that the Inn did not resume functions until 1810, when its license was renewed. A mansard roof and wide front porch were added later in the century, and the barroom was redecorated. Although Chadds Ford Inn no longer provides lodging, it continues to offer solace in the form of substantial fare and strong spirits. Route One remains heavily traveled, perhaps not so well traveled as when it existed as the major highway between Florida and New England, but State Police are kept busy. One does well to pause at Chadds Ford for a hearty meal (all entrees under eight dollars) or a bottle of beer (Bud about seventy-five cents). Most mixed drinks sell for a dollar to a dollar-twenty. Ambience during the day is quiet and cheerful. After supper, particularly on weekends, the old barroom is kept jumping. Chadds Ford is a favorite afterhours saloon for Wilmingtonians, as Delaware bars close early. Chadds Ford Inn is open every day except Sunday, from eleven thirty a.m. until two a.m. The stories we could tell.

Try Chadds Ford Tavern, about two miles north of Chadds Ford on Route One, for boozing in a more raucous setting. Tavern caters to Chadds Ford's hipper sensibility, i.e. coke and Dalmane with a margarita chaser, jukebox high as the hemorrhoids will allow, and parabolas of chaotic strut. Less expensive than Chadds Ford Inn and guaranteed to weed your garden.

Also, Anvil Inn, between Chadds Ford and Kennett Square on Route One, for old-fashioned, nineteen-sixties roadhouse rock. Good bands every night except Sunday, two dollar minimum or thereabouts, but worth it if you're seeking a spot to get it on mightily. The rockabilly Roseland of Pennsylvania's mushroom *Provence*.

DELAWARE

Hagea's

#2 Main Street, Henry Clay (Wilmington)

A worker's tavern in the old powderman's hamlet of Henry Clay, Hagea's commands a picturesque stretch of Brandywine Creek several hundred yards south of Henry Clay factory (now Hagley Museum) and the original du Pont powder works. Henry Clay hamlet was ghosted in 1921 when du Pont shut down its Brandywine powder mill after a last, grisly explosion. Powder mishaps were common along the Brandywine—averaging one every fourteen months, three persons killed per blast. Workers' houses were constructed of stone with triple-thick walls to guard against disaster. Many of these old houses survive and are occupied by descendants of nineteenth-century powdermen. They dot forgotten settlements, like homesteaded bunkers. Hagea's is such a powderman's shelter, fashioned early in the 1800s of thick stone, heavy mortar, and firm resolve.

Du Ponts still own #2 Main, but the Hageas have operated a tavern there since August of 1933. Current proprietor is a seventyish woman whose grandfather emigrated from Ireland to work in du Pont powder mills. Mrs. Hagea's uncle ran a general store and post office at #2 prior to 1933. Du Pont hired a preponderance of Irishmen for its nineteenth-century operations, and clientele at Hagea's reflects Henry Clay's Irish heritage. Irish bands entertain certain evenings and a spontaneous jig may erupt any moment. Mrs. Hagea lives upstairs at #2, as did her ancestors, tending bar with the help of a relative, also seventyish and doddering. Hagea's old barroom is peaceful during the afternoon when du Pont employees in business suits rather than coveralls may be overheard discussing the latest in polyethylenes. They are joined in summer by Brandywine rafters, canoeists, outspoken guzzlers wearing Industrial League softball uniforms or neighborhood bowling shirts, plus an occasional dinner-jacketed hierarch. Hagea's is that sort of homogenized drinking spot where a retired Federal judge may relax in company of an ex-Hell's Angel and journeyman plumber or two. Wilmington mayor Thomas Maloney has been overheard remarking at Hagea's, "This is the only place in town I can go where nobody asks me for a job."

A thin fluted column stands at the center of Hagea's barroom, flanked by a pine-faced bar and numerous heavy wooden tables, topped in formica, with matching heavy wooden ice-cream chairs. An old fireplace has been plastered over, but its lovely mantelpiece remains. An upright piano and gas heater sit in that same corner before a tiny stage. It is here that entertainment transpires on weekends and on special evenings during the work week. Old wooden coat racks are positioned about the room. A pair of antique porcelain lamps rest in two windows facing the Brandywine. They are kerosene fixtures, refitted to electricity. No toilet facilities are readily visible, but a stroll rearward, through storage rooms and dank corridors, reveals the necessary accouterments.

A standard selection of liquors is available at Hagea's pine bar, averaging seventy-five cents a drink. A bottle of Budweiser sells for fifty cents and an ice-cold, old-fashioned, six-and-one-half ounce bottle of Coca-Cola may be purchased for twenty-five. Hagea's is somber as a nineteenth-century riverman's tavern during the day. After dark Hagea's shudders to life—roaring until one a.m. with patrons packed shoulder to shoulder around the makeshift bandstand. Wilmington boasts several comfortable bars . . . Buckley's, Logan House, Gallucio's, George's . . . but none synthesizes the stratified social castes and abominable industrialisms of the old gunpowder boomer like Hagea's.

OHIO

Phoenix Café
641 Walnut Street, Cincinnati

Cincinnati has a downtown area still very much alive after dark, albeit crackerboxed with bright movie marquees, overpriced showbars and flashy surf'n turf restaurants. A March gale caroms off the Ohio River at Cincinnati with a force which shuffles Chicago to second place in the wind-chill derby. Citizens crash along in mini-skirts or open sport jackets with bitter defiance, anxious to be fleeced by cheezy, downtown pleasure emporiums. Cincinnati seems a cross between Minneapolis and Baltimore—many funky tonks, much urban renewal and skyglass architecture—but with a character of its own. Once a great river port and capstone to Booboisie architecture in the frontier East, the "Queen City" is now an aging madame, shabby of heel, ratty of hem, and portly about the midsection.

"Porkopolis" is what they dubbed her in the salad days, world famous for her exported hams and fine German beer. One would hardly guess it, but there are enclaves of the old life still kicking in downtown Cincinnati, and Phoenix Café is a noteworthy example. It sits amongst its glittery neighbors like a Hans Holbein in an exhibition roomful of Jasper Johns. One would miss it entirely if not for the yaffle of old men steaming Phoenix's front window on a chill Saturday evening; in tweed overcoats, beaten felt hats, and twill workpants, crowded the length of Phoenix's old wooden bar.

It's like a John Sloan portrait of McSorley's inside Phoenix; boozy old Germans and Irish, a smattering of young working types, but no women. "No women served at bar" is the cry of Phoenix's barkeep, but what he really means to say is "No women served." One or two gargantuan elderesses may be seen at a side table, but they are so sexless as to be exceptions to the rule. A fiftyish waitress with acrylic hair serves spillover patrons at sturdy formica-top tables to the rear of Phoenix, but key positions are clearly at the oak front bar. A twelve-ounce mug of Hudepohl light (Cincinnati's finest) may be had there for an astonishing twenty-five cents and conversation is of course bizarre. There is an Art Deco back bar at Phoenix (since the thirties) with a steamboat lantern at its center and customary paddle fans overhead. A pressed tin ceiling caps the whole—as smoke-stained and greasy as an old gent's smile. Phoenix's scarred wooden floor is cluttered, with cuspidors full to overflowing. There is a raucousness to the old saloon which is alarming; Cincinnati oldsters don't look like they'd generate that kind of commotion, but Queen City in her dotage is no maiden aunt, and the old boys like to howl. Antiquated jazz selections, such as "Woodchopper's Ball," crowd Phoenix's juke, with polkas and sentimental ballads in attendance, all kept at high volume. A mining camp atmosphere prevails at Phoenix, more like a Butte, Montana, saloon than the last gasp of a withering Porkopolis. Yet Phoenix's fear factor is negligible: Old geezers in white beards and gray fedoras pulled rakishly over an eye, grungy decor, colored lights, brassy waitresses, folks conversing passionately, jukebox on fire . . . all adding up to a hit of smoky warmth and a hint of recollection in an otherwise unremarkable American downtown.

Jack Abrams Café
824 Elm Street, Cincinnati

Both Phoenix and Jack Abrams cafés are "poor man's clubs" in the classic tradition of nineteenth-century saloon life: A man does his work, goes home to dinner, then slips to his corner bar for an evening of relaxation with mates. Or, if retired, he starts early. Alone. One tippler may prefer the bustle of Phoenix . . . shoulder to shoulder, haunch to haunch guzzling . . . another the absolute order of Jack Abrams Café, where a white-aproned waiter never stops straightening, and the strangest commotion is from a tote-along TV.

Jack Abrams is Porkopolis's epitome of a clean well-lighted place; there is not a salt shaker or beer coaster out of synch, and the joint is *clean*. A large draft and Jack Daniels on the rocks comes to eighty cents, and if you can beat that price anywhere in this country, wire me collect. Hudepohl draft is served, well-chilled and properly tapped. Drinks are more than generous. An overweight bartender, himself in floor-length apron, serves patrons via Abrams' waiter. Both men look to be in their seventies, and clientele varies in age from mid-twenties to the nearly embalmed. "Your idea of a great bar," a companion fumed, "is a roomful of old men talking to themselves and peeing in their pants." A certain truth to that remark. But where an old man can feel comfortable, *anyone* can feel good; where an old man does not complain exists a peaceful spot.

A lovely Exposition-style back bar, of the St. Louis school, encircles the mirror at Abrams. Eighty years old, at least. An AFL-CIO "Union House" tag dangles haphazardly from one of the back bar's medallions. An old wooden front bar serves whatever patrons wish to stand or sit astride ancient stools. Formica tables, scrupulously polished, serve whoever wishes to sit. Or is unable to stand.

Jack Abrams opens early—boxes of Rice Krispies are for sale behind the bar—and closes late enough for the oldest insomniac. Some food is served: chili, sandwiches, wurst. A sign over the steam tray reads:

OH YES

MR. OLSON

DRINKS

OUR COFFEE.

Oldsters hack and fart into the night, younger clients such as myself, sip Abrams's cheapest of drinks and muse; about order, warmth, the ache of a restless spirit which no single room can appease.

Tony Packo's

Corner of Front and Consaul Streets, Toledo

Humble Toledo is the second largest port on the Great Lakes and ninth in the Nation, with thirty-five miles of natural harbor along Lake Erie and the Maumee River. Teeming one imagines, with high-class nautical saloons. In truth, it is difficult to find *any* high-class saloons at Toledo, except for those along Front Street on the southeast side of the river: Ship'n Shore, Seatime, others of their ilk, seedy and uninspiring, but with classic any-port-in-a-storm vitality.

Amongst these, on a cold corner facing Craig Memorial Bridge, is Tony Packo's—a cocky Hungarian joint which has blossomed since its founding in 1932, into a Toledo tradition and something of a gastronomical landmark. It's not the Falstaff on tap, at seventy-five cents a twelve-ounce glass, which grabs you at Packo's, nor is it Dixieland music on weekends (no cover, no formalities, just a good semi-pro band) . . . it's Packo's heavyduty sandwiches and blue plate specials: stuffed cabbage, pickerel, Hungarian sausage, frogs' legs, ham baked in wine, "Tony's Wife's Homemade Chili," vegetable soup with Hungarian dumplings, strudel, and the "World Famous Hungarian Hot Dogs."

It's those dogs which nearly got me in trouble. Rolls, actually. Interior design at Packo's is fairly standard for a thirties saloon—Art Deco front and back bar, stained-glass insets, a large mirror, booths, checkered tablecloths, paddle fans, old Wurlitzer, a modicum of 1930s formica, some nice wooden cabinets underneath the back bar with silver dollar medallions, antique memorabilia, pressed tin ceiling, player piano, Victorian statues over the back bar and cut glass doors out front—but a side partition is lined with what appear to be small wooden drawers, similar to those found in the card catalogue of any large library. I had been conducting research along Front Street for a good part of that afternoon, and I'd had a few drinks. For the life of me I couldn't figure out what a Dewey decimal system was doing in Tony Packo's Hungarian Saloon. It was necessary to climb over several anxious patrons, seated in booths beneath Packo's card catalogue, before I could unravel the puzzle. Packo's card catalogue was a series of autographed hot dog rolls, horizontally arranged on brown formica plaques, all in a row, the length of the partition. Tony's "World Famous Hot Dog" rolls had been autographed by any number of show business characters; including Tony Randall, Jack Klugman, Louis Jourdan, Pat Paulson, and Hubert Humphrey. A letter of thanks from Burt Reynolds was framed and hanging not far from the hot dog collection. *Can't wait to get back to Tony Packo's and Toledo,* Reynolds had written, or something to that effect. "Tony attracts the show business crowd," a waitress explained. "Lot of summer stock around Toledo, and these people ain't got no real place to go."

There is something of a show business atmosphere to Packo's, though on a basic Toledo level. If Packo's is Toledo's answer to Marti's in New Orleans, or Roy's Place in Gaithersburg, it is still very much a Toledo saloon. Neighborhood blacks wander in and out, some not even bothering to sit, but purchasing food at the take-out counter—as blacks carry home seafood at Gordon's in Baltimore. A young crowd is comfortable at Packo's, as are well-dressed, middle-aged swingers. The place has a goodtime frontier atmosphere. It is not overly expensive. A Jack Daniels on the rocks was a dollar-fifteen, and ladies' cocktails varied from a dollar-thirty to a dollar-ninety. Sandwiches ranged from a buck twenty-five to two dollars. A pitcher of Falstaff could be had for three seventy-five, and a plethora of pitchers was circulating that Saturday evening.

Packo's, despite its virtues, seems headed for a self-consciousness which may prove disconcerting in future years: Tony Packo mugs are already for sale, as are records of the Packo band. A certificate of appreciation from Toledo's Chamber of Commerce hangs next to the bar, and that is an inauspicious sign. Still, Tony Packo's is the afterhours action in Toledo, well worth a saloon hopper's time on any Great Lakes tour.

MARYLAND

Peabody Bookshop and Beer Stube
913 North Charles Street, Baltimore

Peabody is located near once fashionable Mount Vernon Place, a few yards from Peabody Conservatory of Music, Walters Art Gallery, and Baltimore's George Washington Monument. Peabody is one of the three Great American Bars situated in the shadow of a Washington monument—other two being Old South Mountain Inn at Boonsboro, and Old Ebbitt Grill at Washington, D.C. Peabody, upon first glance, seems nothing more than a musty second-hand bookshop of the type commonly seen about college neighborhoods before proliferation of the paperback. Indeed, Peabody's roots are in another small bookshop once located on Centre Street behind Peabody Conservatory. Hugo Weisberger, a Viennese, founded this shop in 1912. Not until 1919 did Weisberger move to the basement of a mid-nineteenth century, red brick row house, Peabody's present digs. Siegfried Weisberger, Hugo's brother and a seaman, came ashore about this time and began refitting Peabody's carriage house for the sale of spirits. As this was during Prohibition, entranceway to the old carriage house at the rear of Hugo's bookshop was camouflaged by a revolving bookcase. Liquor was served in tea cups. By 1923, Siegfried's beer stube was a popular trysting spot, attracting likes of the redoubtable H. L. Mencken. In 1933 when Prohibition was repealed, the Weisbergers decided to maintain things *status quo*, uniting beer stube and bookshop under one flag.

Hugo died in 1935, but Siegfried Weisberger ran both bookshop and beer stube until 1954, when he retired. Siegfried is still alive. Charlie Lancaster, Peabody's current manager, describes Siegfried as cordial but aloof, reluctant at age eighty-one to reveal details of Peabody's early operation. Siegfried "affects a bushy mustache, and resembles Albert Schweitzer," Charlie says. Siegfried is largely responsible for the character of Peabody, an establishment that has changed very little since his day.

During Prohibition, a patron either knew enough to push through Siegfried's revolving bookcase or he did not; Siegfried is not remembered to have encouraged pre-Repeal tippling in perfect strangers. Today, Siegfried's bookcase is long gone and the dimly lit passageway is crowded with extra tables and chairs, a dog's water dish, and scores of photographs. Numerous celebrities have visited the old speakeasy. Peabody has been conscientious to photograph as many as possible: Jack Palance is pictured seated at Peabody's upright piano, a bemused expression on his face. Mickey Mantle, Whitey Ford, Gil McDougald, and assorted Yankees crowd about a side table; Dustin Hoffman mugs, Godfrey Cambridge grins maniacally; Mitch Miller, Peter Ustinov, and others cavort at back tables with soppy abandon.

The beer stube itself is a cantilever-roofed affair, about the size of a garage. An upright piano sits to the left as one enters past the kitchen, flanked by ten or twelve modest tables with accompanying chairs. Both tables and chairs are vintage, initialed by generations of Peabody topers. A caribou head hangs over a wide fireplace, where of an afternoon in winter, a fire is kept burning. Pictures of every description clutter the walls; busts crowd the shelves, a pair of ballet slippers dangles from a chandelier, sheet music for singalongs is stacked on a rear table, illustrations from period magazines such as *Smart Set* hang here and there, joined by more than one photograph of H. L. Mencken. Walls are pine paneled but so damaged with soot and dinge that their nature is nearly indecipherable. Beer Stube's clientele runs to regulars: students from Peabody, Johns Hopkins, or Maryland; professors, seamen, or businessfolk from older sections of town. They congregate nightly in Peabody's dim clutter, dining on eight-ounce T-bones, crab cakes, knockwurst . . . sipping a variety of potations and studying the inimitable Dantini, who performs his magic each evening at ten, twelve on weekends.

Dantini is an eightyish gentleman with flowing gray hair and a belt-length beard, who was born in Fells Point, Baltimore (of Polish parents), but who left home at sixteen to seek out Houdini in New York and learn secrets of the magic trade. Houdini is said to have instructed Dantini. The young Baltimorean soon found work and for many seasons was a staple on America's vaudeville circuit, touring with a troupe of twenty magicians. Dantini has appeared regularly at Peabody for over a decade, never failing to amuse beer stube clientele with his performances. After Chinese rings, scarf, card, and golf ball tricks, the turbaned master passes a silver plate for contributions. It is a rare evening when he fares poorly, even with regulars who have seen his act a hundred times.

The bulk of Peabody's entertainment is provided by customers themselves however, who delight in singing to the rickety piano of

Professor Eddy Mitnick, another octogenarian who has been playing around Baltimore since 1914. Professor Eddy got his start accompanying silent movies and still may be coaxed into backing up an occasional decrepit film, shown on an overhead screen at a rear corner. Mostly though, he plays an outrageously out-of-synch medley of standards which are joyously sung along to by Peabody's enthusiasts. The whole act is so off the wall it is not even corny; jaded veterans of a thousand singalong bars relax and give in to this chaos readily. In Baltimore, people always seem to be singing in saloons. One recalls that Francis Scott Key composed much of "The Star-Spangled Banner" in a Baltimore tavern, and set his verses to the tune of a popular drinking song.

Rose Pettus, Peabody's current owner, added an upstairs room in 1969 which offers entertainment of a different bent: folk singers, serious pianists, trios, that sort of thing. But nothing formal. The upstairs room is just as cluttered with memorabilia, and nearly as consoling. There is a bar, plus more spacious seating arrangements. Rose Pettus took over Peabody in 1957, having bought it from Josephine Birmingham Adler, an Englishwoman who acquired it from Siegfried Weisberger in 1954. Mrs. Adler, upon first visiting Peabody as a minor, was carded by Siegfried and refused service. "Can't imagine why you're treating me this way," Mrs. Adler is supposed to have said. "Someday I shall own this tavern." Rose Pettus, of Armenian heritage, had traveled to Baltimore from Virginia as a girl, and had obtained work as a waitress in Little Italy; she was fired after two weeks' service in a restaurant there for innocently going out with customers. Her subsequent association with Peabody has been gracious and fruitful. The old speakeasy has prospered while changing in character very little.

The bookshop section of Peabody is not fake, nor has it been since its establishment. Customers spend many hours browsing through old volumes, some of which are quite valuable. Peabody has always bought and sold a great many books; Hugo Weisberger operated a branch on Monument Street near Johns Hopkins Hospital which specialized in medical texts. Today, a goodly amount of antiquish junk has been added to Peabody's stock, and the bookshop does a fair trade in gewgaws. Work of Baltimore artists is displayed. Charlie Lancaster, manager of both bookshop and beer stube, came to Peabody in 1969. Charlie had frequented the place as a customer for years. Scion of an old St. Mary's County family, Charlie had worked as a commercial fisherman, was in fact president of a lower

Chesapeake Bay commercial fisherman's association when Rose asked him to take over Peabody's bookshop. "Rose's regular manager was sick," Charlie remembers, "had been for some time. I was passing through Baltimore on my way down from New York. Rose said why don't you try it for a few days; here I am six years later." Like Siegfried before him, Charlie had come ashore after a varied life in the maritime. Charlie is a tall, bearded fellow with a bookish air and a sailor's gait, who looks completely at home in the old bookshop. "Enlisted in the Coast Guard when I was seventeen," Charlie expounds. "Stayed in for some years, then took a B.A. in history. Had a variety of teaching offers but decided to fish. Spent a good deal of time around Gulf Coast waters. Shucked oysters in New Orleans, old Half Shell Bar. Was a nine-a-minute man; one fellow we had there could shuck fourteen. And oysters down south are difficult to open. Don't freeze up like Chesapeake oysters, which means their musculature never relaxes. Commercial fishing—we took a little bit of everything. Suppose I was ready to come ashore though. This job has been a decidedly pleasant experience." Charlie, more than Rose or others of the current staff, sets Peabody's tone. He more than anybody seems in lineal descent from Siegfried and Hugo Weisberger.

Prices at Peabody have been kept down, in some instances to nearly Prohibition level: fifty cents a draft during the day, seventy-five after eight, with drinks a dollar to a dollar and a half. Pastries are available for seventy-five cents, as are assorted cheeses at one dollar. Peabody's T-bone is a best buy at two forty-nine. Sandwiches of salami, ham, braunschweiger, knockwurst, sardine, and crab cake are all under two dollars. The old speakeasy is not a bad place to plan on having dinner; it is a must for afternoon or after-hours tippling.

Helen's

Thames Street at Broadway (Fells Point), Baltimore

Helen's waterfront saloon is so close to the harbor that a departing patron is often startled to find his passage blocked by the rusted belly of some Norwegian freighter, moored yards away. Jacob Bochenski, Helen Christopher's father, bought the old saloon in 1915 when Fells Point was still referred to as Sailor Town. Seamen from all over the world jammed Fells Point's waterfront hotels, hiring its prostitutes and drinking in its fancy saloons. Helen's was founded in 1900 and its Exposition-style back bar, large mirror and mahogany front were well known by the time Bochenski acquired them. Fells Point had been a ship building center since its establishment in 1726. Baltimore became famous for its broad-hulled clipper ships manufactured at Fells Point; warehouses and ship chandlers' offices dotted the neighborhood, and commerce was everywhere afoot. America's first warship, the *U.S. Frigate Constellation*, was built at Fells Point, as were 600 other ships between 1726 and the Civil War. Both World Wars effected booms, and the old neighborhood was kept bustling until 1968 when a world-wide decline in shipping saw a blunting of the Point. Vacated buildings and lower rents coaxed artists to the area, and many old saloons were refurbished to accommodate fresher clientele. A mid-seventies boom is currently underway; lower Broadway is once again Baltimore's liveliest night district, lined with hotspots, most of which have been redone with flair, if not decorum. In the midst of this new insanity rest numerous pre-Prohibition saloons which remain virtually unchanged.

A white granite step before Helen's is tiled with the name of Jacob Bochenski and the date, 1916. Helen's short mahogany bar, with matching side cabinets, is situated to the right as one enters. Helen's back bar, framing a ten-foot mirror, is of some stained veneer and hung with Victorian lamps, all original. Front bar is worn but still handsome. A brass trough runs the length of its foot, reminder of days when plumbing was less bother. A pressed tin ceiling overhead; clippings concerning Fells Point about the walls. A nineteen-forties AMI jukebox of ornate design fills a far corner. Gene Krupa's "After You've Gone," Al Jolson's "Back in Your Own Backyard," Jimmy Dorsey's "So Rare," plus assorted tunes from the bands of Duke Ellington, Harry James, and Buddy Clark are but a few of the old juke's selections. Plain wooden chairs and two or three tables crowd Helen's rear wall. It is a small barroom, quiet but for the yapping of a tiny dog, and eminently peaceful. Drinks are sensibly priced: fifty cents for most bottle beers, seventy-five cents for bar whisky. Seamen and Port Authority workers frequent Helen's, but in the evening a younger crowd predominates. Helen's venerable mahogany accepts all of it stoically.

"I was offered four thousand dollars for that bar during World War Two," Helen comments. "Who knows what I could get for it today?"

Zieppies Five Point Tavern
Thames Street at Ann (Fells Point), Baltimore

During salad days of Sailor Town, Zieppies operated as the down-stairs bar of a waterfront hotel which sported a twelve-foot electric flag on its roof—visible for miles· around Baltimore Harbor. What the hell is that, sailors would wonder upon docking, and beeline for the gaudy bait. Zieppies' statuesque fixtures and fair prices never let them down; and the old barroom managed to acquire something of a reputation in a neighborhood sodden with exquisite saloons. Today, oldtimers lounge about Zieppies swilling coffee, eating fresh hard-boileds or sipping the first of the afternoon. Zieppies' mahogany bar set, fashioned by Ruse and Company of Baltimore some one hundred years ago, provides a modicum of order to the old seamen's day. Mahogany, though marred, is finely crafted in a Romanesque style with embossed filigree, fat columns, wide arches and a gener-ous expanse of plate glass. Matched side cabinets flank it, stocked with Copenhaver snuff and oddments of the maritime trade. Blue-water men still frequent Zieppies' old saloon, as do pilots, river cap-tains, and tugboaters; they may be observed relaxing at comfortable side tables beneath pictures of merchant ships. After supper, locals from the largely Polish neighborhood drift in; they are joined by art-ists, tourists, and whoever else happens to be at the Point. A quarter will buy you three polkas on Zieppies' jukebox, or a game of eight ball. Herbert Zientak, in partnership with his brother Leonard, has owned Zieppies for the past twenty-five years. Things have changed very little in that time: a masonry façade was added during the fif-ties, Zieppies' bar trough was covered to provide a footrest, and the price of beer jumped once or twice. But not drastically. Draft Na-tional Bo sells for thirty cents a glass, Bud for fifty-five. Bar drinks hover around sixty-five cents. Zieppies during daylight hours has a more comfortable air to it than most Fells Point barrooms. Its situa-tion at a northeast corner overlooking the harbor provides it with good afternoon light. Old seamen huddle at tables toward Zieppies' front, as close to sunlight and bustle as they can get. Herb Zientak maintains a lively patter, pulling beer and hawking half pints from behind the counter. For these and other kindnesses, the old men seem grateful.

Other noteworthy saloons near the foot of Broadway in Fells Point are: Pete's Hotel Bar, Chios Greek Tavern, Waterfront Hotel Bar, River Drive Inn, Leadbetter's (liveliest of all afterhours), plus ten or fifteen more. On weekends, patrons spill out onto sidewalks and the old bohemian neighborhood enjoys a carnival atmosphere redolent of the sixties. Broadway Market is jammed, restaurants and raw bars are busy, art galleries and bookstalls overflow . . . the place is a gold mine of chaos, not to be skipped.

Capt'n Sam Bailey's
Route 520, River Springs

Capt'n Sam's is a crabhouse and oysterman's bar on White Neck Creek, near the mouth of the Wicomico River, in a sector of St. Mary's County virtually unchanged since the seventeenth century. Capt'n Sam's was founded in 1880 by Captain Kenelm Cheseldine, who erected a bar and general store on ground already used for centuries by Mattepany Indians as a trading site. Cheseldine was a shipwright renowned for his sturdy Chesapeake Bay schooners and skipjacks, so that he took this knowledge to the construction of his bar. The twenty-four by thirty-two-foot building he erected withstood hurricanes and high water until 1949, when it was destroyed by fire. Captain Matt Bailey had bought the old bar from Cheseldine in 1903, and had operated it virtually unchanged in function and design until 1949. After the fire, Bailey's son-in-law Raynor Blair purchased the business and rebuilt the old tavern, adding a restaurant and restoring the pier Sam Bailey had constructed.

Today, Capt'n Sam's is slightly more genteel than in its pre-fire days, but a similar raft of oystermen congregates in the plain barroom, swilling draft beer at thirty cents a glass and warming their insides with Bailey's marvelous crab soup. Capt'n Sam's pier hosts one or two disreputable-looking gas pumps, and in summer a few tourist boats can be seen docked before the bar. White Neck Creek and its neighboring rivers were the scene of oyster wars during the latter part of the nineteenth century, when dredgers from the Eastern Shore pirated Southern Maryland waters, and police boats hunted the trespassers with guns and nooses. Captain Douglas Russell was one of the legendary figures around the old tavern, a vigilante oysterman who nearly always got his man. Nautical skirmishes could be observed from the back room at Capt'n Sam's upon many a slow afternoon, and the cry "Fetch the glasses" was the signal that action was brewing on the creek. Captain Sam Bailey himself was skipper of the notorious *Mattie Dean*—a balsawood model of which can be seen today behind the back bar.

Seafood is fantastic at Capt'n Sam's and quite inexpensive. Drinks are cheap, and if you want a feel of old Southern Maryland and the best of lower Potomac and Chesapeake Bay seafood, less than two hours south of Baltimore, Bailey's is the bar to hit.

Duffy's
Route 5, Point Lookout, St. Mary's County

The highway ends at Duffy's. It breaks off into the Chesapeake Bay in great jagged chunks of concrete and macadam, and there is Duffy's. The shoreline before the old saloon is crowded with wrecks of automobiles and trucks: Engine blocks, frames, axles, cabs of models you have not seen since you were a child. This is Duffy's breakwater. For years the State promised Duffy a seawall, but they have never come through. You can sit at Duffy's big bayside window and watch waves break back and forth over the engine blocks, and there is a certain poetry to it. Duffy's is the last bar on the last point of land in this part of Maryland. Hotels have come and gone, rental cabins, beach concessions, all washed into the bay, their foundations eroded by time and an incessant pounding of waves. Duffy's has endured.

God knows, Point Lookout is a desolate enough spot. In winter, whitecaps and wind blow off Chesapeake with gale force, covering the highway, eating away at the land. The point itself is a series of marshes and sandbars, never intended for habitation by man. In summer, both temperature and humidity reach the hundred-degree mark, and mosquitoes are heavy as napalm. The Union Army manned a prison facility at Point Lookout, during the Civil War, which was said to have rivaled Andersonville in terror and squalor. Over 3,000 prisoners of war died at Point Lookout, most of them from exposure and beatings. There are two monuments to Confederate dead at the site of the old prison, one erected by the Federal

Government, one by the state of Maryland. Neither is so eloquent a testament to the spirit of Point Lookout as Duffy's, nor a more fitting remembrance of those prisoners who survived.

For survival is what Duffy's is about. It's a ramshackle place, extending in several directions, with rickety appendages which don't look as if they'd weather a heavy rain, let alone Point Lookout's winter. Yet Duffy's has been a bar since the twenties. Mr. Duffy is a fat old man in a tent-sized Hawaiian sportshirt, who is constantly tinkering with physical artifacts of the establishment. Mr. Duffy possesses a waistline suggestive of his irregular breakwater—lumps like engine blocks or discarded clock radios protruding from beneath his shirt. Mrs. Duffy is likewise fattish, around sixty years old and darkhaired, with an Ace bandage on one ankle. Neither of the old couple looks much more sturdy than the barroom; still, they persevere year after year, running Duffy's more as a labor of love than for financial reward. They sleep in a crowded apartment toward the rear of the building, so that their overhead is not outrageous. The backbone of Duffy's clientele is local, with some tourists in summertime, a few fishermen, and campers. In the old hotel days, music and dancing were the order every Saturday night. But the ballroom at the back of Duffy's is closed, used only for an occasional crabfeast. The Duffys ran a rental cottage business until the Chesapeake swept it away. So the old bar is all that's left.

ICE

BREAKFAST

SANDWICHES

AND

DINNERS

a chalked-over blackboard reads, outside Duffy's front entrance. The old screen door rattles as you open it, and precaution must be taken not to pull it off its hinges. Mr. Duffy is on his knees before an ancient Wurlitzer, examining twenty-year-old Teresa Brewer discs and the apparatus which is supposed to make them spin. Mrs. Duffy is sweeping out, but she offers a cold can of Gunther for forty cents and a stool before Duffy's hand-fashioned bar. "The paneling we got from Point Lookout Hotel," Mrs. Duffy explains. "It was on the bay side from here. All that land's gone now. They had to tear it down and we bought the paneling. My, but there were times at that hotel. We had some business then." Duffy's front bar is faced in rough pine, and paneling from Point Lookout Hotel has been tacked up around the barroom. Old straw hats, steerhorns, bric-a-brac, non-specific beach junk hangs from the ceiling. A collection of cute signs and sayings lines Duffy's back bar. The entire room is crowded with churlish artifacts; the Duffys are like a pair of childish packrats, hoarding everything they find which amuses them, eventually hanging it in Duffy's for display. Drinks are cheap at Duffy's, and booze-to-go is for sale. Food is good, Chesapeake specialties such as crab-cake sandwiches prepared by Mrs. Duffy herself. Salt and pepper is served in Rolling Rock pony bottles with pin holes poked through the caps. Every so often in summer, the Duffys will relent and hire a band—some maudlin local group with a female singer and two electric guitarists chording, neither with energy enough to pick a single string lead.

But geography and interior design are perennially the attractions at Duffy's. There is a Barthian feel to this part of Southern Maryland, and one can only think of *Floating Opera* or *End of the Road* when sitting at Duffy's bayfront window, sipping a Gunther, eavesdropping on farmers and crabbermen, and gazing at an inexorable tide washing over breakwater wreckage of a true end of the road saloon.

Zanzibar

501 South Baltimore Street, Ocean City

Zanzibar is situated in Ocean City's oldest building, around the corner from Rayne's Store, a small bentwood teashop and restaurant, reminiscent of a nineteenth-century ice-cream parlor. Although far from bentwood, Zanzibar retains a comparable atmosphere, minus tea cups and sweets. Plus, of course, booze. JR Truitt, Zanzibar's proprietor and retired charter-boat mate, runs to the sauce himself and his coterie of commercial fishermen, off-duty deepwater guides, and heavy equipment operators speaks eloquently for Ocean City's roots as an eighteen-seventies boomer. Zanzibar is open year-round; one is as likely to see the same faces in March as in June. The old barroom is kept cool in summer and toasty warm in winter. Tourists inflict modest damage during summer months, but nothing like a spoilage. JR and friends are too hipped on their own highfalutin to permit that.

A silver-capped marlin bill from a three hundred and two pound blue is tacked up behind JR's back bar. JR caught it. Pictures of various launches JR has worked are displayed about the barroom. One shows JR in the company of Governor Marvin Mandel, a sizable marlin between them. "Governor caught that one, and one more t'other time we went," JR says. "He ain't caught no more since. I told him, Governor, better pull on that fish if you want it, you ain't up t'Annapolis signing papers." Grouper, blue marlin and other fish hang about Zanzibar's walls. Prints of ships add to JR's collection of nautical memorabilia. Couple of tidewater folks wearing International Harvester caps pitch darts over by the jukebox. A canoe paddle marked REST ROOMS points the way. A touch of fishnet is displayed overhead. Located several blocks from Ocean City's charter boat docks, Zanzibar is the tippler's logical choice.

An icy Bud draft may be had for sixty cents, Jack Daniels on the rocks for a dollar twenty-five. Bar stock goes for ninety cents a shot. A handsome formica counter is maintained by an efficient barmaid who fields fishermen's jokes good naturedly. Little formica table and chair sets are placed at comfortable intervals about the room. JR slaps a back and lurches into another story about his days as a Cape Hatteras guide. The old barroom is remarkably peaceful. John Denver strikes up from the juke, "Gee, it's good to be back home again . . ." The bustle of contemporary Ocean City is for a moment lost as JR's clientele impatiently calls for another.

Staub's Lunch
Corner Routes 109 and 28, Beallsville

Staub's is a crossroads country store (between Monacacy Cemetery and a filling station) which serves Beallsville and outlying acres as post office, Western-wear emporium, restaurant, and beer parlor. It was founded in 1925 by the father of the current owner. In the twenty years that I have stopped at Staub's it has not changed one bit, and probably never has. The same polished wooden tables are in evidence, the same bentwood ice-cream chairs, the same fieldstone fireplace burning constantly in winter. When I was a boy, we would lunch at Staub's during hunting trips up into the country, my father and his friends drinking beer at the short counter, me eating hamburgers and ice cream before a stuffed turkey and deer's head with a red Christmas tree ball on his nose, situated over Staub's mantelpiece. It was a cheery country atmosphere which has lingered into the seventies—threatened by an insurgence of middleclass developers and entrepreneurs of the impending megalopolis—but so far untainted by their presence.

Mr. Staub is a lean fellow in his forties, bearing an uncanny resemblance to pianist Mose Allison. Mr. Staub's hair is dark, his mustache salt and pepper, and he affects a Western air shored up by cowboy boots from his store's selection, stockman's pants and slash-pocketed, snap-cuffed shirts. Staub's ancestors were wheelwrights who settled near Beallsville in the eighteenth century. Hard-working people, whom Staub emulates in his triple role as postmaster, short order chef, and bartender. There is a gas pump outside the old store, and Staub even takes a hand at that. The town of Beallsville has a ghostly quality—Darby's Store sits vacant across Route 28, its empty shelves, tall windows, and stark Victorian façade a grim portent—quickly relieved by a step inside Staub's lunchroom.

On any given day, hunters, fishermen, country lawyers and physicians, laborers, farmers, farm women, and daytrippers can be seen at Staub's old counter or before the fieldstone fireplace. Beer is cheap at forty cents, and food, though not of the quality of Titus's Tasty Cupboard in neighboring Poolesville, is adequate and eagerly prepared by Mr. Staub himself. Whisky is not served, nor is wine. Beer is sold to go . . . but liquid provender is not really what Staub's is about. It's a quiet goodtime place, with a country music jukebox and friendly clientele who depend upon Staub's for vital services. The mood is of vanishing America; specifically that era when carriages changed to motor cars, and gasoline joined beer and bacon as necessary commodities at the corner market.

Red Fox Inn

4940 Fairmont Avenue, Bethesda

Red Fox has hosted some of the finest bluegrass musicians in the country, and continues to be Bethesda's best shot for bluegrass entertainment on a nightly basis. It's an informal spot, with tables and stage up front, formica bar and pool table toward the rear. There is a cover charge of two dollars most nights, but Monday is free, with hootenanny entertainment sponsored by the Washington Folklore

Society. Mondays are favorite evenings at the Fox, because of the absolute variety of entertainment that stumbles across the stage. It's not just a teenager's hoot, though teenagers are welcome, but a professional's opportunity to showcase new material. The most satisfying musical experiences of a Washington week can be had at the Fox on Mondays, so don't pass by what you might deem to be a corny inclusion in a "serious" schedule.

The Fox has featured bluegrass entertainment for at least ten years, and has been something of a Bethesda fixture much longer than that. My parents drank at Red Fox in the thirties and forties; it was a redneck local tavern then, with sailors from Bethesda Naval Hospital among the flotsam and jetsam. Although Red Fox has tried recently to upgrade its clientele into a dinner/music crowd, a stable of working locals still calls the old bar home. They can be seen any evening in Pepsi Cola jackets, American Oil coveralls, or old men's gabardines, usually lined up at the bar or clustered around the pool table, watching their fellows shoot. Music of the Rosslyn Mountain Boys, the Country Gentlemen, Seldom Scene, Mike Auldridge, Grass Menagerie, or Hickory Wind may be enthralling patrons toward Red Fox's front, but working locals will be conversing quietly or shooting pool among themselves. Not that the music clientele is a bunch of flighty intellectuals glomming the people's music; factions are blurred: one third freak, one third workingman, one third retirees and business folk.

Beer and wine is served at Red Fox, no liquor, and drinks tend to be slightly overpriced: ninety cents for a ten-ounce draft, three-sixty a pitcher (four twenty-five mixed with Guiness stout), and wine is a dollar-ten the glass, twenty cents more for wine cooler. Sandwiches are between two and three dollars, and some dinners are available. A fear factor is practically nonexistent.

The Red Fox moved from Wisconsin Avenue, near the old ice house, to its present location in 1962 or '63—current owner, Walt Broderick, is not sure which. Walt has had Red Fox since 1971, and it is his perseverance which has made the establishment a musical success. People come from all around the Washington area to hear Walt's bluegrass. "We're a Beltway bar," Walt says, "with a majority of our clientele from Montgomery County and Northwest Washington." Which is not to downgrade hardcore Bethesda locals, who continue to lounge near Red Fox's pool table, lending the venerable tavern much of its old Bethesda character. Bethesda has been transformed, over the past twenty years, from a quiet suburban village to another vestige of the urban megalopolis. Red Fox (with McDonald's Raw Bar, Bethesda Crab House, and Trav's Inn—Glen Echo) is what's left of old Bethesda, and Metropolitan Washington is less dreadful for its survival.

VIRGINIA

Hillbilly Heaven
Route 1, Woodbridge

Hillbilly Heaven is a country music dance hall in the hurdy-gurdy tradition of all frontier societies where men outnumber the women, and a pretty girl is something to be shared. In early days of the American West, hurdy-gurdies existed without women, and whiskered miners in calico dress would dance all night with their boozy mates as blushing belles of the ball. Later, when camp girls arrived, hurdy-gurdies charged a silver dollar a dance and got it—miners lined twenty or thirty deep for a spin around the floor. This spirit of share-and-share-alike, which, in theory, promised order and insured profit for the establishment, is extant at Hillbilly Heaven, where country gentlemen ask for a dance with cotillion-like formality, and retire when the music has stopped with reluctant aplomb.

But:

There is the loudest goddam country music you ever heard at Hillbilly Heaven, plus the gaggingest collection of greasers, plowboys, bouffant waitresses, and farmwives, all jelly-bopping and love-hunching about Heaven's premises every Friday and Saturday night until two a.m. The place is jammed; there is a twenty-foot dance floor, surrounded by two tiers of tables and a plywood bandstand which threatens to collapse as the big beat quickens.

First time I visited Hillbilly Heaven, I ran into a little housewife named Ginger who got me so wiped out on cough syrup I had to enjoin my TWA friend Stoney to pilot me back to D.C. at a hundred m.p.h. along drunk-congested Route One. Ginger, like most girls at Hillbilly Heaven, had humped me on our first dance like she'd known me all her life, then retired discreetly to her table once the song had finished. I'd incurred a good deal of wrath from share-her boys when I followed, but at that time I wasn't aware of how the game was played. You hugdance from the hip at Hillbilly Heaven, your partner stuck to you tighter than Saran Wrap; you rub and nuzzle, and when the song stops you say so-long. Somebody else gets a shot. At the end of the evening, if you're lucky, you can cut something out.

There are a lot of military people at Hillbilly Heaven, from Fort

267

Belvoir and Quantico, and they get just as drunk as they possibly can, harassing country folk and generally making asses out of themselves. Hillbilly Heaven is the sort of tangentially military establishment where you wouldn't be surprised to find a recruiting sergeant in the men's room—card table beside the urinal, patriotic poster over the sink—offering fountain pens and urging re-ups as delirious soldiers vomit onto the wall. It usually costs two dollars to get into Hillbilly Heaven on weekends, and beers are seventy-five cents a can. The atmosphere is *carpe diem*, and nobody seems to be counting his pennies. Performers include Marcel Twitty: "Conway Twitty's Nephew" . . . and "Dolly Parton's Sister-in-Law," advertised as such on prominent signs outside the front door. Locals like "Miss Rocky Top," an obese vocalist whose favorite number is an Osborne Brothers hit of the same name, and "Cookie," a twelve-year-old who plays drums during intermission, are regularly featured. Hillbilly Heaven, as one might expect, has an extraordinary country jukebox, and Cookie plays along adeptly as an occasional couple sways to the recorded strains.

There used to be a wonderful bluegrass bar adjacent to Hillbilly Heaven, called Ruby's; but as of late, Ruby's has reverted to its old role of truck-stop café, and has dropped entertainment. In the early seventies, one might hear on any given evening: Bill Monroe, the Country Gentlemen, Osborne Brothers, Cliff Waldron, or the Grass Menagerie. When Ruby's closed, one could stagger across the parking lot to Hillbilly Heaven for some electric Nashville music. I treated Hunter and Sandy Thompson to Ruby's one evening in 1972, while Hunter was covering the presidential campaign for *Rolling Stone*, and Hunter declared it to be the only bar in Washington for which he felt affection. I was afraid to take Hunter into Hillbilly Heaven—but *Voice* editor Richard Goldstein once accompanied me there, and pronounced it "Amazing. I have never seen people act this way in my life."

And it *is* amazing. There exists at Hillbilly Heaven an energy reminiscent of hurdy-gurdy dance halls at their wildest; an energy unmatched by any establishment of the ilk that I have encountered. Hillbilly Heaven's beat, its volume, its country glitter, beer, and patrons . . . all add up to a genuine frontier experience, not to be missed by any bar person within a hundred miles of Washington, D.C.

Gatsby's

1300 East Cary Street, Richmond

Gatsby's is situated in the historic riverfront/tobacco warehouse district of Shockoe Slip, one of few restored neighborhoods in scarifying Richmond, and the only such dedicated to restitution of old bars. *Bar*, it should be stated categorically, as Gatsby's is sole survivor in original garb. Despite its rimjob moniker, Gatsby's is a genuine saloon complete with wooden booths, pressed tin ceiling, paddle fans, wood and glass cabinets, a marble raw bar, wooden front counter, and antique hairpin chairs. For years Gatsby's existed as Carl's, a corner dive which served warehousemen beer and fried-chicken sandwiches. It has been a saloon at least since Prohibition, probably before that.

Carl wouldn't recognize many of his old clientele today, but he'd be delighted to encounter Gatsby's slinky waitresses in floor-length white gowns . . . black cloths draping his scarred wooden tables, peacock feathers in slim vases, potted plants, and an all-out effort to render his pre-Pro saloon Art Deco as day after tomorrow. Carl's was already somewhat Art Deco, as chiaroscuro paneling on his wooden booths suggests. But nothing like the transformation of late.

Gatsby's is recently opened, and one can only wish the fledgling management well. Certainly Carl's old saloon deserves to be preserved, and should be as popularity of Shockoe Slip blossoms. Downtown Richmond reverts to Condition Ominous after five p.m. when a mass exodus shudders toward the vanilla suburbs. Shockoe Slip, with its cheerful saloons—Warehouse, Sam Miller Exchange in the old Richmond Grain Exchange, and J. W. Rayle further west on Cary—provides blessed solace.

Gatsby's offers a simple menu of prime ribs, New York strip, and kosher corned beef; but primary emphasis is on seafood from Virginia tidewaters. Cherrystone clams, oysters Christopher, Virginia oyster stew, fried oysters, stuffed shrimp, fried shrimp, and gumbo are listed, averaging about four dollars per portion. Cocktails are generous, if slightly overpriced: a mint julep is two dollars and fifty cents, but a Coke just twenty-five cents. Whisky hits the dollar-fifty mark, and Gatsby's pours only the best—Jack Daniels, Smirnoff, Cutty Sark—no cheapjack under-the-counter swill.

Fixtures at Gatsby's are worth your trip. Dinner is served late, drinks until small hours. A tonier spot in funky old Richmond you're not likely to tabulate.

Vienna Inn
120 Maple Avenue (Rt. 123), Vienna

The Vienna Inn is an antique frame building encased in brick, and broken, where cars have crashed into its façade from the parking lot. It's kind of a redneck soulfood joint, open six a.m. on weekdays, seven and nine on weekends. A workingman's bar. It's the last funky old Vienna hotspot on Route 123, and squats alongside plastic Ernesto's and Roy Rogers' food emporiums like an open sore.

Inside, tacky wooden booths are lined up like bus seats, with the Inn's menu and luncheon specials chalked on an overhead blackboard. A stand-up wooden bar serves customers on three sides of its rectangular space: jovial heavy-equipment operators in hooded sweatshirts and Red Wing boots, indifferent merchants studying classified ads and swilling cold Bud on tap for thirty-five cents a glass, and doubleknit CIA employees from headquarters in Langley or the secret, underground installation at Tysons Corner Mall. There is a modest fear factor at Vienna during slack hours, but at lunch and dinner the atmosphere is relaxed, even cordial. Cadaverous waitresses carry your food at a clip, and clear the table with dispatch once you have paid. There is a leisurely feel to Vienna's barroom, however, and customers may nurse a beer for hours without sensing pressure. An old-fashioned, sawdust shuffleboard game stands against a far wall, and a country juke with all the oldest hits is kept busy. Tables in the barroom are for lounging, and a group of eight or ten old men can usually be seen there passing afternoon hours. Pictures of football players—high school heroes and Washington Redskins—grace Vienna's walls, and there is a patriotic feel to the barroom. A bus leaves from Vienna Inn every Sunday during football season, for JFK Stadium and the Redskins' home games. Ex-jocks gone to pot can be found around the old bar on any afternoon, and in summer, young men in mustaches and sponsor's softball jerseys crowd the stools.

Pal Stoney and I used to lunch at Vienna—after long afternoons of drinking, eating, and chasing women into the sunset. There was usually a girl, a ketch on the Chesapeake, a point-to-point race, or bluegrass festival somewhere down the road. Vienna Inn was a convenient stopping point; more often than not it was our destination. You could not beat Vienna's draft beer for thirty-five cents, the fish sandwich for fifty, chili mac with onions and cheese for one-fifty, grilled pepper steak with two vegetables for one thirty-five, soft-shell crab or the kielbasa sandwich (Polish sausage) for sixty cents, and Vienna's homemade soups for thirty-five. Vienna Inn was open until midnight and served food until ten, so the hours were right. On early mornings coming back from the country, a ham and egg sandwich on rye toast with a frosty mug was just the ticket to start our day. For the girls there was "Bloody Marie," a special wine cooler at fifty-five cents.

The Vienna Inn has been in its present location longer than anyone cares to remember—owner Mike Abraham has been proprietor some fifteen years now. Last winter, Vienna's mayor proclaimed February 25 "Mike Abraham Day," issuing a citation which praised Mike for offering his establishment as refuge from plastic Vienna. The document has been framed and hangs proudly on a pillar at the center of the room, where Mike can keep an eye on it from behind his bar. The Inn has been known to host entertainment on weekends—shitkicker locals plucking bluegrass or lonesome Western ballads—but showtime has never been Vienna's forte. It's a quiet place during most hours, where one can get away from the jiveass hustle of Northern Virginia and remember when towns like Vienna were small Southern settlements on the road to Georgetown.

DISTRICT
OF COLUMBIA

Bill Bode's letter concerning the closing of Donnelly's in Iowa City, Iowa, reached me on the eve of our nation's Great Bicentennial:

. . . for us boys who frequented the bar, the closing (urban renewal demolishment) had been vaguely imminent for about a year and a half so it was only during the last week of its existence that the fact that there wouldn't actually *be* a Donnelly's anymore finally struck home. Harold Donnelly, who of course (besides the physical, aesthetic quality of his bar) was a main reason Donnelly's was so irreplaceable, had started to show a bit of the strain of knowing that the end was actually a reality. Harold was an authority figure who kept his bar on its no-fights, no beer-swilly bullshit keel. In the last couple of months he was ornery, would get drunk once in a while, which was an extreme rarity before. This isn't to say he started feeling sorry for himself. He just got a little more cantankerous. He always was a tough no-bullshit man. He just became a little quicker to react. The last week there was a definite feeling of knowing the end of a legitimate institution was at hand. Also there was the edge to it that we knew it wasn't his choice but the choice of absurd, nebulous business interests, which wanted to turn the downtown into some big plastic, futuristic shopping center. In a way there could be no saying good-bye to a man, his place, who was prepared to say that he was ready to stop the ten-to twelve-hour days, that he wanted to enjoy the relaxation of a gracious retirement. Perhaps he would never have done it that way, but for a man with as much character as he has, and his place had, it was rather unfortunate that it wasn't really in his hands to do it the way he wanted to. A quote from the last few weeks' graffiti on the men's can in Donnelly's by a fellow named Ray Burnhardt stated it sort of well—

> Roll on man in the moon roll on
> Roll on man in the moon roll on
>
> If ever I pass this spot
> And Donnelly's is an empty lot
> I'll know urban renewal's
> Done me wrong

—to the tune of the "Whiffenpoof Song." A bit more background to that quote is that after about three years of downtown demolishment everything is either a parking lot or just untouched lots.

Donnelly's closed on Monday, December 9 [1974], which was when Harold's beer license ran out. He could've stayed open a couple more weeks but it wasn't worth renewing the license. Friday and Saturday were both packed days-and-nights at Donnelly's. Saturday night, about forty of the younger regulars gave Harold an inscribed gold watch, and Charley (who had worked for twenty-six years as Harold's trusted lieutenant) a silver inscribed cordial and plate set. A big standing-on-the-bar-by-the-pool-table presentation. The final afternoon, Monday, a television station, KCRG Cedar Rapids, came in and interviewed both of them. It was on the six o'clock news. The last day the entire proceeds went to Charley as a parting bonus from Harold. The place was packed all day with regulars, plus people who had been in the place a few times. The place was a combination workingman, college poolplaying, intellectual talking bar. The supposed ending was when the beer ran out. Harold's son and daughters, one from California, and wife and Charley took care of handling the bar. Pictures were taken by quite a few people. Everyone was getting drunk and there was a feeling that the end was going to be morose. But at nine o'clock Harold closed the taps and then the whole crowd watched the ten o'clock news to see if the interview would be on. The last thing was everyone cheering when the TV showed Harold saying (politic as he was) what a great town and customers he'd had to work with. Ending jubilance. He handled it as a man of his character would.

Papers from Cedar Rapids, Davenport, Iowa City, and Des Moines carried stories on the closing. Donnelly's was an institution in their sense. However, basically, the bar was Harold's trip, and only people who knew him as the white-haired, proud man that he was understood how difficult it would be to replace what was so much an extension of him.

Most of us pool players went to another bar, not as pleasant aesthetically but as low-keyed. The final touch was a picture in the Iowa City *Press Citizen* showing Harold watching a huge bulldozer with a long unicorn-like probe tearing the building to rubble. He looked like he thought it was absurd but he could handle it. A final irony is that no one knows now—the way the economy is— whether federal urban renewal money will be available to put something in the hole which remains.

That's the end of Donnelly's as I remember it. It definitely was a bar worthy of a three-day, Dylan Thomas drunk.

PS: The old front and back bar set is in storage at Mount Vernon, a town about twenty miles north of here. Harold sold it to the owner of Bushnell's Turtle, a restaurant which is temporarily located in a module in Iowa City. If they ever get a permanent place built through urban renewal, they're going to set up the whole works in a new bar, presumably Bushnell's Turtle. . . .

It was cold in Washington, one of those bleak December twilights which kept tourists shut in hotel rooms and pigeons fluffed over cornices or tucked inside volutes of the city's more elaborate Victoriana. I had an appointment at Old Ebbitt Grill * to interview a retired chief bosun's mate named Herman Brody—a regular there before the 1850s mahogany since 1928. It was Herman Brody's custom to spend his evenings at Old Ebbitt, busing in each day from Prince George's County, then busing back out. Old Ebbitt's manager had told me of Herman, indicating he was considered a fixture about the place, as familiar to staff and clientele as Old Ebbitt's walrus or the Alexander Hamilton bear. Herman Brody was a gourmet chef who on Sundays would bus in entire feasts for the Old Ebbitt family. Today was Sunday. There had been no parking space before 1427 F, none below Washington Hotel on the Elipse, and I had been forced to stow my world-weary Volks in a PMI lot above Lafayette Square. As I passed the little building at 601 Fifteenth Street . . . old Rhodes Tavern, where Admiral Cockburn and General Ross had toasted the burning of Washington, August 14, 1814, and watched the White House fry . . . I noted that a souvenir shop had sequestered its ground floor, was doing a brisk business in Watergate T-shirts and eight-year-old Dump the Hump buttons. F Street further along was deserted. Old Ebbitt's brass epaulets flickered dully under exterior gas lanterns, and Garfinckel's next door looked as if it had never known a customer, let alone a friend.

Herman Brody was seated at the near corner of Ebbitt's bar, beneath a stuffed alligator. He was pug-nosed, round of face, and smoked a thin cigar. He wore a dark raincoat. A shopping bag crowded the floor between Ebbitt's brass rail and his feet. He seemed to be drinking gin. He was absolutely the last link, and I needed him desperately.

Old Ebbitt's manager introduced us and we turned quickly to a discussion of the saloon's past. Herman Brody spoke quietly; he was articulate. He had begun patronizing Old Ebbitt two years after its

* See Introduction, p. *xxi*.

move (1926). He remembered all the intervening owners and many of the staff: "A. R. Lofstrand was first proprietor here, a Swedish fellow who served heavy German-style food, hamburgers which he did up in hot dog rolls, delicious, also ten-cent soup, steamship rounds of beef, baked beans, and a glass of beer which sold for ten cents. It was near-beer all through Prohibition, but with Lofstrand's food you didn't mind. He'd been headwaiter at Ebbitt Hotel, had bought these fixtures when that establishment closed, and set up shop here. The floor at Ebbitt Hotel must have been raked, because, until recently, this bar was higher at one end than the other. I mean it was chest high. They rubbed it in those days, too. After 1970 with that change of management, they cut it down, sanded the top, and in my opinion ruined it.

"Old Lofstrand was a character. He invented things—one of the early dishwashing machines, and a soldier's crutch, that elbow crutch first used during World War II. He had a little shop here on the third floor. During the Depression you could eat for practically nothing at Old Ebbitt, and the food was good. Lofstrand retired in 1946 and sold the place to George Pappas. Pappas was partners with a notorious gambler named Buzzer Ryan, a bodyguard to Jimmy Fontaine who ran a big joint out near Bladensburg. A criminal lawyer named Charley Ford I think also was involved in that partnership. Pappas made no changes and carried everyone over, colored waiters, bartenders, and kept the same food. All Lofstrand's animal heads, his paneling, et cetera came originally from Ebbitt Hotel. Those sorts of fixtures were common in the 1870s. Pappas did add one thing, though—a fully rigged sailing ship, beautiful. It became too coated with grease finally, and they got rid of it.

"Contrary to what you may have heard, there never was gambling here. The place was owned by gamblers but they always were very careful not to let anything go on. Must have kept the place as a tax shelter. I don't know. But they kept it well.

"Were some great bartenders, too. One fellow I remember was a stonecutter at National Cathedral, also over at Immaculate Conception; a guy who made thousands a month, but who worked here in the evenings for sixty bucks a week. He just liked the place and he liked people. He was related to Pappas. There were other great ones: Buck, Smitty, a longtimer, Otto, a German fellow. I never knew them by anything but their first names. You understand I went to sea when I was fifteen—Merchant Marine, Coast Guard, Navy—so I was around only so often. I always tried to bring something back though. Over the years I brought back water jugs from the Amazon, carvings from East Africa, pressed butterfly wings, that photo there behind the bear, *Iron Men and Wooden Ships*. They'd display this stuff around the walls. Most of it's gone now. A Nazi helmet I brought back from Normandy invasion sat on that Walrus's head for, hell, twenty-five years. It's gone. You remember? Sort of made him look like the Kaiser, right? People got a kick out of that. I brought it in.

"Pete Bechas removed a lot, I think. Also Stuart Davidson, the current owner. Bechas took over from Pappas in 1960. He kept things the same at first, but by the time he'd lost it in 1970, he'd sold some stuff. Bechas was in debt regularly from playing the horses. IRS finally closed him down for back taxes. They were going to auction off the joint, piece by piece, but Davidson bid for the entire kit and got it. You can say what you want about Davidson's handling of the place, but he saved it. You have to give him that."

In June 1970, the Internal Revenue Service had closed Old Ebbitt Grill, Inc. (Pete Bechas, president, director and treasurer) for failure to pay $10,995.15 in federal taxes dating to 1965. A public auction of Old Ebbitt's fixtures had been held, June 16, and individual bidding rose to a mere $6,639 before those sales were wiped out by Stuart Davidson, who won the aggregate with a bid of $11,250. "I'd gone down there to buy that mahogany bar," Davidson told me, "but bidding was so ridiculously low I couldn't resist going for the whole place." Davidson, founder of Clyde's in Georgetown and a true entrepreneur in the neo-Saloon business, had allowed Old Ebbitt to remain closed four months before reopening October 13, 1970. "We replaced that oak floor downstairs, polished everything, particularly brass and paneling, and cleaned up the animals. The bar was falling through the floor. We cut it down from fifty-four inches, so you could sit at it without eating under your chin. It was a lovely old thing, but how could you make a buck with it high as that. I took several of the nicer steins for myself, but everything else is pretty much as we found it. The two-hundred-year-old clock over the doorway, 'still running with its original wooden wheels,' we found did not run and does not have wooden wheels. We opened the omelette room upstairs a year or so ago, and that's doing well. Old Ebbitt is really the only spot left downtown where people can gather post-theater. We draw a lot of business from National Theater and the Kennedy Center. Dustin Hoffman came in every night when he was here last year. Oh, lots of other people. Susan Ford used to sneak around the corner for a glass of beer. Katharine Hepburn's in town now, I'll have to ask whether she's been by . . . not sure Old Ebbitt's really her sort of spot."

When Stuart Davidson bought Old Ebbitt, he'd rescued just its fixtures: "American Security Corporation owns the building. We're permitted a five-year lease with a six months' cancellation clause. That means they can close us anytime with just six months' notice. They own nearly the entire block. They're dying to put an office building in here, so eventually I suppose we'll have to go."

American Security Corporation had purchased the property "for its ground value," John Neal, Executive Vice President, had told me. "Economy being what it is, we haven't moved yet on replacing it with a larger commercial structure; I can't say how or when we will." John Neal referred me to Richard Huhn, a lawyer in the neighborhood who had represented the Ann Burchell estate, from which American Security Corporation had purchased Old Ebbitt. Mr. Huhn was a soft-spoken man with a slight Southern accent, who had talked with me briefly about Anders Rudolph Lofstrand and the early history of Old Ebbitt:

"I acted as Mr. Lofstrand's attorney," Huhn had said, "and was close friends with him for many years. He was a wonderful story-teller—I do wish you could have met him; we tried to get him to tape some of his anecdotes but he never would. I remember him telling me about his acquisition of 1427 F. Mr. Lofstrand was employed up the street at Ebbitt Hotel, which was slated to be torn down. One afternoon he was walking past 1427 F and overheard a woman who was tenant there arguing with her landlord. Apparently she couldn't pay her back rent. Mr. Lofstrand knew he had to vacate Ebbitt Hotel, so he offered to pay this woman's rent if she'd give him her lease. He cleared the deal, went in to talk with my old senior partner Mr. Ogleby, and worked it out with Mrs. Burchell. There were so many stories. Mr. Lofstrand was just a great old man. He met the competition of government restaurants during the Depression, brought all his sandwiches down to five cents apiece, and had lines waiting round the corner. He invented that elbow crutch and a dishwashing machine, which incidentally, Peoples Drugstore still carries, using the third floor at 1427 as a workshop. One day we were having lunch together at Normandy Farm and he began tinkering with one of their dishwashing machines. 'Get away, you might break that!' a busboy had screamed. 'I merely invented it,' Mr. Lofstrand replied."

Stuart Davidson had not been the first to acquire Ebbitt's venerable fixtures via public auction. A. R. Lofstrand must have struck a similar tack, for by May 10, 1925 (*Washington Post*), Ebbitt House's furnishings had been sold to the highest individual bidders. Mr. Lofstrand took Ebbitt's storied mahogany bar, an arch from the hotel's Dutch Room, paneling from its English Room, the Alexander Hamilton bear, Ebbitt's collection of steins, the two-hundred-year-old clock, plus assorted stuffed animals and heads. Ebbitt House closed its doors May 1, 1925, ending a reign of sixty-odd years, the likes of which Washington might never enjoy again.

Ebbitt House had its beginnings in an 1837 hostelry, near the southeast corner of Fourteenth and F, known as Frenchman's Hotel. A Mrs. Smith ran a boarding house there for some years, but by 1856 William Ebbitt had bought the property, christening it Ebbitt House. In 1863, Mr. Ebbitt transferred ownership to his son-in-law Albert H. Craney, who in 1865 sold the property to Caleb C. Willard. All trace of William Ebbitt had been lost at this point, but Caleb C. Willard would become a force to be reckoned with in the Washington hotel business.

Caleb Willard was something of a romantic—a native of Vermont who had emigrated West, fumbled over a hotel career in Chicago, bartended on Hudson River steamers, and journeyed to Washington during the 1840s to assist his brothers, E. D. and H. A. Willard, in an already successful hotel venture. Willards' Hotel, situated at the northwest corner of Fourteenth Street and Pennsylvania Avenue, had not yet expanded to include the entire frontage of Fourteenth, but had prospered as the City Hotel since about 1818. Caleb Willard seems not to have gotten along with his elder brothers; or perhaps felt the goad of wanderlust, for in 1849 he drifted to Boston, then again West; but after a time he returned East, bought and rebuilt the Hygeia Hotel at Old Point Comfort, Virginia, which he ran until 1862, when it was commandeered by the Union government and razed. Caleb Willard next became involved with New York's Girard House, but by 1865 he'd returned to Washington and purchased the Ebbitt.

In 1858 Henry A. Willard had extended his hotel from Pennsylvania Avenue to F Street, along its western side. Caleb Willard's sibling rivalry must have been piqued, for he frantically desired a caravansary that would not merely compete with, but would in fact stifle his brother's venture. By 1866 he'd acquired the southeast corner building at Fourteenth and F, a four-story structure with a grocery occupying the first floor, run by Bushrod Reed. Reed had built the house in 1826 and held out for some years, but by 1866 Caleb Willard had busted him, hung his sign EBBITT HOUSE out over the coveted corner, and commissioned Mathew Brady to photograph it.

A grocer named N. W. Burchell continued to occupy Ebbitt's ground floor until 1872 when Caleb Willard finally remodeled—putting into effect his dream of hosting Washington's most fashionable hostelry. Willard had bolstered Ebbitt's reputation during the Civil War, whilst his establishment became a favorite of naval and military officers, newspapermen, politicians, even President Lincoln. Gath's *Washington, Outside and Inside,* published 1874, described Ebbitt as "one of the largest and decidedly the best-looking [hotel], architecturally, at the Capital." Willard had added a mansard roof, hiking Bushrod Reed's original structure to six stories. "The taste of the proprietor, Caleb C. Willard," Gath continued, "is displayed in the elegant French pavilions and broken lines of the roof, and in the series of classical window moldings, which liken the establishment to the purer class of the public edifices." A photograph of 1874 Ebbitt House survived today at the rear wall of Old Ebbitt's taproom. The earlier Brady photograph could be viewed upstairs, in Old Ebbitt's omelette room. Caleb Willard eventually extended his hotel the entire block between F and Pennsylvania, as his brother Henry had *across* Fourteenth Street in 1858. But as Gath.related, "Beneath [Ebbitt's] dining room is the historic line of offices known over the whole country as Newspaper Row. The newspaper correspondents had pitched upon this block before a hotel was devised on account of its immediate proximity to the telegraph offices, the Treasury, all lines of city communications, and as it was centrally situated to the White House and the great departments. When the Ebbitt was rebuilt the proprietor reserved the basement stage for newspaper offices, and for the length of the whole block lights can be seen shining at every night in the week. . . ." During its years as a newspaperman's hostelry, Ebbitt hosted Mark Twain, Ben Perley Poore, and James Whitcomb Riley, to say nothing of political figures such as Presidents Lincoln, Johnson, Grant, Cleveland, McKinley, Roosevelt, Taft, and Harding; Generals Sherman and Hancock; Admirals Farragut, Porter, Scott, Rowan, and Stenble. General George Armstrong Custer stopped at Ebbitt House before starting West on his final campaign. Ebbitt's list of notables was lengthy. John Howard Payne, author of "Home, Sweet Home," had been a longtime resident.

Caleb Willard's installation of the oblong Crystal Ballroom had afforded much excitement to Washingtonians of the day. It ran lengthwise along Fourteenth Street and was two stories high. "The lofty ceiling is beautifully frescoed," Gath wrote, "while the windows are given nearly the loftiness of the hall, thus bathing the apartment in the exquisite light of this latitude." Certainly A. R. Lofstrand must have overseen this "spacious dining and dancing salon," indeed, must have furbished his future digs with fixtures from its ruins. No mention had I found of an Ebbitt House bar—excepting John Clagett Proctor's note in a November 1, 1942, *Washington Star* essay, recalling a stairway from Crystal "which led to the basement, where other things beside soda water were served."

By 1923 when Caleb Willard's estate had put Ebbitt House on the auction block, it had drawn from F. H. Smith Company "a record $2,500,000," the *Star* reported. Two years later Ebbitt had closed, and on January 6, 1926, razing had begun—ironically, to make way for a National Press Club building.

Old Ebbitt Grill remained—Old Ebbitt with a six-months' cancellation clause, a few oldtimers like Herman Brody, and a troop of longhaired waiters whom Stuart Davidson shuttled in prefab with cocky manners, surly attitudes, and always the elbow in your side whenever they passed you seated uncomfortably at the lowered bar. Davidson hired them because they worked cheap, and he held them in line with lie detector tests. That's right. Every few months his entire staff underwent the humiliation of a professionally administered polygraph, to ascertain whether they'd been stealing, giving away free drinks, or perhaps masturbating in the toilet room. They all looked very paranoid. Davidson kept women behind the bar . . . Georgetownish women in tight slacks who mixed drinks so ineptly, served them so slowly and with such little grace that it caused a battered saloon-head like me to nearly retch. "Food here is shit, too," Herman Brody added. "Try a little of this Swedish tea loaf. I brought it in: Raisins, cherries, whole butter, fruit, nuts. You ought to try my Tugboat Cake some evening, that's the specialty. That's what really lets you know you're alive."

On October 12, 1937, A. R. Lofstrand had celebrated Ebbitt's "gala eighty-first anniversary." He'd composed a brief history for the occasion (reprinted and available upon request), scattered with factual errors but replete with pride. This brief history had been included on Lofstrand's anniversary invitations, facing a note from the old maitre d' which read: "You may find this hard to believe, but

. . . all the food is going to be on the house . . . THE FOOD WILL BE FREE. And who mentioned drinks???? They can't be given away under the law, but it will be just like old times for beer will cost you only five cents and you may purchase any of the other drinks on our Wine and Liquor List for HALF PRICE."

Now, Stuart Davidson had been known to host a free party—at Clyde's, at Clyde's in Columbia, but to my knowledge never at Old Ebbitt. Point being that tonight an Ebbitt cheeseburger sold for two dollars and sixty cents, a hot roast-beef sandwich for three twenty-five, tossed salad a dollar-ten, cheesecake one dollar . . . and draft beers: Heineken's, Guinness, Andaeker, Bass, ranged from seventy-five cents to a dollar and a half. Omelettes upstairs averaged about three dollars, which was fair, but *one glass* of table wine sold for a dollar-twenty. The spirit of old Lofstrand was not with us. But then Stuart Davidson had graduated from Harvard Business, not "the most gracious and elegant caravansary at the capital."

"All of them are gone," Herman remarked. "Caruso's, the Bavarian, Ender's, Hamill's, Cy Ellis's, Harvey's, Hall's. Washington's a disaster area. Personally, I am glad Davidson's hiked the prices. It keeps the trash away. Look what's going on a couple blocks north of here. I mean Fourteenth Street used to be a swell neighborhood."

And one of Washington's oldest. F Street, from Ninth to the Treasury, had been the earliest section in L'Enfant's Ten-Mile Square to have been developed. For many years it marked the city's boundary; acreage northward consisting mainly of farms and forest. It was seeded residentially at first—Aaron Burr, John Quincy Adams and others owning stately houses hereabouts—but gradually waxed commercial with the advent of one-horse trolley cars in 1864, the attendant excitement of Civil War, the establishment of nineteen out-of-town newspaper offices, and the bustle of numerous saloons and hostelries. Harvey's, for example—where in 1948 my father had met Ernest Hemingway—in 1858 existed as Washington's first oyster bar, conducting business from a repainted blacksmith's shop at Eleventh and C Streets, with bare planks for a counter and a steaming iron pot at the center of the room. During the Civil War, Harvey's had supplemented Army of the Potomac's diet with five hundred barge loads of oysters a week. The steamed oyster was said to have first come into popularity at Harvey's. Walt Whitman had dined there. So had everyone else. Harvey's was long gone from the neighborhood, but survived, plastic as any Howard Johnson's, at 1001 Eighteenth. Henry Adams had lived round the corner on Lafayette Square, where he'd built a great mansion and compiled his *Education*. GW himself had dined next door to Ebbitt at Rhodes Hotel. There were so many reasons to feel good about Old Ebbitt. It was fitted like a casket, dark paneling, polished brass, the mother *was* a casket in many ways; but that's how I wanted to go.

Herman Brody was reminiscing about Galveston in the good old days, Balboa, Brooklyn—a bar there beneath Brooklyn Bridge known as "Frank's House of a Thousand Assholes." I had my fist wrapped around Bill Bode's letter concerning the death of Donnelly's; was thinking about Washington. A few post-Prohibition saloons here were worth frequenting. Notably:

Martin's Tavern, 1264 Wisconsin Avenue, Georgetown, featuring Albert Faina tending bar superbly, as he had for forty years; shucking oysters, serving Martin's simple food in the darkly paneled barroom. William G. Martin, founder, had played with the 1916 Braves, year they took the Series. My father had drunk beer at Martin's as a boy. Billy Martin's son, current proprietor, had been a corpsman of my father's at Bethesda Naval. Martin's Tavern was the last serious drinking spot in Georgetown.

Charing Cross, 3027 M Street, Georgetown, was new but possessed a hundred-year-old front bar of West Coast fir, coupled with a turn-of-the-century back bar of marble, mahogany, and milk glass from an apothecary shop in Virginia. (Old Ebbitt itself had once been a drugstore, 1901, with a chiropodist's office upstairs. A photograph had told me.)

Childe Harold, 1610 Twentieth Street, NW, hosted some of the finest music in the nation on a small saloon basis, and was run by a true gentleman-prankster, William A. Heard, Jr. Childe Harold had been the home of Dr. Charles Augustus Simpson, a friend of my Grandfather Thompson and professor to my father at George Washington University Medical School. My grandfather had been a guest many evenings in the same front room where Bruce Springsteen, Mose Allison, Elvin Jones, Ramblin Jack Elliot, and hundreds of others now performed. Bill Heard kept the upstairs elegant: William Jordan Company, a small contractor in Georgetown had fabricated Heard's back bar from scraps of Simpson mantel, bedroom trim, walnut, oak, and good mahogany. Before Heard redesigned Childe Harold in 1975, the upstairs had possessed an extraordinary old-saloon feel. It was still the best place in town to hear music and drink standing at a bar, but it had changed. Better spot now to hear music than to drink.

The Pilgrimage, in Childe Harold's English basement, had been Dr. Simpson's dermatological office. It was tastefully designed, but as a bar not much.

Admiral Benbow, next door at 1636 Connecticut Avenue, NW, was a post-Prohibition dive both my father and grandfather had patronized. Friendly during the afternoon, it was terribly desolate most evenings; last Easter I'd been standing at Benbow's bar and two seven-foot blacks in full bunny-drag had pranced in, offering painted eggs and jellybeans from straw baskets they carried over their arms. Admiral Benbow *could* be cheerful.

Columbia Station, 1836 Columbia Road, NW, had recently opened and looked promising; lent a North Beach-Sausalito ambience to Washington's SoHo/Habana quarter. Poetry readings, hanging out, artiste mufti.

Pig Foot, 1812 Hamlin Street, NE, Bill Harris had just established as a welcome addition to Washington's jazz scene. Harris's jazz guitar-work featured. Fantastic energy. Wonderful soul food.

Blues Alley, behind 1073 Wisconsin Avenue, Georgetown, in a converted carriage house, had been filling the Washington jazz gap since 1964. Many big names, plus a small barroom where the poorer enthusiast might sit without paying a cover, and still hear the music.

Bassin's GW Inn, 832 Twentieth Street, NW, was post-Pro and the last of that Pennsylvania Avenue string which had included La-Salle Grill and Brownley's. Decidedly not a college joint, it offered Washington drinkers a Midwestern atmosphere, that of a Chicago pump, say, specifically at its Art Deco bar and accompanying booths.

Le Jour et Nuit, 1204 Thirtieth Street, Georgetown, for its simpatico Frog jukebox.

Garvin's, 2619 Connecticut Avenue, NW, near the Shoreham Hotel, for late night snacks and in summer, pleasant sidewalk drinking.

Capitol Hill held its share . . . The Tune Inn, along Pennsylvania Avenue SE, past Congressional Library, Supreme Court, the Capitol . . . check the yellow pages; take a stroll, ask a cop. I could guarantee you nothing like Old Ebbitt.

Five years at the most, six months cancellation any time. What the hell. I needed to piss. Herman Brody was fascinating company, but I'd scheduled a rendezvous with old friend S. Jack at a new hotspot in College Park—"decorated like something out of Tolkien," I'd heard, very seventies—"unique." One year earlier, S. Jack, British philosopher Alan White, and I had enjoyed a hopeful evening at Old Ebbitt prior to my departure for this last bout of research. Everything had looked so promising: Alaska, Hawaii, the Carolines . . . "When you get round to England," White had laughed, "I'll show you our London discos." In the *continental U.S.* I'd barely scratched the surface. Pressure on my bladder proved insistent. Bill Bode's letter was sweat-damp against my thigh as I turned and caught a long-haired busboy's tray, hard, just below the ribs.

"You sonofabitch," I said, coming off my stool very slowly, "you God-damned sonofabitch."

Index

285